# BELF

## STREET ATLAS & GUIDE

CU00701946

# CONTENTS

| | |
|---|---|
| LAYOUT OF MAP PAGES | (ii) |
| LEGEND | (iii) |
| MAPS | 1 - 27 |
| ALPHABETICAL STREET INDEX | 28 - 41 |
| NUMERICAL STREET INDEX | 42 - 48 |
| PUBLIC TRANSPORT | 51 - 57 |
| PLACES OF INTEREST | 58 - 62 |
| THEATRE, MUSIC, CINEMA | 63 - 66 |
| RESTAURANTS & PUBS | 67 - 78 |
| SPORT & LEISURE | 79 - 82 |
| SHOPPING | 83 - 86 |
| WHERE TO STAY | 87 - 88 |
| EXPLORING NORTHERN IRELAND | 89 - 92 |
| DIARY OF EVENTS | 93 |

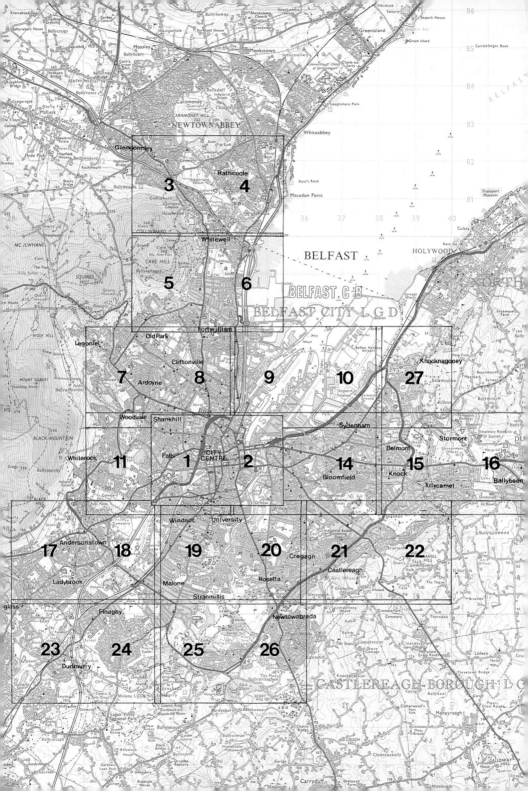

Scale of main map pages is 1:15,000 (4.2 inches to 1 mile)

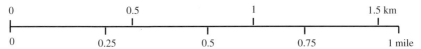

# LEGEND

| City Centre Security Zone(restricted access) | | Built-up Areas | |
| Main Routes | | Named Buildings | |
| Other Roads | | Church | + |
| One Way Street | → | Public Car Park | P |
| Banned Turn | | Parks | |
| Ulsterbus/Citybus Routes | 23   49 | Pedestrian Precinct | |

Printed in Northern Ireland by The Universities Press (Belfast) Ltd.

Edited by Paul Slevin. Published by Causeway Press (N.I.), Enterprise House, Balloo Avenue, Bangor BT19 7QT. Phone (01247) 271525. Fax (01247) 270080.

ABERCORN BASIN

J9

CORPORATION STREET
GREAT GEORGE'S ST
LANCASTER ST
LITTLE AFRICA STREET
GREAT PATRICK STREET
DUNBAR LINK
CORPORATION ST
GPO
DONEGALL STREET
FREDERICK STREET
YORK LANE
Gov't Office
Tourist Board
ROYAL AVENUE
ROSEMARY ST
HIGH STREET
WARING STREET
TALBOT STREET
GORDON ST
ACADEMY
DUNBAR ST
HILL STREET
Clarendon Dock
Harbour Office
+ Presb
Isle of Man Ferry Terminal
Stranraer SeaCat Terminal
LAGAN BRIDGE
M3 MOTORWAY
DONEGALL QUAY
DARGAN BRIDGE
Custom House
DONEGALL QUAY
QUEEN'S QUAY
QUEEN'S SQ
PRINCE'S STREET
VICTORIA STREET
ANN ST
QUEEN ELIZABETH BRIDGE
QUEEN'S BRIDGE
CANAL QUAY
OXFORD STREET
Bus Station
LAGANBANK ROAD
Court Ho
VICTORIA SQUARE
CHICHESTER STREET
HMSO
163A 300
CASTLE PL
CASTLE LANE
ANN STREET
ARTHUR ST
GLOUCESTER ST
MAY STREET
CITY HALL
DONEGALL SQ N
DONEGALL SQ S
DONEGALL PL
CROMAC SQUARE
Royal Courts of Justice
EAST BRIDGE STREET
ALBERT BRIDGE
CENTRAL STATION
Leisure Centre
BEDFORD STREET
ADELAIDE STREET
FRANKLIN ST
CLARENCE STREET
ORMEAU AVENUE
CROMAC STREET
HAMILTON STREET
GRACE ST
FRIENDLY STREET
ELIZA STREET
RAPHAEL ST
BOND ST
McAULEY STREET
STEWART ST
Comm Centre
LAGAN
RIVER
Rupert Stanley College of Further Education
BMX Cycle Track
Recreation Centre
Playing Field
ORMEAU EMBANKMENT
Playing Field
All Weather Pitch
Playing Fields
Bowling Green
Tennis Court
Park Educational Resource Centre
BANKMORE STREET
HARDCASTLE STREET
MARYVILLE STREET
LINDSAY ST
APSLEY STREET
CHARLOTTE ST
DONEGALL PASS
ELM ST
PINE WAY
WALNUT ST
VERNON STREET
COOKE STREET
COOKE MEWS
SHAFTESBURY AVENUE
Old People's Home
Playing Field
Recreation Centre
CROMWELL ROAD
WOLSELEY STREET
ESSEX STREET
INDIA ST
MCCLURE ST
EBLANA ST
North of Ireland Sports Ground

BRIDGE END
MIDDLEPATH STREET
Bridge End Flyover
BALLYMACARRETT
SHORT STRAND
MOUNTPOTTINGER LINK
MOUNTPOTTINGER ROAD
Laganside Walkway
WOODSTOCK LINK
BALLARAT ST
BENDIGO STREET
DUNVEGAN ST
CARRINGTON ST
RICHARDSON ST
DONARD STREET
LONDON STREET
RAVENHILL
DELAWARE ST
LONDON ROAD
FLORIDA DRIVE
WATT ST
IMPERIAL STREET

QUEEN'S QUAY ROAD
MACART ROAD
SYDENHAM ROAD
OLD CHANNEL ROAD
Bridge End

J6

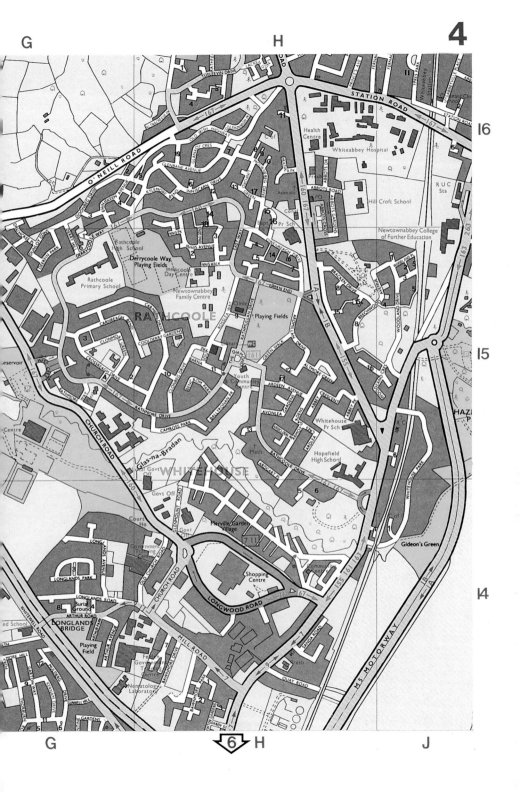

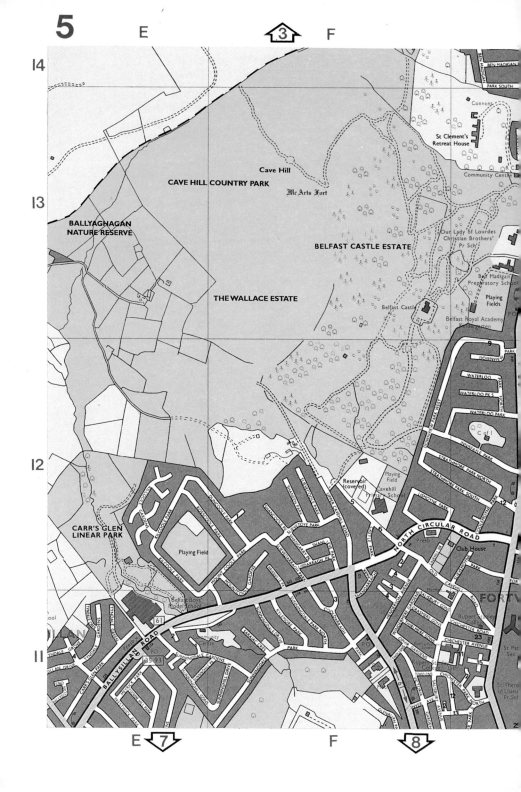

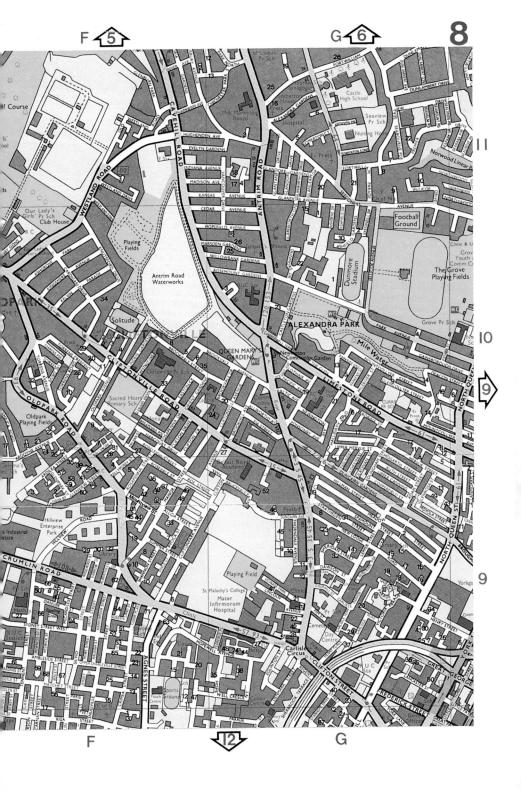

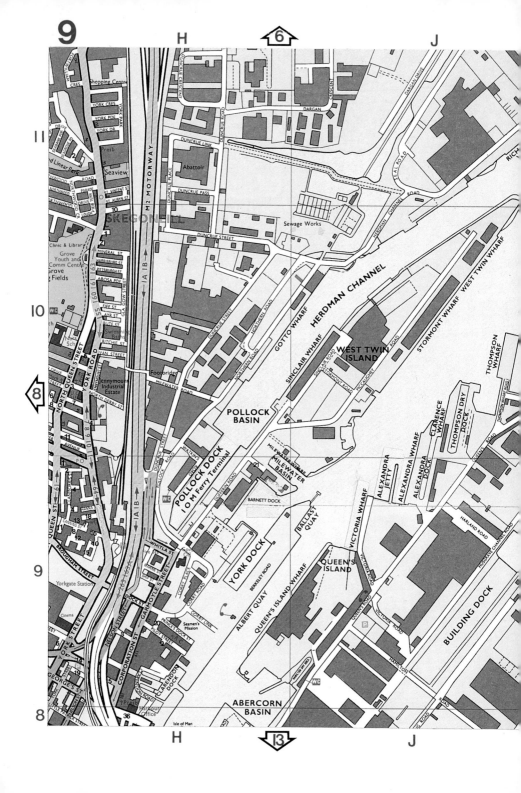

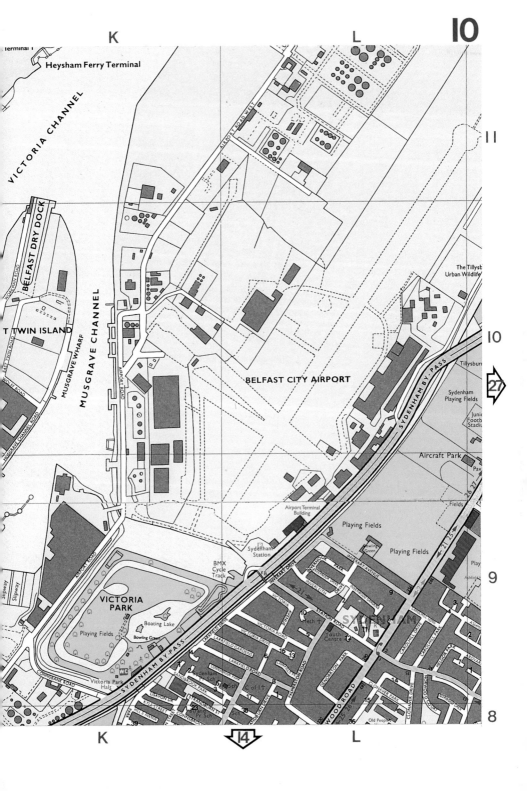

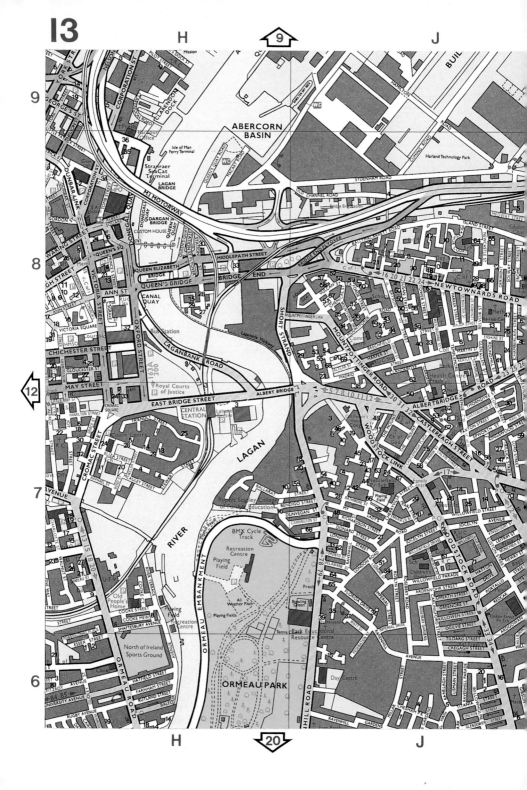

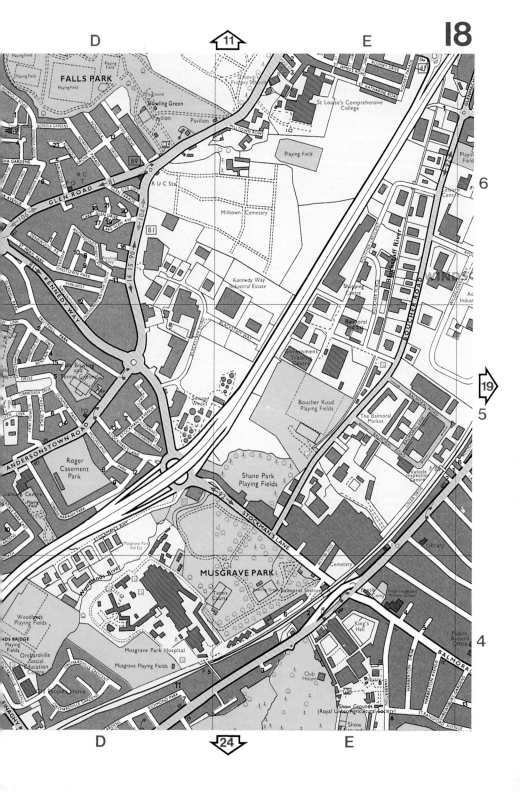

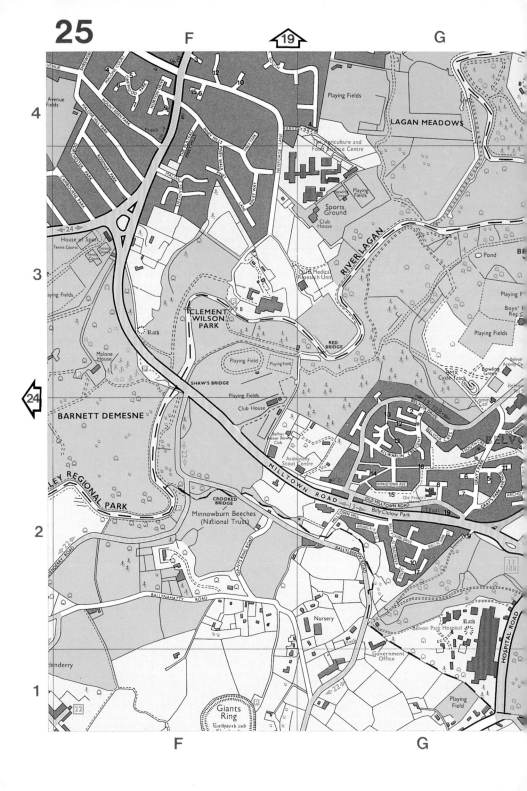

Due to insufficient space, some streets and/or their names have been omitted from the street map. These streets are indexed with an additional number shown in brackets. The number appears in black on the street map and indicates the location of the street.

The name of a street which has been so numbered can be found by referring to the NUMERICAL STREET INDEX on pages 42-48.

**ABBREVIATIONS**

Av. - Avenue
Br. - Bridge
Cent. - Central
Cotts. - Cottages
Cres. - Crescent
Ct. - Court
Dr. - Drive
E. - East
Gdns. - Gardens
Gve. - Grove
Hts. - Heights
Lit. - Little
N. - North
Pde. - Parade
Pk. - Park
Pl. - Place
R'about - Roundabout
Rd. - Road
S. - South
St. - Saint, Street
Terr. - Terrace
Wk. - Walk
W'way - Walkway

16  Abbey Court  **P7(26)**
4  Abbey Court  **J16(6)**
4  Abbey Crescent  **H15**
7  Abbey Dale Cres  **D10**
7  Abbey Dale Drive  **D10**
7  Abbey Dale Gdns  **D10**
7  Abbey Dale Pde  **D10**
7  Abbey Dale Park  **E10**
15  Abbey Gardens  **N7**
16  Abbey Gardens  **P7(29)**
15  Abbey Park  **N7**
16  Abbey Park  **P7**
4  Abbey Park  **H15**
15  Abbey Road  **N7**
4  Abbeyville Place  **J16**
4  Abbots Cross  **H16**
4  Abbots Drive  **H16**
4  Abbots Gardens  **H16**
4  Abbots Road  **H16**
19  Abbercorn Street  **G6(3)**
1  Abbercorn St N  **F7(40)**
1  Abbercorn Walk  **F7(31)**
1  Aberdeen Street  **F8(77)**
24  Aberfoyle Gardens  **D2(2)**

24  Aberfoyle Park  **D2**
14  Abetta Parade  **K7**
14  Abetta Parade  **K7(13)**
1  Abingdon Drive  **F7**
24  Aboo Court  **D4(4)**
1  Abyssinia Street  **F7(39)**
1  Abyssinia Walk  **F7(26)**
12  Academy Street  **G8**
8  Acton Street  **F9**
8  Adam Street  **G9**
8  Adela Place  **G9(22)**
8  Adela Street  **G9(42)**
19  Adelaide Avenue  **F5**
19  Adelaide Park  **F5**
2  Adelaide Street  **G7**
23  Aghery Walk  **B2(13)**
20  Agincourt Avenue  **H6**
20  Agincourt Street  **H6(19)**
8  Agnes Court  **F9(15)**
8  Agnes Street  **F9**
20  Agra Street  **H6**
14  Aigburth Park  **K8**
20  Ailesbury Crescent  **H5**
20  Ailesbury Drive  **H5**
20  Ailesbury Gardens  **H5**
20  Ailesbury Road  **H5**
11  Ainsworth Avenue  **E8**
11  Ainsworth Drive  **E8**
7  Ainsworth Parade  **E9(4)**
11  Ainsworth Pass  **E8**
11  Ainsworth Street  **E8**
10  Airport Road  **K9**
10  Airport Road West  **L11**
17  Aitnamona Cres  **C6**
21  Alanbrooke Road  **K6**
1  Albany Place  **F8(1)**
1  Albany Square  **F8(37)**
2  Albert Bridge  **H7**
12  Albert Court  **G8(51)**
21  Albert Drive  **K5**
2  Albert Square  **H8**
1  Albert Street  **F8**
1  Albert Terrace  **F8(32)**
13  Albertbridge Road  **J7**
8  Albertville Drive  **F9**
12  Albion Lane  **G7(51)**
12  Albion Street  **G7(97)**
22  Alder Close  **N6(1)**
23  Alder Close  **C1**
6  Alexander Court  **G12(8)**
21  Alexander Road  **K6**
8  Alexandra Av  **G10(13)**
8  Alexandra Gardens  **G11**
8  Alexandra Park Av  **G10**
16  Alford Park  **P7(23)**
2  Alfred Street  **H7**
23  Alina Gardens  **B2(10)**
7  Alliance Avenue  **E10**
7  Alliance Crescent  **E10**
7  Alliance Drive  **E10**
7  Alliance Gardens  **E10**
7  Alliance Parade  **E10**
7  Alliance Road  **E10**
8  Alloa Street  **F9**
8  Allworthy Avenue  **G10**
13  Altcar Street  **J8**
11  Altigarron Court  **D7(29)**
4  Altmore Green  **H15**
25  Altnacreeva Avenue  **G2**
25  Altnacreeva Close  **G2(10)**
4  Altnacreeve Park  **H16**
12  Alton Court  **G8(8)**
12  Alton Street  **G8(67)**
8  Ambleside Street  **F9**

11  Amcomri Street  **E7**
12  Amelia Street  **G7**
13  Ampere Court  **J7(37)**
13  Anderson Court  **J8(53)**
18  Andersonstown Cr  **D6**
18  Andersonstown Dr  **D6(9)**
18  Andersonstown Gdns  **D6(10)**
18  Andersonstown Gve  **D6(12)**
18  Andersonstown Pde  **D6(8)**
18  Andersonstown Park  **D6**
18  Andersonstown Pk  **D6(11)**
18  Andersonstown Park S.  **D6**
18  Andersonstown Pk W.  **D6**
18  Andersonstown Rd  **D5**
2  Ann Street  **H8**
20  Annadale Avenue  **H4**
20  Annadale Crescent  **H5**
20  Annadale Drive  **H5(4)**
19  Annadale Embank.  **G5**
20  Annadale Flats  **H5**
20  Annadale Gardens  **H5(3)**
20  Annadale Green  **H5(5)**
20  Annadale Grove  **H5(2)**
19  Annadale Terrace  **G5(1)**
8  Annalee Court  **F9(48)**
8  Annesley Street  **G9(28)**
1  Annsboro' St  **F8(16)**
8  Antigua Court  **F9(59)**
8  Antigua Street  **F9**
3  Antrim Road  **G14**
19  Apollo Road  **K6**
18  Appleton Park  **D4**
12  Apsley Street  **G7**
8  Arbour Street  **F10(9)**
25  Archdale Grove  **G2**
25  Archdale Park  **G2**
3  Archvale Park  **F16**
16  Ardara Avenue  **Q7(4)**
8  Ardavon Park  **G11**
16  Ardcarn Drive  **P7**
16  Ardcarn Green  **P7(4)**
16  Ardcarn Park  **P7(3)**
16  Ardcarn Way  **P7**
4  Ardcloon Park  **H15**
4  Ardeen Avenue  **H15**
4  Ardeen Gdns  **H15(17)**
20  Ardenlee Avenue  **J6**
20  Ardenlee Drive  **J6**
20  Ardenlee Gardens  **J6**
20  Ardenlee Parade  **J6**
20  Ardenlee Street  **J6**
13  Ardenvohr Street  **J7**
13  Ardfarn Close  **H15(13)**
4  Ardgart Place  **H15**
14  Ardgowan Dr  **K7(10)**
13  Ardgowan Street  **J7**
15  Ardgreenan Cr  **M8(10)**
15  Ardgreenan Drive  **M8**
15  Ardgreenan Gdns  **M8(9)**
15  Ardgreenan Mt  **M8(6)**
15  Ardgreenan Pl  **M8(7)**
8  Ardilea Court  **F10(25)**
8  Ardilea Drive  **F10(12)**
8  Ardilea Street  **F9**
21  Ardkeen Crescent  **L5(7)**
4  Ardlea Crescent  **H15**
8  Ardmillan  **G11(25)**
4  Ardmillan Drive  **H15**
4  Ardmillan Gdns  **H15(12)**
7  Ardmonagh Gdns  **D7**
11  Ardmonagh Way  **D7(11)**
20  Ardmore Avenue  **H5**
23  Ardmore Avenue  **D4**

24  Ardmore Court  **D4(8)**
17  Ardmore Drive  **D4**
17  Ardmore Park  **C4**
18  Ardmore Park S  **D4(1)**
1  Ardmoulin Av  **F8(79)**
1  Ardmoulin Cl  **F8(66)**
12  Ardmoulin Pl  **G8(59)**
1  Ardmoulin St  **F8(96)**
1  Ardmoulin Terr  **F8(97)**
8  Ardoyne Avenue  **F10**
8  Ardoyne Ct  **F10(23)**
8  Ardoyne Pl  **F10(24)**
7  Ardoyne Road  **E10**
8  Ardoyne Wk  **F10(13)**
21  Ardpatrick Gdns  **K6**
27  Ardvarna Cres  **M9(1)**
27  Ardvarna Park  **M9**
23  Areema Court  **B3(9)**
23  Areema Drive  **B2**
1  Argyle Court  **F8(56)**
1  Argyle Street  **F8**
1  Argyle Street  **F8(60)**
8  Ariel Street  **F9(11)**
18  Arizona Street  **D6**
23  Arlington Park  **C4(5)**
14  Armitage Cl  **K8(25)**
4  Armoy Gdns  **H15**
20  Arney Close  **J5**
12  Arnon Street  **G8(1)**
9  Arosa Parade  **H10**
13  Arran Court  **J8(3)**
13  Arran Street  **J8(55)**
20  Artana St  **H6(18)**
4  Arthur Avenue  **G14**
2  Arthur Lane  **H8(20)**
4  Arthur Park  **G14**
2  Arthur Place  **H8(19)**
4  Arthur Road  **G14**
2  Arthur Square  **H8(17)**
12  Arthur Street  **G8**
1  Arundel Courts  **F7(45)**
1  Arundel Walk  **F7(46)**
22  Ascot Gardens  **M6**
22  Ascot Mews  **M6(22)**
22  Ascot Park  **M6**
15  Ashbourne Court  **M8(18)**
10  Ashbrook Crescent  **L9(3)**
10  Ashbrook Drive  **L9(4)**
27  Asburn Green  **M9(4)**
12  Ashburne Mews  **G7(93)**
12  Ashburne Place  **G7(94)**
14  Ashdale Street  **K8**
8  Ashdene Drive  **G10(15)**
8  Ashfield Court  **G10(10)**
8  Ashfield Crescent  **G10(1)**
8  Ashfield Drive  **G10**
8  Ashfield Gardens  **G10**
27  Ashford Green  **M9(2)**
8  Ashgrove Park  **F10**
23  Ashlea Bend  **B1**
19  Ashleigh Manor  **F6(5)**
19  Ashleigh Avenue  **F6**
19  Ashley Drive  **F6**
6  Ashley Gardens  **G12**
23  Ashley Park  **B2**
1  Ashmore Place  **F8(30)**
1  Ashmore Street  **F8**
27  Ashmount Grove  **M9(3)**
27  Ashmount Park  **M9**
27  Ashmount Place  **M9(5)**
23  Ashton Green  **C4**
23  Ashton Park  **C4**
23  Aspen Park  **B3**
23  Aspen Walk  **B3(8)**

15 Aston Gardens **M8(8)**
15 Astoria Gardens **M7(3)**
12 Athol Street **G7**
12 Athol Street Lane **G7(6)**
8 Atlantic Avenue **G10(19)**
23 Auburn Place **C2(11)**
23 Auburn Street **C2(4)**
23 Aughrim Court **B1(11)**
12 Aughrim Park **G7(86)**
20 Ava Avenue **H6**
20 Ava Crescent **H5**
20 Ava Drive **H5**
20 Ava Gardens **H5**
20 Ava Parade **H6**
20 Ava Park **H5**
20 Ava Street **H5**
8 Avoca Street **F9**
8 Avonbeg Close **F9(49)**
14 Avondale Street **K7**
14 Avoniel Drive **K7**
14 Avoniel Parade **K7(19)**
13 Avoniel Road **K7**
4 Avonlea Gardens **H15**
14 Avonorr Drive **K7(28)**
9 Ayr Street **H10**
1 Azamor Street **F8**
13 Back Mount Street **J7(11)**
12 Bain's Place **F7**
11 Bainesmore Drive **E8**
20 Balfour Avenue **H6**
7 Balholm Drive **E9**
1 Balkan Court **F8(23)**
1 Balkan Street **F8**
17 Ballaghbeg **C6(3)**
13 Ballarat Court **J7(19)**
2 Ballarat Street **H7**
23 Ballybog Road **B1**
25 Ballycairn Close **G2**
25 Ballycairn Drive **G2**
8 Ballycarry Street **F10(31)**
8 Ballycastle Court **F10(26)**
8 Ballyclare Street **F10(7)**
8 Ballyclare Way **F10(7)**
11 Ballygomartin Drive **D8**
7 Ballygomartin Park **E9(2)**
11 Ballygomartin Road **D7**
22 Ballygowan Road **M4,M5**
16 Ballyhanwood Road **Q6**
25 Ballylesson Road **G2**
13 Ballymacarrett Road **J8**
14 Ballymacarrett W'way **K8(7)**
11 Ballymagarry Lane **D8**
8 Ballymena Court **F9(4)**
27 Ballymiscaw Road **N9**
8 Ballymoney Street **F9**
11 Ballymurphy Cres **D7(15)**
11 Ballymurphy Drive **D7**
11 Ballymurphy Pde **D7(16)**
11 Ballymurphy Road **D7**
11 Ballymurphy Street **E7**
25 Ballynahatty Road **F2**
8 Ballynure Street **F10**
8 Ballynure Way **F10(7)**
16 Ballyregan Road **Q8**
4 Ballyronan Park **H15**
11 Ballyroney Hill **G14(11)**
5 Ballysillan Cres **E11**
5 Ballysillan Road **E11**
18 Balmoral Avenue **F4**
18 Balmoral Court **E4(2)**
18 Balmoral Drive **E4(5)**
18 Balmoral Gdns **E4(4)**
18 Balmoral Link **E5**
19 Balmoral Mews **F4(11)**
18 Balmoral Road **E5**
18 Baltic Avenue **G10**
14 Banbury Street **K8(44)**
8 Bandon Court **F9(33)**
12 Bank Street **G8**
12 Bankmore Square **G7(54)**
12 Bankmore Street **G7**
8 Bann Court **F9(18)**
20 Bannagh Corner **J5**
11 Bantry Street **E8**

21 Bapaume Avenue **K5**
23 Barbour Gardens **C3**
4 Barna Square **H15**
9 Barnett Dock Road **H9(21)**
15 Barnett's Cres **N7(5)**
15 Barnett's Green **N7**
15 Barnett's Road **N7**
20 Baroda Drive **H6(9)**
20 Baroda Parade **H6(10)**
20 Baroda Street **H6**
12 Barrack Street **G8**
1 Barrington Gdns **F7(27)**
13 Baskin Street **J8(13)**
14 Bathgate Drive **L8(33)**
14 Bately Street **K7**
11 Battenberg Street **E8**
19 Bawnmore Ct **F5(13)**
4 Bawnmore Drive **H14**
4 Bawnmore Gve **H14(1)**
4 Bawnmore Park **H14**
4 Bawnmore Pl **H14(2)**
19 Bawnmore Road **F5**
4 Bawnmore Terr **H14(3)**
17 Bearnagh Drive **D5**
17 Bearnagh Glen **D6(15)**
23 Beattie Park Central **C2**
23 Beattie Park North **C2(8)**
23 Beattie Park S. **C2(10)**
23 Beattie Park Terr **C2(7)**
26 Beaufort Avenue **H3**
26 Beaufort Crescent **H3**
26 Beaufort Gardens **H3(6)**
26 Beaufort Grove **H3(7)**
26 Beaufort Park **J3**
12 Bedford Street **G7**
23 Beech Grove **B1**
21 Beech Park **K5**
13 Beechfield Court **J8(39)**
13 Beechfield Street **J8**
21 Beechgrove Avenue **K4**
21 Beechgrove Cres **K4(2)**
20 Beechgrove Drive **J4**
21 Beechgrove Gdns **K4**
21 Beechgrove Park **K4**
21 Beechgrove Rise **K4**
26 Beechill Avenue **J2**
26 Beechill Court **J2(7)**
26 Beechill Park **J3(12)**
26 Beechill Park Av **J2**
26 Beechill Park East **J3**
26 Beechill Park North **J3**
26 Beechill Park South **J2**
26 Beechill Park West **J3**
26 Beechill Road **J2**
19 Beechlands **G5**
23 Beechlawn Avenue **C2**
23 Beechlawn Park **C3**
11 Beechmount Avenue **E7**
11 Beechmount Cres **E7(19)**
11 Beechmount Drive **E7**
11 Beechmount Grove **E7**
11 Beechmount Parade **E7**
18 Beechmount Park **D4(7)**
11 Beechmount Pass **E7**
11 Beechmount Street **E7**
8 Beechnut Place **F9(44)**
8 Beechpark Street **F9(45)**
23 Beechtree Court **B2(14)**
11 Beechview Park **E7**
11 Beechwood Avenue **H15**
2 Beechwood Grove **H8**
16 Beechwood Manor **Q7(13)**
11 Beechwood St **K8(19)**
14 Beersbridge Road **K7**
12 Beggs Street **G7(104)**
1 Beit Street **F7**
1 Belair Street **E8(20)**
19 Belgravia Avenue **F6(9)**
9 Bell Close **F9(54)**
13 Belle Bashford Ct **J7(3)**
14 Bellevue Drive **F14(1)**
3 Bellevue Park **F15**
1 Bellevue Street **F8**
14 Belmont Avenue **L8**

14 Belmont Av. W. **L8(9)**
15 Belmont Church Rd **M8**
14 Belmont Close **L8(22)**
14 Belmont Court **L8(8)**
15 Belmont Drive **M8(24)**
14 Belmont Grange **L8(21)**
14 Belmont Mews **L8(24)**
14 Belmont Park **L8**
15 Belmont Place **M8**
15 Belmont Road **M8**
27 Belmont Road **N9**
4 Belmore Gdns **H15(11)**
20 Belmore Street **H6(2)**
19 Belvedere Park **G4**
25 Belvoir Close **G2(1)**
25 Belvoir Crescent **G2**
25 Belvoir Drive **G2, H3**
25 Belvoir House **G2(18)**
26 Belvoir Road **H3**
13 Belvoir Street **J8**
26 Belvoir View Pk **H3(5)**
3 Ben Madigan Hts **G14(10)**
3 Ben Madigan Park **G14**
5 Ben Madigan Park S. **G14**
11 Benares Street **E8(12)**
17 Benbradagh Gdns **C5(13)**
19 Benburb Street **F6**
4 Benmore Park **H15**
13 Bendigo Street **J7**
24 Benmore Court **D3(21)**
24 Benmore Drive **D3**
24 Benmore Walk **D3(9)**
8 Bennett Drive **F10(5)**
18 Benraw Gardens **D5(4)**
18 Benraw Green **D5(15)**
18 Benraw Road **D5**
18 Benraw Terrace **D5(3)**
7 Bentham Drive **F7**
9 Bentinck Street **H9(12)**
7 Benview Parade **E11**
7 Benview Park **E11**
7 Benwee Park **B4**
26 Berkley Court **H3(8)**
19 Berkley Court **F6(10**
9 Berkley Road **H9**
1 Berlin Street **F8**
7 Berry Street **G8(69)**
7 Berwick Road **E10**
14 Bethany Street **L8(15)**
1 Beverley Street **F8**
7 Bilston Road **D10**
17 Bingnian Drive **C5**
14 Bingnian Way **C5(10)**
23 Birch Green **B1**
8 Bisley Street **F9**
11 Black Mountain Gve **D8(4)**
11 Black Mountain Pde **D8(19)**
11 Black Mountain Pk **D8(6)**
11 Black Mountain Pl **D8(7)**
11 Black Mountain Wk **D8(1)**
11 Black Mountain Way **D8(2)**
23 Black's Road **C4**
18 Blackstaff Road **D5**
12 Blackstaff Square **G7(109)**
18 Blackstaff Way **E5**
1 Blackwater Way **F7(18)**
20 Blackwood Street **H6**
19 Bladon Court **G4**
19 Bladon Drive **F4**
19 Bladon Park **F4**
12 Blakely Terrace **G7(35)**
8 Blaney Street **F9(14)**
7 Bleach Green **D11(21)**
11 Bleach Green Court **D7(25)**
11 Bleach Green Terr **D7(26)**
21 Blenheim Drive **K6**
12 Blondin Street **G7(53)**
14 Bloomdale St **K8(30)**
14 Bloomfield Avenue **K7**
14 Bloomfield Court **K7(26)**
14 Bloomfield Cres **K7(4)**
14 Bloomfield Drive **K7**
14 Bloomfield Gardens **K7**
14 Bloomfield Parade **K7**

14 Bloomfield Park **K7**
14 Bloomfield Pk W. **K7(11)**
14 Bloomfield Road **K7**
14 Bloomfield Street **K7(25)**
12 Blythe Street **G7**
1 Bombay Street **F8(89)**
2 Bond Street **H7**
7 Boodles Hill **D11(9)**
7 Boodles Lane **D11(8)**
8 Bootle Street **F9**
6 Botanic Avenue **G6**
19 Botanic Court **G6(22)**
18 Boucher Crescent **E6**
18 Boucher Place **E6**
18 Boucher Road **E5, E6**
12 Boundary Street **G8**
12 Boundary Walk **G8(13)**
12 Boundary Way **G8(12)**
8 Bowness Street **F9**
12 Boyd Street **G8**
12 Boyne Court **G7(59)**
4 Bracken Drive **H15**
7 Bracken Street **E9**
14 Bracken Way **H15(15)**
24 Brackenwood Lane **E2(1)**
12 Bradbury Place **G7**
20 Bradford Place **J4(8)**
2 Bradford Square **H8(3)**
12 Brady's Lane **G8(26)**
7 Brae Hill Crescent **D11**
7 Brae Hill Link **D11(28)**
7 Brae Hill Parade **D11**
7 Brae Hill Park **D11**
7 Brae Hill Road **D11**
7 Brae Hill Way **D11(27)**
3 Braemar Court **E16(11)**
11 Braemar Street **E7(4)**
22 Braeside Grove **M6**
14 Bramcote Street **K7**
14 Brandon Parade **K8**
14 Brandon Terrace **K8(5)**
14 Brandra Street **K8(6)**
22 Braniel Crescent **M6**
22 Braniel Park **M6(17)**
22 Braniel Way **M6(14)**
7 Brantwood Street **G10(4)**
1 Brassey Street **F7(16)**
7 Bray Close **E9**
7 Bray Court **E9(13)**
7 Bray Street **F9**
1 Bread Street **F8(39)**
26 Breda Avenue **J3**
26 Breda Crescent **J3(9)**
26 Breda Drive **J3**
26 Breda Gardens **J3**
26 Breda House **H2(7)**
26 Breda Parade **J3**
26 Breda Park **J3**
26 Breda Road **J3**
26 Breda Terrace **J3**
17 Brenda Park **C5(8)**
14 Brenda Street **K7**
21 Brentwood Park **L6**
26 Brerton Crescent **H2**
26 Brerton Grove **H2(6)**
4 Bresk Hill **G14(9)**
1 Brethan Drive **F7**
5 Brianville Park **F12**
22 Briarwood Park **N6**
2 Bridge End **H8**
13 Bridge End Flyover **J8**
12 Bridge Street **G8**
13 Bright Street **J8(46)**
7 Brighton Street **E7(2)**
6 Bristol Avenue **G12**
16 Bristow Drive **P6**
24 Bristow Park **E3**
12 Britannic Drive **G7(58)**
12 Britannic Park **G7(44)**
12 Britannic Terrace **G7(71)**
11 Britton's Court **E7(11)**
11 Britton's Drive **D7**
11 Britton's Lane **E7**
11 Britton's Lane **D8(17)**
11 Britton's Parade **E7**

| | | | |
|---|---|---|---|
| 1 Broadway **F7** | 26 Cairnshill Drive **J3(8)** | 12 Castle Lane **G8** | 22 Cherryvalley Pk W **M6(11)** |
| 11 Broadway Court **E7(10)** | 26 Cairnshill Gardens **J3(7)** | 21 Castle Mews **L5(6)** | 13 Cherryville Street **J7** |
| 19 Broadway Parade **F6** | 26 Cairnshill Green **J3(6)** | 5 Castle Park **F12** | 20 Chesham Crescent **J6(4)** |
| 8 Bromley Street **F9(61)** | 26 Cairnshill Park **J3** | 12 Castle Place **G8** | 20 Chesham Drive **J6(7)** |
| 7 Brompton Park **E9** | 20 Cairo Street **H6** | 12 Castle Street **G8** | 20 Chesham Gardens **J6(8)** |
| 22 Brook Meadow **N6(13)** | 11 Caledon Court **E8(13)** | 26 Castleboy Avenue **H3** | 20 Chesham Grove **J6(3)** |
| 17 Brooke Close **C4(8)** | 11 Caledon Street **E8** | 26 Castlecoole Park **H3** | 20 Chesham Parade **J6** |
| 17 Brooke Crescent **C4** | 12 California Close **G8(14)** | 26 Castlecoole Walk **H3(4)** | 20 Chesham Park **J6** |
| 17 Brooke Drive **C4** | 20 Callan Way **J5** | 2 CastleCourt Centre **G8** | 20 Chesham Terrace **J6(9)** |
| 23 Brooke Park **C4** | 12 Callender Street **G8** | 26 Castledillon Road **H3** | 5 Chester Manor **G11(23)** |
| 7 Brookfield Place **E9(5)** | 13 Calvin Street **J7** | 15 Castlehill Drive **N8** | 20 Chesterfield Park **J5** |
| 7 Brookfield Street **E9(9)** | 8 Camberwell Terrace **G10** | 15 Castlehill Manor **N8** | 8 Chestnut Gardens **F10** |
| 7 Brookfield Walk **E9(6)** | 25 Cambourne Park **F3** | 15 Castlehill Park **N8** | 23 Chestnut Park **B3** |
| 8 Brookhill Avenue **G10** | 4 Cambrai Park **J16(2)** | 15 Castlehill Park W. **N8(3)** | 14 Cheviot Avenue **K8** |
| 23 Brooklands **B4(11)** | 7 Cambrai Street **E9** | 15 Castlehill Road **N8** | 14 Cheviot Street **K8(43)** |
| 19 Brookland Street **F5** | 9 Cambridge Street **H9(8)** | 26 Castlehume Gdns **H2(1)** | 5 Chichester Avenue **G11** |
| 23 Brooklands Grange **B3** | 19 Camden Street **G6** | 15 Castlekaria Manor **N8(5)** | 5 Chichester Close **G11(11)** |
| 7 Brookmill Way **D11(30)** | 12 Cameron Street **G7** | 21 Castlemore Avenue **L5** | 5 Chichester Court **G11(12)** |
| 11 Brookmount Gdns **E8(3)** | 21 Cameronian Drive **L6** | 21 Castlemore Park **L5** | 5 Chichester Gdns **G11(15)** |
| 1 Brookmount Street **F8** | 21 Camlough Place **L5(1)** | 15 Castleorr Manor **N8(4)** | 8 Chichester Mews **F11(2)** |
| 8 Brookside Court **F10(35)** | 15 Campbell Court **M8(13)** | 14 Castlereagh Parade **K7** | 5 Chichester Park **G11** |
| 8 Brookvale Avenue **G10** | 15 Campbell Pk Avenue **M8** | 21 Castlereagh Place **J7** | 5 Chichester Pk Cent **G11(13)** |
| 8 Brookvale Court **G10(35)** | 8 Campbell's Row **G8** | 21 Castlereagh Road **K6** | 5 Chichester Park N. **G11** |
| 8 Brookvale Drive **G10** | 4 Camross Park **H15** | 13 Castlereagh Street **J7** | 8 Chichester Park S. **G11** |
| 8 Brookvale Fold **F10(8)** | 13 Canada Street **J7** | 26 Castlerobin Road **H3** | 5 Chichester Road **G11** |
| 8 Brookvale House **G10(24)** | 3 Canberra Park **E16** | 9 Castleton Av **H10(3)** | 2 Chichester Street **H8** |
| 8 Brookvale Parade **F10(6)** | 20 Candahar Street **H6** | 8 Castleton Gardens **G10** | 7 Chief Street **E9** |
| 8 Brookvale Street **F10** | 1 Canmore Court **F8(7)** | 26 Castleview Court **M6(20)** | 24 Chippendale Ct **D3(18)** |
| 7 Broom Street **E9** | 1 Canmore Street **F8** | 15 Castleview Road **N7** | 24 Chippendale Gdns **D3(19)** |
| 19 Broomhill Close **F4(1)** | 9 Canning Place **H9(7)** | 14 Castleview Terr **L5(2)** | 19 Chlorine Gdns **G6** |
| 19 Broomhill Court **F4(2)** | 9 Canning Street **H9** | 26 Castleward Park **H3(3)** | 14 Chobham Street **K8(18)** |
| 19 Broomhill Manor **F4(14)** | 8 Canning's Court **F8(5)** | 6 Catherine Row **H13(3)** | 1 Christian Place **F8(35)** |
| 19 Broomhill Park **G4** | 19 Canterbury Street **G6(23)** | 2 Catherine Street **H7(32)** | 23 Church Avenue **C2** |
| 19 Broomhill Pk Cent **G4(1)** | 13 Canton Court **J7(25)** | 2 Catherine Street N. **H7(6)** | 3 Church Crescent **F16** |
| 9 Brougham Street **H9** | 20 Cappagh Gardens **J5(3)** | 5 Cavanmore Gdns **C5** | 3 Church Drive **F16** |
| 20 Broughton Gardens **J6** | 13 Cappy Street **J7(62)** | 11 Cavehill Drive **F12** | 16 Church Green **Q7** |
| 20 Broughton Park **J6** | 19 Capstone Street **F5(6)** | 8 Cavehill Road **F11** | 2 Church Lane **H8** |
| 12 Brown Street **G8** | 8 Cardigan Drive **F10** | 11 Cavendish Court **E8(11)** | 3 Church Park **F16** |
| 12 Brown's Row **G8(7)** | 14 Carew Street **K8** | 1 Cavendish Square **F7(52)** | 21 Church Road **L5** |
| 12 Brown's Square **G8** | 12 Cargill Street **G8** | 11 Cavendish Street **E7** | 20 Church Road **J4** |
| 12 Bruce Street **G7** | 4 Carlan Close **G15(2)** | 11 Cawnpore Street **E8** | 4 Church Road **G15** |
| 8 Brucevale Court **G9(46)** | 13 Carlingford Street **J7** | 19 Ceara Court **G6(19)** | 1 Church Row **G8(64)** |
| 8 Brucevale Park **G9** | 8 Carlisle Circus **G9** | 8 Cedar Avenue **G10** | 12 Church Street **G8(70)** |
| 12 Brunswick Street **G7** | 8 Carlisle Parade **G9** | 27 Cedar Grove **N10** | 3 Church Way **F16** |
| 8 Bruslee Way **G9(19)** | 8 Carlisle Road **G9** | 26 Cedarhurst Court **J2(17)** | 22 Church Wynd **N6(9)** |
| 8 Brussels Street **F9(56)** | 8 Carlisle Square **G9(29)** | 26 Cedarhurst Rise **H2(5)** | 8 Churchill Street **G9** |
| 13 Bryansford Place **J7(29)** | 8 Carlisle Terrace **G9** | 26 Cedarhurst Road **H2** | 8 Churchview Ct **F9(28)** |
| 13 Bryson Court **J8(43)** | 8 Carlisle Walk **G9(20)** | 11 Central Arcade **H8(31)** | 21 Cicero Gardens **K6** |
| 13 Bryson Gardens **J8(44)** | 1 Carlow Street **F8** | 11 Centurion Street **E8** | 27 Circular Road **M9** |
| 13 Bryson Street **J8** | 19 Carmel Street **H6** | 11 Centurion Way **F8(83)** | 12 City Walk **G7(45)** |
| 17 Bunbeg Park **B5(9)** | 9 Carnalea Place **H9(4)** | 8 Century Street **F9(62)** | 12 City Way **G7(70)** |
| 19 Buncrana Gdns **B5(12)** | 21 Carnamena Avenue **K5** | 11 Ceylon Street **E8(19)** | 8 Clanchattan St **G10(5)** |
| 20 Burmah Street **H6** | 21 Carnamena Gdns **K5(3)** | 13 Chadolly Street **J8(66)** | 13 Clandeboye Drive **J8(62)** |
| 1 Burnaby Court **F7(13)** | 21 Carnamena Park **K5(4)** | 19 Chadwick Street **F6** | 13 Clandeboye Gdns **J8** |
| 1 Burnaby Park **F7(35)** | 1 Carnan Street **F8** | 13 Chamberlain Street **J8** | 13 Clandeboye Street **J7(56)** |
| 1 Burnaby Place **F7(12)** | 17 Carnanmore Gdns **B4(4)** | 13 Chambers Street **G7(102)** | 9 Clanmorris Street **H9** |
| 1 Burnaby Walk **F7(8)** | 17 Carnanmore Park **B4** | 14 Channing Street **K7** | 14 Clanroy Parade **L8** |
| 1 Burnaby Way **F7(6)** | 21 Carncaver Road **L5** | 12 Chapel Lane **G8(76)** | 14 Clara Avenue **K7** |
| 26 Burnside Avenue **J3** | 5 Carncoole Park **F12(1)** | 12 Charles Street South **G7** | 14 Clara Cres Lower **K7(6)** |
| 26 Burnside Park **J3** | 21 Carney Crescent **L5** | 19 Charleville Av **F8(5)** | 14 Clara Cres Upper **K7(7)** |
| 21 Burntollet Way **K5** | 13 Carnforth Street **J8(26)** | 8 Charleville Street **F9(23)** | 14 Clara Park **L7** |
| 20 Burren Way **J5** | 11 Carnmore Place **D7(23)** | 2 Charlotte Street **H7** | 15 Clara Road **M7** |
| 9 Bute Street **H10** | 17 Carnnamona Ct **C6(10)** | 8 Charnwood Avenue **F11** | 13 Clara Street **K7** |
| 8 Butler Place **E9(7)** | 4 Carnreagh Bend **G15** | 22 Charters Avenue **N6(6)** | 14 Clara Way **L7(8)** |
| 7 Butler Walk **E9(7)** | 4 Carnreagh Gdns **G15(3)** | 8 Chater Street **K8(8)** | 14 Clarawood Crescent **L7** |
| 7 Cabin Hill Court **M7(7)** | 20 Carolan Road **H5** | 13 Chatsworth Street **J7** | 14 Clarawood Drive **L6(2)** |
| 15 Cabin Hill Gdns **N7** | 10 Carolhill Drive **L9** | 14 Chelsea Street **K8** | 14 Clarawood Grove **L6(1)** |
| 15 Cabin Hill Mews **N7(9)** | 10 Carolhill Gardens **L9** | 26 Cheltenham Gdns **J5(6)** | 14 Clarawood Park **L6** |
| 15 Cabin Hill Park **M7** | 10 Carolhill Park **L9** | 20 Cheltenham Park **J5** | 14 Clarawood Park **L7(8)** |
| 13 Cable Close **J8(19)** | 1 Carolina Street **F8(44)** | 13 Chemical Street **J8** | 14 Clarawood Walk **L7(9)** |
| 19 Cadogan Park **F5** | 12 Carrick Hill **G8** | 23 Cherry Close **B3(6)** | 4 Clare Gardens **H5(10)** |
| 20 Cadogan Street **H6(5)** | 17 Carrigart Avenue **B5** | 23 Cherry Court **B3(4)** | 19 Claremont Court **G6(24)** |
| 27 Cairnburn Avenue **M9** | 13 Carrington Street **J7** | 23 Cherry Drive **B3** | 19 Claremont Mews **G6(4)** |
| 27 Cairnburn Crescent **M9** | 5 Carr's Glen Park **E11** | 23 Cherry Gardens **B3** | 19 Claremont Street **G6** |
| 27 Cairnburn Dell **M9(6)** | 21 Casaeldona Cres **L5** | 23 Cherry Park **B3(3)** | 12 Clarence Pl Mews **G7(9)** |
| 27 Cairnburn Drive **M9** | 21 Casaeldona Drive **L5(4)** | 23 Cherry Road **B3** | 12 Clarence Street **G7** |
| 27 Cairnburn Gardens **M9** | 21 Casaeldona Gdns **L5** | 23 Cherry Tree Walk **M7(8)** | 14 Clarence Street W. **G7(16)** |
| 27 Cairnburn Park **M9** | 21 Casaeldona Park **L5** | 23 Cherry Walk **B3(5)** | 14 Clarendon Avenue **K7** |
| 27 Cairnburn Road **M9** | 21 Casaeldona Rise **L5** | 19 Cherryhill **G5(7)** | 14 Clarke's Lane **G8(5)** |
| 1 Cairndale **D10(13)** | 12 Castle Arcade **G8(45)** | 16 Cherryhill Gardens **R8(4)** | 13 Claun Place **J7** |
| 3 Cairngorm Cres **E16** | 6 Castle Avenue **G12** | 15 Cherrytree **N6(10)** | 19 Cleaver Avenue **G5** |
| 1 Cairns Street **F8(11)** | 21 Castle Court **L5(5)** | 15 Cherryvalley **G5** | 19 Cleaver Court **G5(6)** |
| 26 Cairnshill Avenue **J2(3)** | 6 Castle Drive **G12** | 15 Cherryvalley Gdns **N7** | 19 Cleaver Gardens **G5** |
| 26 Cairnshill Court **J2(9)** | 6 Castle Gardens **G12** | 15 Cherryvalley Green **M7(2)** | 19 Cleaver Park **G5** |
| 26 Cairnshill Crescent **J2(6)** | | | 15 Cherryvalley Park **M7** | 12 Clementine Drive **G7(68)** |

12 Clementine **Gdns** G7(72)
12 Clementine Park G7(67)
26 Clevely Park J3
8 Clifton Crescent F10
8 Clifton Drive F10
8 Clifton Street G9
7 Cliftondene Cres E10
7 Cliftondene Gdns E10
7 Cliftondene Park E10
8 Cliftonpark Avenue F9
8 Cliftonville Avenue G10
8 Cliftonville Drive F10(2)
8 Cliftonville Parade F10(3)
8 Cliftonville Road F10
8 Cliftonville Street F10(4)
26 Cliveden Crescent J3
16 Cloghan Crescent P7(25)
16 Cloghan Gardens P7(2)
24 Cloghan Gardens E3(2)
16 Cloghan Park P7
14 Clonallon Gardens L8
14 Clonallon Court L8(43)
14 Clonallon Park L8
1 Clonard Court F8(52)
1 Clonard Crescent F8(48)
1 Clonard Gardens F8
1 Clonard Heights F8(50)
1 Clonard Place F8(51)
1 Clonard Rise F8(82)
1 Clonard Street F8
10 Clonaver Cres N. L9(14)
10 Clonaver Cres S. L9(15)
10 Clonaver Drive L9
10 Clonaver Park L9
4 Clonbeg Drive H15
18 Clondara Parade E6(3)
18 Clondara Street E6(2)
21 Clonduff Drive L5
17 Clonelly Avenue C5
12 Clonfadden Cres ,G8(55)
12 Clonfadden St G8(54)
14 Clonlee Drive L8
4 Clonmore Green G15
4 Clonmore Walk G15(4)
23 Cloona Avenue B4
23 Cloona Crescent B4
23 Cloona Park B3
19 Cloreen Park G6(9)
17 Closnamona Court C6(15)
11 Clovelly Street E8(14)
27 Cloverhill Gardens N9
15 Cloverhill Park N8
11 Clowney Street E7
13 Cluan Place J7(50)
13 Clyde Court J8(29)
12 Coar's Lane G8(6)
13 Coburg Street J7(51)
17 Cois Cluana C5(20)
26 Colby Park J3
1 Colchester Park F7(28)
2 Cole's Alley H8(12)
19 Colenso Court G6(11)
19 Colenso Parade G6
26 Coleshill Gardens H3(1)
23 Colin Road B4
23 Colindale Park B3
11 Colinpark Street E8(23)
6 Colinton Gardens G13
23 Colinview B1(3)
11 Colinview Street E8
11 Colinward Street E8
12 College Avenue G8(75)
12 College Court G8
19 College Gardens G6
19 College Green G6
19 College Park G6
19 College Park G6(13)
19 College Pk Avenue G6(21)
19 College Park East G6(20)
12 College Place N. G8(36)
12 College Square E. G8
12 College Square N. G8
12 College Street G8
12 College St Mews G8(37)
1 Colligan Street F7

17 Collin Gardens C5(11)
20 Collinbridge Av H6(7)
3 Collinbridge Close E15(5)
3 Collinbridgre Court E15(6)
3 Collinbridge Drive E15
3 Collinbridge Gdns E15
3 Collinbridge Park E15
3 Collinbridge Road F15
20 Collingwood Road H6(22)
3 Collinwald Avenue F15
3 Collinward Crescent F16
3 Collinward Drive F16(2)
3 Collinward Gdns F16
3 Collinward Grove F16
3 Collinward **Park** F15(4)
3 Columbia Street E9
14 Colvil Street K8
13 Comber Court J8(45)
13 Comber Gardens J8(32)
12 Combermere St G7(84)
18 Commedagh Drive D5
12 Commercial Court G8(20)
26 Commons Brae J3
12 Conduit Street G7
20 Coneen Way J5
8 Coniston Close F9(69)
1 Connaught Street F7
10 Connsbank Road K9
14 Connsbrook Avenue K8
14 Connsbrook Drive K8
14 Connsbrook Park L9
14 Connswater Grove K8(49)
14 Connswater Mews K8(50)
14 Connswater Street K8
13 Constance Street J7(1)
13 Convention Court J8(42)
13 Convention Walk J8(9)
1 Conway Court F8(55)
1 Conway Link F8(47)
1 Conway Square F8(84)
1 Conway Street F8
1 Conway Walk F8(63)
2 Cooke Court H7
2 Cooke Mews H7
2 Cooke Place H7(8)
2 Cooke Street H7
5 Cooldarragh Park F11
5 Cooldarragh Pk N. F11(3)
5 Coolderry Gardens H15
1 Coolfin Street F7
19 Coolmore Street F6
23 Coolmoyne House B2(11)
5 Coolmoyne Park G12
17 Coolnasilla Avenue C5
17 Coolnasilla Close C5(15)
17 Coolnasilla Drive C5
17 Coolnasilla Gardens C5
17 Coolnasilla Park C6(16)
17 Coolnasilla Park E. C5
17 Coolnasilla Park S. C5
17 Coolnasilla Park W. C5
4 Coolshannagh Park H16
8 Coombe Hill Park H11
8 Copperfield Street G9
17 Corby Way C5
22 Cormorant Park M5(2)
12 Corn Market G8
16 Coronation Park Q7
2 Corporation Square H8(36)
2 Corporation Street H8
17 Corrib Avenue B5
23 Corrina Avenue B3
23 Corrina Park B3
9 Corry Link H9
9 Corry Place H9
9 Corry Road H9
8 Cosgrave Court G10(11)
8 Cosgrave Street G9(5)
8 Cotlands Green B3(11)
26 Cotswold Avenue J3
8 Court Street F9(16)
14 Courtrai Street F9(46)
2 Coyle's Place H7(27)
2 Coyle Street H7(21)
1 Craig's Terrace F8(13)

12 Craigmore Way G7(48)
7 Cranbrook Court E10(5)
7 Cranbrook Gdns E10(4)
8 Cranburn Street G9(21)
24 Cranfield Gardens D3(7)
19 Cranmore Avenue F5
19 Cranmore Gardens F5
19 Cranmore Park F5
7 Craven Street F8(8)
21 Crawford Park L5(3)
23 Credenhill Park B3
17 Creeslough Gdns B5(14)
17 Creeslough Park B5
17 Creeslough Park B5(25)
17 Creeslough Walk B5(13)
18 Creeve Walk D5
22 Creevy Avenue M6
22 Creevy Way M6(12
21 Cregagh Court K6(6)
21 Cregagh Park K5
21 Cregagh Park East K5
21 Cregagh Road K6
20 Cregagh Street J6
23 Creighton Road B3
19 Crescent Gardens G6(1)
12 Crescent Lane G7(56)
26 Crevenish Walk H3(2)
19 Cricklewood Cres G4(3)
19 Cricklewood Park G4
8 Crimea Close F9(13)
21 Crimea Court F8(67)
8 Crimea Street F9
17 Croaghan Gdns C5(12)
1 Crocus Street F7
16 Crofthouse Court P7(28)
2 Cromac Square H7
2 Cromac Street H7
17 Cromwell Road G7
12 Crosby Street G8(28)
20 Cross Parade H6
1 Crosscollyer St G10(14)
8 Crossland Court F8(9)
1 Crossland Street F8(6)
13 Crossley Street J7(16)
4 Crossreagh Drive G15
12 Crown Entry G8(48)
7 Crumlin Gardens E9
7 Crumlin Road D10
14 Crystal Street K7
7 Cuan Parade E8
13 Cuba Walk J8(10)
7 Cullingtree Road F7
17 Culmore Gardens B5(16)
9 Cultra Street H9(2)
16 Cumberland Av Q7(2)
16 Cumberland Close Q7(9)
16 Cumberland Drive Q7
16 Cumberland Park Q7
16 Cumberland Road Q7
1 Cumberland Street F8(24)
1 Cumberland Walk F8(15)
13 Cuming Road J8
1 Cupar Street Lower F8
1 Cupar Street Upper E8
1 Cupar Way F8
1 Curtis Street G8
20 Curzon Street H6(6)
19 Cussick Street F6
2 Custom House Sq H8(6)
23 Cypress Close C1
14 Cyprus Avenue L7
14 Cyprus Gardens L7
14 Cyprus Park L7
11 Dairy Street E7(1)
11 Daisyfield Street F9(51)
11 Daisyhill Court D7(28)
17 Dalebrook Avenue C4
17 Dalebrook Park C4
16 Dalry Park P7(6)
2 Dalton Street H8(33)
20 Damascus Street H6
14 Dandy Street H14
13 Dann's Row J7(18)
8 Danube Street F9
7 Daphne Street F7

9 Dargan Crescent J11
9 Dargan Drive J11
6 Dargan Road J11
1 David Street F8
8 Dawson Street G9
12 Dayton Street G8(30)
8 Deacon Street G10
14 Dean Crooks Fold L7(15)
8 Deanby Gardens F10
24 De Beere Court D3(22)
14 Dee Street K8
4 Deerfin Park G15
7 Deerpark Drive E10
7 Deerpark Gardens E10
8 Deerpark Grove F10(1)
7 Deerpark Parade E10(1)
7 Deerpark Road E10
14 Dehra Grove L8(4)
21 Delamont Park L5
13 Delaware Street J7
20 Delhi Parade H6
20 Delhi Street H6
18 Denewood Drive D6(7)
18 Denewood Park D6
8 Denmark Street G9
20 Dennet End J5(11)
10 Denorrton Park L9
27 Depot Road M10
20 Deramore Avenue H5
25 Deramore Court G4(4)
19 Deramore Drive F4
20 Deramore Gardens H5
19 Deramore Park F4
19 Deramore Park South F4
20 Deramore Street H5(12)
1 Derby Terrace F8(42)
20 Derlett Street H6(20)
18 Derrin Pass D5(2)
4 Derry Hill G15
3 Derry Road E16
4 Derrycoole Park H16(14)
4 Derrycoole Walk H16(18)
4 Derrycoole Way G15
19 Derryvolgie Avenue F6
13 Derwent Street J8
1 Devenish Court F8(68)
14 Devon Drive K8(2)
14 Devon Parade K8
12 Devonshire Close G8(2)
12 Devonshire Place G7(1)
7 Devonshire Street F7
12 Devonshire Way G7(3)
8 Dewey Street F9
11 Dhu-Varren Crescent E8
11 Dhu-Varren Parade E8
11 Dhu-Varren Park E8
24 Diamond Avenue D4(2)
24 Diamond Gardens D4
21 Dill Road K6
7 Disraeli Court E9(11)
7 Disraeli Street E9
7 Disraeli Walk E9(12)
7 Distillery Street F7
1 Distillery Court F7(21)
1 Distillery Way F7(22)
12 Divis Court G8(74)
18 Divis Drive D6
12 Divis Street G8
11 Divismore Crescent D7
11 Divismore Park D7
11 Divismore Way D7(4)
9 Dock Street H9
7 Donaldson Crescent E9
13 Donard Street J7
12 Donegall Arcade G8(57)
19 Donegall Avenue F6
19 Donegall Gardens F6
12 Donegall Lane G8(4)
19 Donegall Parade F6(8)
24 Donegall Park D4
6 Donegall Park Av G12
12 Donegall Pass G7
12 Donegall Place G8
2 Donegall Quay H8
1 Donegall Road F7

12 Donegall Square East **G8**
12 Donegall Sq Mews **G7(10)**
12 Donegall Square N. **G8**
12 Donegall Square S. **G7**
12 Donegall Square West **G8**
12 Donegall Street **G8**
2 Donegall Street Pl **G8(21)**
19 Donnybrook Street **F6**
8 Donore Court **G9(23)**
8 Donore Place **G9(8)**
21 Donovan Parade **K6**
17 Doon Cottages **B4(14)**
24 Doon End **D3(4)**
17 Doon Road **B4**
4 Doonbeg Drive **G16**
25 Dorchester Park **F3**
14 Douglas Court **L8(16)**
12 Dover Court **G8(29)**
12 Dover Place **G8**
12 Dover Street **G8**
12 Dover Walk **G8(27)**
17 Downfine Gardens **C6(2)**
18 Downfine Park **D6(4)**
18 Downfine Walk **D6(2)**
25 Downhill Avenue **G2**
25 Downhill Walk **G2(3)**
1 Downing Street **F8(41)**
14 Downpatrick Street **K8(45)**
21 Downshire Parade **K5(2)**
21 Downshire Park Cent. **K5**
21 Downshire Park East **K5**
21 Downshire Park N. **K5**
21 Downshire Park S. **K5**
12 Downshire Place **G7(33)**
21 Downshire Road **K5**
6 Downview Avenue **G12**
6 Downview Crescent **G12**
6 Downview Drive **G12**
6 Downview Gardens **G12**
5 Downview Lodge **G13(8)**
6 Downview Park **G12**
5 Downview Park West **F12**
5 Downview Park W. **G12(9)**
17 Drenia **C4(4)**
20 Dromara Street **H6(17)**
20 Dromore Street **J6**
26 Drumart Drive **H2**
26 Drumart Gardens **H2(2)**
26 Drumart Green **H2(4)**
26 Drumart Square **H2(3)**
25 Drumairn Walk **G2(4)**
25 Drumcairn Close **G2**
4 Drumcor Court **G15(6)**
4 Drumcor Green **G15(1)**
4 Drumcree Place **G15**
20 Drumkeen Court **J4(5)**
20 Drumkeen Manor **J4(7)**
24 Drummond Park **E4(1)**
24 Drummond Park **E3(12)**
20 Drumragh End **J5(2)**
14 Dub Lane **E3**
12 Dublin Road **G7**
13 Dublin Street **J7(33)**
13 Dudley Street **H6**
9 Dufferin Road **H9**
7 Duffield Park **D9**
13 Duke Street **J8(50)**
2 Dunbar Street **H8**
14 Dunblane Avenue **E10**
11 Dunboyne Park **D8**
8 Duncairn Avenue **G9**
8 Duncairn Gardens **G9**
8 Duncairn Parade **G9**
8 Duncoole Park **F12**
9 Duncrue Crescent **H11**
9 Duncrue Link **H11**
9 Duncrue Pass **H11**
9 Duncrue Place **H11**
9 Duncrue Road **H11**
9 Duncrue Street **H9**
9 Duncrue Street **H10**
1 Dundee Street **B8(76)**
14 Dundela Avenue **L8**
14 Dundela Close **L8(39)**
14 Dundela Court **L8(20)**

14 Dundela Crescent **L8**
14 Dundela Drive **L8(11)**
14 Dundela Flats **L8(12)**
14 Dundela Gardens **L8**
14 Dundela Manor **L8(31)**
14 Dundela Park **K8**
14 Dundela Street **L8**
14 Dundela View **L8(10)**
16 Dundonald Heights **Q7(7)**
7 Duneden Park **E10**
17 Dungloe Crescent **B5**
17 Dungore Gardens **B4**
7 Dunkeld Gardens **E11**
8 Dunlambert Avenue **G11**
8 Dunlambert Drive **G11**
8 Dunlambert Gardens **G11**
8 Dunlambert Park **G11**
1 Dunlewey Street **F8(101)**
1 Dunlewey Walk **F8(10)**
4 Dunloy Gardens **G15**
4 Dunluce Avenue **F6**
18 Dunmisk Park **D5**
18 Dunmisk Terrace **D5(5)**
8 Dunmore Cres **G10(22)**
8 Dunmore Drive **G10**
7 Dunmore Street **F8**
11 Dunmoyle Street **E8(1)**
24 Dunmurry Lane **D2**
7 Dunowen Gardens **F10**
4 Dunowen Pass **G16(3)**
14 Dunraven Avenue **K7**
14 Dunraven Crescent **K7**
14 Dunraven Drive **K7(27)**
14 Dunraven Gardens **K7**
14 Dunraven Parade **K7**
14 Dunraven Park **K7**
26 Dunseverick Avenue **H2**
13 Dunvegan Street **J7**
1 Dunville Street **F7**
12 Durham Court **G8(32)**
12 Durham Street **G8**
20 Earl Close **G9(34)**
20 Earl Haig Crescent **J6(5)**
20 Earl Haig Gardens **J6(11)**
20 Earl Haig Park **J6**
11 Earlscourt Street **E7**
14 Earlswood Court **L8(19)**
14 Earlswood Grove **L8(32)**
14 Earlswood Park **L8(13)**
14 Earlswood Road **L8**
14 East Bread Street **K7**
2 East Bridge Street **H7**
16 East Link Road **Q7**
10 East Twin Road **K10**
4 East Way **H15**
14 Eastleigh Crescent **L7**
15 Eastleigh Dale **M8(14)**
14 Eastleigh Drive **L8**
14 Easton Avenue **F10(33)**
8 Easton Crescent **F10**
19 Eblana Street **G6**
19 Ebor Drive **F6**
19 Ebor Parade **F6**
19 Ebor Street **F6**
14 Ebrington Gardens **L8**
8 Eccles Street **F9**
25 Edenderry Road **F2**
8 Edenderry Street **F9(27)**
17 Edenmore Drive **C5**
14 Edenvale Court **L8(25)**
14 Edenvale Crescent **L8**
14 Edenvale Drive **L8**
14 Edenvale Gardens **L8(5)**
14 Edenvale Grove **L8(26)**
23 Edenvale Meadows **C3(5)**
14 Edenvale Park **L8(6)**
23 Edenvale Park **C3**
13 Edgar Street **J8**
14 Edgecumbe Drive **L8(3)**
14 Edgecumbe Gardens **L8**
14 Edgecumbe Park **L8(37)**
14 Edgecumbe View **L8(36)**
19 Edinburgh Street **F6**
13 Edith Street **J7(30)**
8 Edlingham Street **G9**

8 Edlingham Street **G9(31)**
2 Edward Street **H8**
8 Edwina Street **F8(85)**
1 Egeria Street **F7**
19 Eglantine Avenue **G6**
19 Eglantine Gardens **G6(8)**
19 Eglantine Place **F6(3)**
19 Eglinton Street **G9**
12 Egmont Gardens **G7(5)**
8 Eia Street **G10**
19 Eileen Gardens **F5(1)**
19 Elaine Street **G6**
21 Elesington Court **K6(3)**
20 Elgin Street **H6**
8 Elimgrove Street **F10(11)**
2 Eliza Street **H7**
2 Eliza Street Close **H7(4)**
2 Eliza Street Terr **H7(34)**
23 Elm Corner **B2**
12 Elm Court **G7(57)**
14 Elm Court **E16(12)**
12 Elm Street **G7**
14 Elmdale Street **K7**
3 Elmfield Avenue **F15**
3 Elmfield Crescent **F15**
3 Elmfield Drive **F15**
3 Elmfield Park **F15**
3 Elmfield Road **F15**
7 Elmfield Street **E9**
7 Elmfield Street **E9(11)**
19 Elmwood Avenue **G6**
19 Elmwood Mews **G6**
6 Elmwood **H6(15)**
11 Elswick Street **E8(24)**
13 Emerald Street **J7**
1 Emerson Street **F8**
1 Empire Drive **F7(51)**
1 Empire Parade **F7**
1 Empire Street **F7**
7 Enfield Drive **E9(20)**
7 Enfield Parade **E9(19)**
7 Enfield Street **E9**
14 Enid Drive **L7**
14 Enid Parade **L7**
14 Enniskeane Avenue **G16**
13 Epworth Street **J7**
12 Erin Way **G7(92)**
24 Erinvale Avenue **D3**
24 Erinvale Drive **D3**
24 Erinvale Gardens **D3(12)**
24 Erinvale Park **D3(11)**
17 Errigal Park **C5(7)**
17 Erris Grove **B4**
7 Erskine Street **J8**
7 Erskdale Gardens **E10**
8 Esmond Street **E8(9)**
21 Espie Way **L5**
20 Essex Street **H6**
8 Esther Street **G10**
7 Estoril Park **E10**
14 Ethel Street **F6**
8 Etna Drive **E10**
7 Eureka Drive **G7**
13 Euston Parade **J7**
1 Euterpe Street **F7(49)**
14 Evelyn Avenue **K8**
8 Evelyn Gardens **F11**
13 Eversleigh Street **J7(32)**
24 Everton Drive **K5**
8 Evewilliam Park **G11(5)**
8 Evolina Street **G9**
12 Exchange Place **G8(19)**
12 Exchange Street **H8(2)**
12 Exchange St West **G8(18)**
1 Excise Walk **F7(24)**
7 Faburn Park **D10**
7 Factory Street **K7(1)**
8 Fairfax Court **F9(29)**
6 Fairhill Gardens **G12(3)**
6 Fairhill Park **G12**
6 Fairhill Walk **G12**
6 Fairhill Way **G12(4)**
24 Fairview Avenue **E3**
8 Fairview Street **G9(27)**
24 Fairway Crescent **E3(5)**

24 Fairway Drive **E3(6)**
24 Fairway Gardens **E3**
22 Fairway Gardens **M6**
3 Fairyknowe Drive **F15(1)**
3 Fairyknowe Gdns **G15(5)**
3 Fairyknowe Park **G15**
17 Falcarragh Drive **B5**
19 Falcon Road **F5**
1 Falls Court **F8(46)**
11 Falls Road **E7**
11 Fallswater Drive **E7(6)**
11 Fallswater Street **E7**
19 Fane Street **F6**
23 Farmhill **C4(6)**
22 Farmhurst Green **N6**
22 Farmhurst Way **N6(4)**
3 Farmley Crescent **E16**
3 Farmley Gardens **E16**
3 Farmley Mews **E15(7)**
3 Farmley Park **E16**
3 Farmley Road **E16**
20 Farnham Street **H6**
3 Farrier Court **E16(13)**
7 Farringdon Court **E10(2)**
7 Farringdon Gdns **E10(3)**
7 Farringdon House **G10(10)**
14 Fashoda Street **K7**
20 Federation Street **J6**
12 Felt Street **G7**
14 Ferguson Drive **L8(34)**
13 Fern Street **J8(15)**
19 Ferndale Court **F5(3)**
23 Ferndale House **B1(13)**
19 Ferndale Street **F5**
10 Fernvale Street **L9(17)**
20 Fernwood Street **H5**
9 Fife Street **H10**
1 Fifth Street **F8**
24 Finaghy Park Cent. **D4**
24 Finaghy Park North **D4**
24 Finaghy Park South **D3**
18 Finaghy Road North **C4**
24 Finaghy Road South **D3**
24 Finbank Court **E3(15)**
24 Finbank Gardens **E3**
24 Finch Close **E3(10)**
24 Finch Court **E3(26)**
24 Finch Grove **E3**
24 Finch Place **E3(27)**
24 Finch Way **E3(13)**
27 Finchley Drive **M9(7)**
27 Finchley Gardens **M9(8)**
27 Finchley Park **M9**
27 Finchley Vale **M9**
24 Findon Gardens **E3**
24 Findon Grove **E3(25)**
24 Findon Place **E3(11)**
7 Fingal Street **E9(22)**
12 Fingals Court **G8(15)**
6 Finlay Park **H13**
13 Finmore Court **J8(11)**
12 Finn Square **G8(39)**
24 Finnis Close **E3(14)**
24 Finnis Drive **E3**
26 Finsbury Park **J2(5)**
20 Finsbury Street **J6(13)**
14 Finvoy Street **K8**
24 Finwood Court **E3(17)**
24 Finwood Park **E3**
27 Firmount Crescent **N11**
1 First Street **F8**
12 Fisherwick Place **G7(7)**
20 Fitzroy Avenue **H6**
20 Fitzroy Court **H6(8)**
20 Fitzwilliam Avenue **H5**
19 Fitzwilliam Street **G6**
8 Flax Street **F9**
7 Flaxton Place **D11(13)**
8 Fleetwood Street **G9(51)**
14 Flora Street **K7**
3 Floral Gardens **F15**
3 Floral Road **F15**
8 Florence Court **G9(48)**
8 Florence Place **G9**

| | | | | | | | |
|---|---|---|---|---|---|---|---|
| 8 | Florence Square **G9(44)** | 27 | Garnerville Road **M10** | 12 | Glenburn Alley **G7(36)** | 4 | Glenmount Road **H14** |
| 8 | Florence Walk **G9(24)** | 17 | Garnock **C4** | 23 | Glenburn Court **C2(9)** | 18 | Glenmurry Court **D6(22)** |
| 20 | Florenceville Avenue **H5** | 23 | Garnock Hill **C4** | 8 | Glenburn Park **F11** | 8 | Glenpark Court **F9(57)** |
| 20 | Florenceville Drive **H5** | 27 | Garrannard Manor **M9(14)** | 23 | Glenburn Road **C2** | 8 | Glenpark Street **F9** |
| 13 | Florida Drive **J7** | 27 | Garrannard Park **M9** | 23 | Glenburn Road South **C2** | 8 | Glenravel Street **G9(37)** |
| 13 | Florida Street **J7(65)** | 24 | Garron Crescent **D3** | 7 | Glencairn Crescent **E9** | 8 | Glenrosa Link **G9(13)** |
| 20 | Flush Drive **J5(5)** | 4 | Garton Way **G14** | 3 | Glencairn Drive **E16** | 8 | Glenrosa Street **G9** |
| 20 | Flush Gardens **J5(8)** | 17 | Gartree Place **C5** | 7 | Glencairn Park **E16** | 8 | Glenrosa Street S. **G9(2)** |
| 20 | Flush Green **J5** | 14 | Gawn Street **K8** | 7 | Glencairn Pass **D10** | 17 | Glenshane Gardens **C5(9)** |
| 20 | Flush Park **J5** | 16 | Geary Road **P6** | 7 | Glencairn Road **D9** | 21 | Glensharragh Avenue **K5** |
| 17 | Fodnamona Court **C6(14)** | 24 | Geeragh Place **D3** | 7 | Glencairn Street **E9** | 21 | Glensharragh Gardens **K5** |
| 25 | Forest Hill **F4(10)** | 19 | Geneva Gardens **G5(11)** | 7 | Glencairn Walk **D10** | 21 | Glensharragh Park **K5(5)** |
| 23 | Forest Park **B3** | 1 | Genoa Street **F7(47)** | 7 | Glencairn Way **D10** | 23 | Glenshesk Park **C2** |
| 11 | Forest Street **E8** | 8 | Geoffrey Street **F9(66)** | 5 | Glencoe Park **G13** | 21 | Glen Side **K5(6)** |
| 11 | Forfar Street **E8** | 7 | Ghent Place **F9(70)** | 17 | Glencolin Avenue **B5(5)** | 8 | Glenside Drive **D10(2)** |
| 7 | Formby Park **E11** | 25 | Giants Ring Road **F2** | 17 | Glencolin Close **B5(3)** | 7 | Glenside Parade **D10** |
| 8 | Forster Street **F9(12)** | 20 | Gibson Park Av **J6(10)** | 17 | Glencolin Court **B5(22)** | 7 | Glenside Park **D10** |
| 12 | Forsythe Street **G8(28)** | 20 | Gibson Park Drive **J6(6)** | 17 | Glencolin Drive **B5** | 17 | Glenties Drive **B5** |
| 16 | Fort Hill **Q7** | 20 | Gibson Park Gardens **J6** | 17 | Glencolin Grove **B5(23)** | 8 | Glentilt Street **F9(63)** |
| 16 | Fort Road **Q6** | 1 | Gibson Street **F7** | 17 | Glencolin Heights **B5(1)** | 13 | Glentoran Place **J7(42)** |
| 11 | Fort Street **E8** | 22 | Gilbourne Court **N6** | 17 | Glencolin Park **B5(2)** | 7 | Glenvale Street **E9(3)** |
| 11 | Forth Parade **E8(2)** | 22 | Gilnahirk Avenue **N6** | 17 | Glencolin Rise **B5(24)** | 14 | Glenvarlock Street **K7** |
| 7 | Forthbrook Court **D9(8)** | 22 | Gilnahirk Crescent **N6** | 17 | Glencolin Walk **B5(4)** | 17 | Glenveagh Drive **B5** |
| 7 | Forthriver Close **D10(3)** | 22 | Gilnahirk Drive **N6** | 17 | Glencolin Way **B5(6)** | 17 | Glenveagh Park **B5(8)** |
| 7 | Forthriver Cres **D10(7)** | 22 | Gilnahirk Park **N6** | 8 | Glencollyer Street **G10** | 22 | Glenview Avenue **M5** |
| 7 | Forthriver Dale **D10** | 22 | Gilnahirk Rise **N6** | 6 | Glencoole Park **E16(15)** | 8 | Glenview Court **F9(34)** |
| 7 | Forthriver Drive **D10** | 22 | Gilnahirk Road **N6** | 18 | Glencourt **D6(16)** | 22 | Glenview Crescent **M5** |
| 7 | Forthriver Fold **D9(7)** | 22 | Gilnahirk Walk **N6** | 20 | Glencregagh Court **J4(3)** | 22 | Glenview Drive **M5(1)** |
| 7 | Forthriver Green **D10** | 20 | Gipsy Street **H5** | 20 | Glencregagh Drive **J4** | 22 | Glenview Gardens **M5** |
| 7 | Forthriver Link **D10** | 8 | Glandore Avenue **G11** | 20 | Glencregagh Park **J4** | 22 | Glenview Heights **M5** |
| 7 | Forthriver Parade **D10** | 8 | Glandore Drive **G11** | 23 | Glendale **C3** | 21 | Glenview Park **L5** |
| 7 | Forthriver Park **D10** | 8 | Glandore Gardens **G11** | 26 | Glendale Avenue East **J3** | 3 | Glenview Street **F9** |
| 7 | Forthriver Pass **D9(6)** | 8 | Glandore Parade **G10(2)** | 26 | Glendale Avenue N. **J3** | 17 | Glenview Terrace **B4(5)** |
| 7 | Forthriver Road **D9** | 8 | Glanleam Drive **G11** | 26 | Glendale Avenue S. **J3** | 3 | Glenwell Avenue **E15** |
| 7 | Forthriver Road **D10** | 4 | Glanroy Crescent **H16** | 26 | Glendale Avenue W. **J3(1)** | 3 | Glenwell Crescent **E15** |
| 7 | Forthriver Way **D9** | 4 | Glanroy Terrace **H16(19)** | 14 | Glendale Court **K8(26)** | 3 | Glenwell Drive **E15(1)** |
| 1 | Fortuna Street **F7** | 8 | Glantane Drive **G11** | 26 | Glendale Park **J3** | 3 | Glenwell Gardens **E15** |
| 8 | Fortwilliam Court **G11(16)** | 8 | Glantrasna Drive **G11(20)** | 27 | Glendhu Grove **M10(10)** | 3 | Glenwell Grove **E15** |
| 8 | Fortwilliam Crescent **H11** | 8 | Glanworth Drive **G11** | 27 | Glendhu Manor **M10** | 3 | Glenwell Park **E15** |
| 5 | Fortwilliam Drive **G11** | 8 | Glanworth Gardens **G10** | 27 | Glendhu Park **M10** | 3 | Glenwell Road **E15** |
| 8 | Fortwilliam Fold **G11(26)** | 9 | Glasgow Street **H10** | 20 | Glendower Street **J6** | 13 | Glenwherry Place **J7(4)** |
| 8 | Fortwilliam Gdns **G11(19)** | 17 | Glassmullan Gardens **C5** | 23 | Glendun Park **C2** | 1 | Glenwood Street **F8(95)** |
| 6 | Fortwilliam Grange **H11(4)** | 5 | Glastonbury Avenue **G12** | 3 | Glenelm Park **F15(3)** | 2 | Gloucester Street **H8** |
| 8 | Fortwilliam Parade **G11** | 23 | Glasvey Crescent **B3(2)** | 12 | Glenfarne Street **F9(22)** | 4 | Glynn Park **G16(1)** |
| 6 | Fortwilliam Park **G11** | 23 | Glasvey Drive **B3** | 12 | Glengall Lane **G7(13)** | 2 | Gordon Street **H8** |
| 6 | Fortwilliam R'about **H11** | 23 | Glasvey Rise **B3** | 12 | Glengall Mews **G7(14)** | 11 | Gortfin Street **E7** |
| 12 | Fountain Lane **G8(44)** | 3 | Glebe Gardens **F16** | 12 | Glengall Street **G7** | 22 | Gortgrib Drive **N6** |
| 12 | Fountain Street **G8** | 3 | Glebe Road **F16** | 17 | Glengoland Avenue **B4** | 15 | Gortin Drive **N7** |
| 19 | Fountainville Av **G6(14)** | 3 | Glebe Road **C2** | 17 | Glengoland Crescent **B4** | 15 | Gortin Park **N7** |
| 14 | Foxglove Street **K7(9)** | 3 | Glebe Road East **F16** | 17 | Glengoland Gardens **B4** | 22 | Gortland Avenue **N6(5)** |
| 8 | Foyle Court **F9** | 3 | Glebe Road West **F16** | 17 | Glengoland Parade **B4** | 22 | Gortland Park **N6** |
| 4 | Foyle Hill **H16(12)** | 3 | Glebe Villas **F16(1)** | 17 | Glengoland Park **B4** | 4 | Gortmore Terrace **H16(5)** |
| 12 | Francis Street **G8** | 3 | Glebecoole Avenue **F16** | 15 | Glengormley Park **F15** | 17 | Gortnamona Court **C6(7)** |
| 13 | Frank Place **J7(15)** | 3 | Glebecoole Drive **F16(3)** | 23 | Glenhead Avenue **C2** | 17 | Gortnamona Hts **C6(6)** |
| 13 | Frank Street **J7(52)** | 3 | Glebecoole Park **F16** | 17 | Glenhill Court **F9(58)** | 17 | Gortnamona Place **C6(9)** |
| 12 | Franklin Street **G8** | 18 | Glen Crescent **D6** | 18 | Glenhill Park **D6** | 17 | Gortnamona Rise **C6(5)** |
| 12 | Franklin Street Pl. **G7(11)** | 27 | Glen Ebor Heights **N10(2)** | 26 | Glenholm Avenue **J3** | 17 | Gortnamona View **C6(8)** |
| 13 | Fraser Pass **J8(7)** | 27 | Glen Ebor Park **M10** | 26 | Glenholm Crescent **J3** | 17 | Gortnamona Way **C6** |
| 13 | Fraser Street **J8(4)** | 18 | Glen Parade **D6** | 26 | Glenholm Drive **J3** | 13 | Gotha Street **J7(34)** |
| 8 | Frederick Street **G9** | 22 | Glen Rise **M6(16)** | 26 | Glenholm Park **J3** | 16 | Govan Drive **P7(21)** |
| 19 | Frenchpark Street **F6** | 17 | Glen Road **C5** | 14 | Glenhoy Drive **K7(14)** | 14 | Grace Avenue **K7** |
| 2 | Friendly Place **H7(25)** | 22 | Glen Road **M6** | 26 | Glenhugh Crescent **J2(1)** | 2 | Grace Street **H7** |
| 2 | Friendly Row **H7(5)** | 27 | Glen Road **M9** | 26 | Glenhugh Park **J2** | 8 | Gracehill Court **F9(35)** |
| 2 | Friendly Street **H7** | 17 | Glen Road Cotts. **C5(22)** | 6 | Glenhurst Drive **G13** | 26 | Gracemount Park **J2** |
| 2 | Friendly Way **H7(7)** | 23 | Glenann Avenue **C2** | 6 | Glenhurst Gardens **G13(7)** | 21 | Graham Gardens **K6(9)** |
| 13 | Frome Street **J8** | 11 | Glenalina Crescent **D7** | 6 | Glenhurst Parade **G13(2)** | 4 | Grainon Way **G16(4)** |
| 18 | Fruithill Park **D5** | 11 | Glenalina Gardens **D7(6)** | 27 | Glenlea Grove **M10(4)** | 14 | Grampian Avenue **K8** |
| 12 | Fulton Street **G7(98)** | 11 | Glenalina Park **D7** | 27 | Glenlea Park **M10** | 14 | Grampian Close **K8(30)** |
| 12 | Gaffikin Street **G7** | 11 | Glenalina Pass **D7(5)** | 27 | Glenloch Gardens **M10(9)** | 14 | Grand Parade **K7** |
| 8 | Gainsborough Drive **G10** | 11 | Glenalina Road **D7** | 27 | Glenluce Drive **M10** | 16 | Grand Prix Park **Q7** |
| 20 | Galwally Avenue **H4** | 13 | Glenallen Street **J8** | 27 | Glenluce Green **M10(3)** | 23 | Grange Avenue **C3(2)** |
| 20 | Galwally Park **J4** | 12 | Glenalpin Street **G7** | 27 | Glenluce Walk **M10** | 23 | Grange Park **C3** |
| 16 | Galway Court **Q7(10)** | 8 | Glenard Brook **F10** | 27 | Glenmachan Avenue **N9(3)** | 24 | Grangeville Drive **D4(3)** |
| 16 | Galway Drive **Q7** | 23 | Glenariff Drive **C2** | 27 | Glenmachan Drive **N9** | 24 | Grangeville Gardens **D4** |
| 16 | Galway Park **Q7** | 24 | Glenarm Square **E3** | 27 | Glenmachan Grove **M9(10)** | 16 | Grangewood Hts **Q8(4)** |
| 16 | Galway Mews **Q7(11)** | 4 | Glenbane Avenue **H16** | 27 | Glenmachan Mews **N9(5)** | 16 | Grangewood Manor **Q8** |
| 12 | Galway Street **G8(61)** | 7 | Glenbank Drive **D10** | 27 | Glenmachan Park **N10(1)** | 16 | Grangewood Park **R8(13)** |
| 2 | Gamble Street **H8(34)** | 7 | Glenbank Parade **D10(5)** | 27 | Glenmachan Place **E6(1)** | 16 | Grangewood Terr **Q8(13)** |
| 12 | Gardiner Place **G8** | 7 | Glenbank Place **D10** | 27 | Glenmachan Road **N9** | 18 | Gransha Avenue **D6** |
| 12 | Gardiner Street **G8** | 3 | Glenbourne Avenue **E16(5)** | 19 | Glenmachan Street **F6** | 18 | Gransha Crescent **D6** |
| 9 | Garmoyle Street **H9** | 14 | Glenbrook Avenue **K7** | 27 | Glenmachan Tower | 18 | Gransha Drive **D6** |
| 27 | Garnerville Avenue **M10** | 7 | Glenbryn Drive **E10** | | **N10(31)** | 18 | Gransha Gardens **D6** |
| 27 | Garnerville Gardens **M10** | 7 | Glenbryn Gardens **E10** | 27 | Glenmillan Drive **M9** | 18 | Gransha Green **D6** |
| 27 | Garnerville Grove **M10(2)** | 7 | Glenbryn Parade **E10** | 27 | Glenmillan Park **M9** | 18 | Gransha Grove **D6(6)** |
| 27 | Garnerville Park **M10** | 7 | Glenbryn Park **E10** | 13 | Glenmore Street **J8** | 4 | Gransha Grove **G16(2)** |

# ALPHABETICAL STREET INDEX

18 Gransha Parade **D6**
17 Gransha Park **D6**
18 Gransha Rise **D6(3)**
16 Gransha Road **Q6**
16 Gransha Walk **Q7(5)**
18 Gransha Way **D6(14)**
16 Granton Park **P7**
17 Granville Place **F7(4)**
5 Grasmere Gardens **F11**
6 Grays Court **H13**
6 Gray's Lane **G13**
25 Gray's Park **G2**
25 Grays Park Avenue **G2**
25 Gray's Park Drive **G2(11)**
25 Gray's Park Gdns **G2(5)**
6 Graymount Crescent **H13**
6 Graymount Drive **H13**
6 Graymount Gdns **G13(4)**
6 Graymount Grove **H13(1)**
6 Graymount Parade **H13**
6 Graymount Park **H13**
6 Graymount Road **H13**
6 Graymount Terr **H13(2)**
2 Great George's Street **H9**
19 Great Northern Street **F6**
2 Great Patrick Street **H8**
12 Great Victoria Street **G7**
15 Green Crescent **M7**
4 Green End **H15**
22 Green Mount **M6(18)**
15 Green Road **M7**
4 Green Side **H15(9)**
4 Green Walk **H15**
17 Greenan **C5(18)**
23 Greenane Drive **C4(12)**
6 Greencastle Close **H13(5)**
6 Greencastle Place **H13(6)**
7 Greenhill Grove **D11(16)**
7 Greenhill Lane **D11(17)**
12 Greenland Street **G8**
22 Greenlea Gardens **M6(19)**
8 Greenmount Place **G9(49)**
8 Greenmount St **G9(43)**
13 Greenore Street **J7**
24 Greenview Park **E3**
14 Greenville Avenue **K7(5)**
14 Greenville Road **K7**
14 Greenville Street **K7**
21 Greenway **K5(1)**
15 Greenwood Avenue **M8**
15 Greenwood Manor **M8(19)**
15 Greenwood Park **M8**
12 Gresham Street **G8**
24 Greystown Avenue **E3**
24 Greystown Close **E3(3)**
24 Greystown Park **E3**
20 Grillagh Way **J5**
8 Groomsport Court **F9(36)**
8 Groomsport Street **F9(37)**
20 Grosvenor Court **F7(9)**
1 Grosvenor Road **F7**
8 Grove Place **H10(5)**
14 Grove Street East **K7**
1 Grove Tree North **F8(80)**
1 Grove Tree South **F7(3)**
13 Grovefield Place **J7(7)**
13 Grovesfield Street **J7(23)**
8 Gunnel Hill **G14**
17 Gweedore Cres **B5(26)**
17 Gweedore Gdns **B5(10)**
20 Haddington Gardens **J6**
1 Haddow Street **F8(28)**
3 Haig Street **J7**
13 Halcombe Street **J7(63)**
8 Halliday's Road **G10**
8 Halliday's Road **G9(39)**
7 Halstein Drive **L7**
21 Hamel Drive **K5**
12 Hamill Street **G8**
9 Hamilton Road **J9**
2 Hamilton Street **H7**
2 Hamilton's Court **H8(11)**
20 Hampton Drive **H5**
20 Hampton Gardens **H5(8)**
19 Hampton Grove **G5(3)**

20 Hampton Manor **H4**
20 Hampton Manor Dr **H4(5)**
20 Hampton Parade **H5(9)**
20 Hampton Park **H4**
20 Hampton Place **H5(7)**
20 Hampton Strand **H5(6)**
9 Hanna Street **H9**
16 Hanwood Avenue **Q7(6)**
16 Hanwood Drive **Q7**
16 Hanwood Farm **Q7(12)**
16 Hanwood Heights **Q7**
16 Hanwood Park **Q7**
18 Harberton Avenue **E4**
18 Harberton Drive **E4**
18 Harberton Park **E4**
8 Harcourt Drive **F10**
23 Harcourt Terrace **B3(10)**
12 Hardcastle Street **G7**
8 Hardinge Place **G9(16)**
14 Harkness Parade **K8**
14 Harland Park **K8**
9 Harland Road **J9**
13 Harland Walk **J8(8)**
15 Harleston Street **G5**
3 Harmin Avenue **E16**
3 Harmin Crescent **E16**
3 Harmin Parade **E16(3)**
3 Harmin Park **E16**
7 Harmony Court **D10(12)**
12 Harmony Street **G7(32)**
13 Harper Street **J8**
23 Harris Crescent **B2(9)**
9 Harrisburg Street **H10**
8 Harrison Walk **F9(43)**
7 Harrogate Street **E7**
20 Harrow Street **H6(16)**
8 Harrybrook Street **F9**
14 Hart Street **K8(14)**
12 Hartington Street **G7(100)**
14 Hartwell Place **G9(6)**
13 Harvey Court **J8(6)**
13 Hatfield Street **H6**
13 Hatton Drive **J7**
8 Havana Court **F10(14)**
8 Havana Gardens **F10(17)**
8 Havana Walk **F10(16)**
8 Havana Way **F10(15)**
2 Havelock Street **H7(9)**
23 Hawthorn Park **B2(8)**
1 Hawthorn Street **F7**
15 Hawthornden Court **M7(5)**
15 Hawthornden Drive **M8**
15 Hawthornden Gdns **M8(1)**
15 Hawthornden Mews **M8(20)**
15 Hawthornden Pk **M8(3)**
15 Hawthornden Road **M8**
15 Hawthornden Way **M8**
12 Haymarket **G8(34)**
20 Haypark Avenue **H5**
20 Haypark Gardens **H5**
20 Haywood Avenue **H5**
20 Haywood Drive **H6**
23 Hazel Avenue **B1**
7 Hazelbrook Drive **D11**
3 Hazeldene Park **G14**
8 Hazelfield Street **F9(53)**
8 Hazelwood Avenue **B4**
3 Hazelwood Park **G14**
4 Heather Drive **H16(11)**
4 Heather Park **H16**
7 Heather Street **E9**
14 Heatherbell Street **K7(24)**
8 Heathfield Court **F10(10)**
12 Hector Street **G8**
22 Helen's Lea **N6(11)**
10 Helgor Park **L9**
10 Helgor Park Mews **L9(7)**
14 Hemp Street **K8(13)**
5 Henderson Avenue **F11**
5 Henderson Av Flats **F12(3)**
5 Henderson Court **F12(4)**
27 Henderson Ct **M10(11)**
2 Henrietta Street **H7(30)**
8 Henry Place **G9**

8 Henry Street **G9**
20 Herat Street **H6**
7 Herbert Street **E9**
9 Herdman Channel Rd **J10**
8 Hesketh Gardens **E10(7)**
8 Hesketh Park **E10**
7 Hesketh Road E10
14 Hewitt Parade **L7**
11 High Gate **D8(12)**
11 High Gate Terrace **D8(13)**
11 High Green **D8**
11 High Link **D8(9)**
11 High Pass **D8(10)**
11 High Side **D8(11)**
2 High Street **H8**
6 High Street **H13(4)**
2 High Street Court **H8(5)**
11 High Way **D8(5)**
11 Highburn Crescent **D8**
11 Highburn Gardens **D8(3)**
7 Highbury Gardens **E10**
11 Highcairn Drive **D8**
11 Highcliff Gardens **D8**
11 Highdene Gardens **D8**
11 Highfern Gardens **D8**
11 Highfield Drive **D8**
11 Highland Parade **D8**
11 Highpark Crescent **D8**
11 Highpark Cross **D8(8)**
11 Highpark Drive **D8**
3 Hightown Court **E16(14)**
3 Hightown Cres **E15(2)**
3 Hightown Drive **E15(3)**
3 Hightown Gardens **E15**
3 Hightown Park **E15(4)**
3 Hightown Rise **E15**
11 Highvale Gardens **D8**
11 Highview Crescent **D8**
2 Hill Green **J2(2)**
1 Hill Street **H8**
23 Hill Street **C3**
14 Hill's Avenue **K8**
21 Hillburn Park **K5**
14 Hillcrest Gardens **L7(5)**
14 Hillfoot Street **K8**
17 Hillhead Avenue **C5**
17 Hillhead Cottages **C5(19)**
17 Hillhead Court **C5(16)**
17 Hillhead Crescent **C4**
17 Hillhead Drive **C4**
17 Hillhead Heights **C5(21)**
17 Hillhead Park **C5**
9 Hillman Street **G9**
24 Hillmount Court **D3(8)**
24 Hillmount Gardens **D3**
22 Hillsborough Drive **K6**
14 Hillsborough Gardens **J7**
14 Hillsborough Pde **K7(22)**
19 Hillside Crescent **G4**
19 Hillside Drive **G4**
19 Hillside Gardens **G4**
19 Hillside Park **G4**
14 Hillview Avenue **L7**
3 Hillview Court **F9(32)**
3 Hillview Drive **E16**
10 Hillview Road **F9**
14 Hind Street **K8(40)**
21 Hindsdale Park **K5(7)**
8 Hogarth Street **G9**
14 Holland Crescent **L7**
14 Holland Drive **L7**
14 Holland Gardens **L7**
14 Holland Park **L7**
14 Hollycroft Avenue **K7**
23 Hollymount **B1**
24 Hollymount **D3**
24 Hollymount Court **D3**
8 Holmdene Gardens **E10**
2 Holmes Court **H7(2)**
8 Holmes Street **G7(29)**
14 Holyrood **G5**
14 Holywood Road **L8**
12 Hope Street **G7**
14 Hopedene Court **L8(41)**
14 Hopedene Mews **L8(40)**

8 Hopefield Avenue **G10**
8 Hopefield Court **G11(17)**
4 Hopewell Avenue **G9**
8 Hopewell Crescent **G9**
8 Hopewell Place **G9(35)**
8 Hopewell Square **G9(38)**
17 Horn Drive **B4(13)**
17 Horn Walk **B4**
14 Hornby Crescent **K8(33)**
13 Hornby Parade **J8(61)**
13 Hornby Street **J8**
25 Hospital Road **G1**
14 Houston Court **L7(16)**
21 Houston Drive **L6**
21 Houston Gardens **L6**
21 Houston Park **L6**
12 Howard Street **G7**
8 Howard Street S. **G7(37)**
2 Howard Street S **H7(17)**
8 Howe Street **F9**
7 Hoylake Park **E11**
19 Hugh Street **F5**
8 Hughenden Avenue **F11**
20 Hughes Court **J5**
11 Hugo Street **E6**
13 Humber Court **J8(31)**
13 Humber Street **K8(24)**
14 Hunter Street **K8**
12 Hunter Park **G7(75)**
12 Hurst Park **G7(73)**
1 Huss Court **F8(4)**
1 Huss Row **F8(2)**
12 Hutchinson Street **G7(4)**
14 Hyndford Street **K7**
8 Ilchester Street **G9**
6 Imperial Court **G10(27)**
13 Imperial Drive **J7**
13 Imperial Street **J7**
14 Ina Street **K8**
19 India Street **G6**
8 Indiana Avenue **F11**
8 Ingledale Park **E10**
10 Inglewood Court **L9(10)**
17 Inishmore Crescent **C5**
24 Inishowen Drive **E3**
12 Innes Place **G7(46)**
4 Innis Avenue **H15**
4 Innis Park **H15**
4 Innis Walk **H15**
16 Inniscarn Drive **H16**
6 Innisfayle Drive **G12(2)**
6 Innisfayle Gardens **G12**
5 Innisfayle Park **G12**
6 Innisfayle Pass **G12(1)**
6 Innisfayle Road **G12**
16 Innish Gardens **H15(1)**
12 Institution Place **G8(68)**
5 Inver Avenue **F11**
10 Inverary Avenue **L9**
10 Inverary Drive **L9**
4 Inveresk Park **H15(3)**
10 Inverleith Drive **L9**
1 Inverna Street **F7**
10 Invernook Drive **L9**
10 Invernook Park **L9**
10 Inverwood Court **L9(2)**
10 Inverwood Gardens **L9**
4 Iona Gardens **H15**
4 Iona Park **H15(2)**
19 Ireton Street **G6**
11 Iris Close **E7**
11 Iris Court **E7(12)**
11 Iris Drive **E7**
11 Iris Grove **E7(13)**
11 Iris Mews **E7(14)**
11 Iris Street **E7**
11 Iris Walk **E8(15)**
11 Irwell Court **E7(15)**
14 Irwin Avenue **K8**
14 Irwin Crescent **L8**
14 Irwin Drive **K8**
11 Isadore Avenue **E8**
11 Island Street **J8**
11 Islandbawn Drive **E7(3)**
11 Islandbawn Street **E7**

14 Isoline Street **K7**
13 Isthmus Street **J7(31)**
9 Ivan Street **H10**
11 Iveagh Crescent **E7**
11 Iveagh Drive **E7**
11 Iveagh Parade **E7**
11 Iveagh Street **E7**
1 Iverna Close **F7**
1 Ivernagh Street **F7(42)**
8 Jaffa Street **F9**
7 Jamaica Court **F10(21)**
7 Jamaica Road **F10**
7 Jamaica Street **E10**
8 Jamaica Way **F10(18)**
8 James Court **G11(18)**
2 Jame's Pass **H7(25)**
12 James Street South **G7**
20 Jameson Street **H5**
8 Jellicoe Avenue **G10**
8 Jellicoe Drive **G11**
8 Jellicoe Parade **G11(10)**
8 Jellicoe Park **G11(9)**
9 Jennymount Street **H10**
8 Jersey Place **F9**
20 Jerusalem Street **H6**
7 Joanmount Drive **E11**
7 Joanmount Gardens **E11**
7 Joanmount Park
13 Jocelyn Avenue **J7**
13 Jocelyn Gardens **J7(71)**
13 Jocelyn Street **J7**
12 John Street **G8**
15 Johnston Court **M7(10)**
14 Jonesboro' Park **K7(12)**
13 Jonesboro' Street **J7(58)**
2 Joy Street **H7**
2 Joy's Entry **H8(8)**
8 Jubilee Avenue **G10(23)**
1 Jude Street **F8(74)**
14 Julia Street **K8**
1 Kane Street **F8(81)**
8 Kansas Avenue **G11**
8 Kansas Av Flats **G11(4)**
11 Kashmir Road **E8**
13 Kathleen Court **J8(22)**
24 Katrine Park **D3**
9 Keadyville Avenue **H10(10)**
13 Keatley Street **J8**
17 Kells Avenue **B4**
8 Kelvin Parade **F10**
17 Kenard Avenue **C5**
13 Kenbaan Court **J7(27)**
13 Kenbaan Street **J7(5)**
8 Kenbella Parade **G11(3)**
1 Kendal Street **F8(12)**
13 Kenilworth Place **J8(1)**
12 Kenmare Park **G7(66)**
18 Kennedy Way **D6**
27 Kennel Bridge **M9(15)**
14 Kensington Avenue **K7**
15 Kensington Court **M7(4)**
15 Kensington Drive **N7**
15 Kensington Gardens **M7**
15 Kensington Gdns S. **M6**
15 Kensington Gdns W. **M6(9)**
15 Kensington Gate **M7(9)**
22 Kensington Manor **N6(12)**
15 Kensington Park **M6**
22 Kensington Road **M6**
12 Kensington Street **G7(82)**
12 Kent Street **G8**
4 Kernan Close **G14(9)**
7 Kerrera Court **E9(15)**
7 Kerrera Mews **E9(16)**
7 Kerrera Street **E9(14)**
19 Kerrington Court **F5(15)**
14 Kerrsland Cres **L7(3)**
14 Kerrsland Drive **L7(1)**
14 Kerrsland Parade **L7(2)**
17 Kerrykeel Gardens **B5**
8 Keswick Street **F9**
26 Kew Gardens **J2**
12 Keyland's Place **G7(12)**
17 Kilbourne Park **B4(3)**
21 Kilbroney Bend **K5**

21 Kilbroney House **K5(9)**
19 Kilburn Street **F6**
5 Kilcoole Gardens **E12**
5 Kilcoole Park **E12**
12 Kildare Place **G8(2)**
12 Kildare Street **G8(64)**
15 Kilhorne Gardens **M7**
21 Killagan Bend **K5**
24 Killard Place **D3(5)**
21 Killarn Close **L6(3)**
17 Kileen Park **C5(6)**
12 Killen Street **G8(35)**
13 Killowen Street **J7**
4 Killowen Terrace **H16(7)**
25 Killynether Gdns **G2(14)**
25 Killynether Walk **G2(15)**
16 Kilmakee Park **P6**
22 Kilmakee Park **N6**
1 Kilmore Close **F8(69)**
1 Kilmore Square **F8(70)**
15 Kilmory Gardens **P7**
8 Kilronan Street **G9**
25 Kilwarlin Crescent **G2**
25 Kilwarlin Walk **G2(12)**
20 Kimberley Drive **H5**
15 Kimberley Street **H5**
14 Kimona Drive **K8(39)**
22 Kimscourt **M6(10)**
20 Kinallen Court **H6(14)**
20 Kinallen Street **H6(4)**
24 Kinbane Way **D3**
14 Kincora Avenue **L8**
16 Kincraig Avenue **P7(20)**
3 Kincraig Park **G14**
12 Kinedar Crescent **M8**
12 King Street **G8**
12 King Street Mews **G8**
15 King's Brae **N7**
19 King's Bridge **G5**
24 King's Court **E4(3)**
15 King's Crescent **M7**
15 King's Drive **M7**
15 King's Link **N7**
15 King's Manor **N7(8)**
15 King's Park **M7**
16 King's Road **P7**
15 King's Road **N7**
15 King's Square **N7**
20 Kingsberry Park **J5**
23 Kingscourt **B2(15)**
13 Kingscourt Street **J7**
15 Kingsdale Park **N7**
22 Kingsden Park **M6(8)**
15 Kingsland Drive **N7(4)**
15 Kingsland Park **N7**
14 Kingsley Court **L8(32)**
8 Kingsmere Avenue **F10**
8 Kingston Court **F10(19)**
23 Kingsway **B2**
23 Kingsway **C3**
15 Kingsway Avenue **N7**
15 Kingsway Close **N7(6)**
15 Kingsway Drive **N7**
15 Kingsway Gardens **N7**
15 Kingsway Park **N7**
15 Kingswood Park **N7**
13 Kingswood Street **J7**
8 Kinnaird Close **G9(45)**
8 Kinnaird Place **G9(10)**
8 Kinnaird Street **G9(11)**
8 Kinnaird Terrace **G9(9)**
24 Kinnegar Road **D3**
16 Kincross Avenue **P7**
11 Kirk Street **E8**
25 Kirkistown Avenue **G2**
25 Kirkistown Walk **G2(16)**
14 Kirkliston Drive **L7**
14 Kirkliston Gardens **L7**
14 Kirkliston Park **L7**
17 Kirklowe Drive **D3(3)**
16 Kirn Park **P7(12)**
19 Kitchener Drive **F6**
19 Kitchener Street **F6**
8 Klondyke Street **F9(16)**
19 Knightsbridge Manor **G4**

19 Knightsbridge Mews **G4(5)**
19 Knightsbridge Park **G4**
20 Knock Eden Crescent **J5**
20 Knock Eden Drive **J5(9)**
20 Knock Eden Grove **J5(1)**
20 Knock Eden Parade **J5**
20 Knock Eden Park **J5**
22 Knock Green **M6(5)**
22 Knock Grove **M6**
22 Knock Link **M6(3)**
22 Knock Road **M6**
22 Knock Way **M6(4)**
20 Knockbracken Park **J4**
20 Knockbreda Drive **J4(6)**
20 Knockbreda Gardens **J4**
20 Knockbreda Park **J4**
20 Knockbreda Road **J5**
15 Knockburn Park **N7**
15 Knockcastle Park **M7**
27 Knockdarragh Park **N9**
15 Knockdene Park **M7**
15 Knockdene Park North **M7**
15 Knockdene Park South **M7**
17 Knockdhu Park **C5**
4 Knockenagh Walk **H16(1)**
15 Knockhill Park **M7**
15 Knockland Park **N7(2)**
15 Knocklofty Court **M8(21)**
15 Knocklofty Park **M8**
27 Knockmarloch Park **N9(1)**
22 Knockmount Gdns **M6(6)**
22 Knockmount Park **M6(7)**
27 Knocknagoney Av **M10**
27 Knocknagoney Dale **M10**
27 Knocknagoney Drive **M10**
27 Knocknagoney Gdns **M10(8)**
27 Knocknagoney Gn. **M10(6)**
27 Knocknagoney Gve **M10(5)**
27 Knocknagoney Park **M10**
27 Knocknagoney Road **M10**
27 Knocknagoney Way **M10(7)**
4 Knockreagh Gdns **H16(6)**
15 Knocktern Gardens **M8**
15 Knockvale Grove **M7**
15 Knockvale Park **M7**
15 Knockwood Crescent **M7**
22 Knockwood Drive **M6(2)**
22 Knockwood Grove **M6(1)**
22 Knockwood Park **M6**
8 Knutsford Drive **F10**
14 Koram Ring **D5**
14 Kyle Street **K8**
16 Kylemore Bend **H16**
11 Kylemore Park **F11**
11 La Salle Drive **E7**
11 La Salle Gardens **E7(7)**
11 La Salle Mews **E7(18)**
11 La Salle Park **E7**
14 Laburnum Court **K8(48)**
8 Laburnum Lane **K8(15)**
11 Laburnum Park **B3(1)**
23 Laburnum Row **B2(1)**
14 Laburnum Street **K8(34)**
23 Laburnum Way **B3(7)**
13 Lackagh Court **J8(2)**
4 Lacken Gardens **H16**
21 Ladas Drive **K6**
21 Ladas Walk **K6(5)**
21 Ladas Way **K6**
7 Ladbrook Drive **E9**
8 Lady Street **F8**
17 Ladybrook Avenue **C4**
17 Ladybrook Crescent
17 Ladybrook Cross **C4(10)**
17 Ladybrook Drive **C4**
17 Ladybrook Gardens **C4(3)**
17 Ladybrook Grove **C4(2)**
17 Ladybrook Parade **C4(1)**
17 Ladybrook Park **C4**
1 Ladymar Court **F8(36)**
1 Ladymar Grove **F8(36)**
1 Ladymar **Park F8(36)**
1 Ladymar way **F8(36)**

2 Laganbank Road **H8**
20 Laganvale Court **H4(6)**
20 Laganvale Manor **H4(7)**
19 Laganvale Street **G5**
2 Laganview Court **H8(27)**
2 Laganview Mews **H8(29)**
18 Lake Glen Avenue **D6**
18 Lake Glen Close **D6(20)**
18 Lake Glen Crescent **D6(17)**
18 Lake Glen Drive **D6**
18 Lake Glen Green **D6(21)**
18 Lake Glen Parade **D6(19)**
18 Lake Glen Park **D6(18)**
24 Lakeside Drive **D2**
11 Lanark Way **E8**
8 Lancaster Street **G9**
21 Lancedean Road **K5**
19 Lancefield Road **F5**
17 Landscape Terrace **F9(6)**
19 Landseer Street **G6**
16 Langholm Row **P7(7)**
15 Langley Street **F9(50)**
6 Lansdowne Drive **G12(10)**
6 Lansdowne Park **G12**
6 Lansdowne Pk N. **G12(7)**
6 Lansdowne Road **G12**
4 Laragh Court **G14(12)**
11 Larch Hill **C1(1)**
23 Larch Grove **C1**
23 Larkfield Avenue **C3**
10 Larkfield Court **L9(8)**
10 Larkfield Drive **K9**
10 Larkfield Gardens **L9**
10 Larkfield Grove **L9(6)**
10 Larkfield Manor **K9(4)**
10 Larkfield Park **L9**
10 Larkfield Road **L9**
18 Larkstone Street **E5(1)**
3 Laundry Lane **E15**
23 Laurel Way **B2**
20 Laurel Wood **H4(4)**
15 Laurelvale **M8(12)**
3 Lauron Court **E16(17)**
7 Lavens Drive **D10**
12 Law's Court **G8(24)**
1 Lawnbrook Avenue **F8**
1 Lawnbrook Drive **F8(86)**
1 Lawnbrook Square **F8(87)**
13 Lawnmount Street **J7(66)**
7 Lawnview Street **E9(23)**
19 Lawrence Street **G6**
7 Lawther Court **G10(6)**
12 Lawyer Gardens **G7(61)**
21 Lead Hill **L5**
21 Lead Hill Park **L5**
21 Lead Hill View **L5(8)**
19 Lecale Street **F6**
14 Lecumpher Street **K7(20)**
13 Ledley Hall Close **J7(60)**
1 Leeson Street **F7**
7 Leestone Terrace **B4(9)**
7 Legann Street **D10(11)**
7 Leganoe Street **D11**
7 Leggagh Court **D11(25)**
7 Leginn Street **D11(22)**
7 Legmail Street **D10(6)**
7 Legnavea Place **D11(32)**
7 Legoniel Place **D11(3)**
13 Leitrim Street **J7**
13 Lelia Street **K8(41)**
1 Lemberg Street **F7**
14 Lena Street **K8(31)**
17 Lenadery Terrace **H16(9)**
17 Lenadoon Avenue **B5**
17 Lenadoon Walk **B4(12)**
26 Lenaghan Avenue **J2**
26 Lenaghan Court **J3(10)**
26 Lenaghan Crescent **J3**
26 Lenaghan Gardens **J3(5)**
26 Lenaghan Park **J3**
13 Lendrick Street **J8**
3 Lennox Avenue **J3**
19 Lennoxvale **G6**
23 Lenwood Drive **C2(12)**
7 Leopold Place **E9(25)**

| | | | |
|---|---|---|---|
| 7 Leopold Street **E9** | 24 Locksley Parade **D3** | 24 Malfin Court **E3(8)** | 13 Mashona Street **J7(22)** |
| 11 Leoville Street **E8** | 24 Locksley Park **D3** | 24 Malfin Drive **E3** | 12 Massareene Path **G8(11)** |
| 8 Lepper Street **G9** | 24 Locksley Place **E3(1)** | 17 Malinmore Park **B4** | 12 Massareene Row **G8(11)** |
| 7 Leroy Street **D10** | 19 Lockview Road **G5** | 24 Malon Drive **E3** | 12 Massareene Walk **G8(11)** |
| 16 Leven Close **P6(2)** | 14 Lomand Avenue **K8** | 19 Malone Avenue **F6** | 27 Massey Avenue **N9** |
| 16 Leven Crescent **P6(3)** | 12 Lombard Street **G8(60)** | 24 Malone Beeches **F4(9)** | 15 Massey Court **N8** |
| 16 Leven Drive **P6** | 14 Lomond Street **K8(42)** | 25 Malone Cottages **E3(28)** | 27 Massey Green **N9(4)** |
| 16 Leven Park **P6** | 13 London Road **J7** | 25 Malone Court **E3** | 27 Massey Park **N9** |
| 16 Leven Place **P6(1)** | 13 London Street **J7** | 25 Malone Court Mews **F4(4)** | 8 Matchet Street **F9** |
| 7 Lever Street **D11(33)** | 20 Long Acre **J4(4)** | 23 Malone Gardens **C2(5)** | 12 Matilda Avenue **G7(76)** |
| 14 Library Court **L8(42)** | 2 Long Lane **G8(57)** | 25 Malone Grange **F4(3)** | 12 Matilda Drive **G7(77)** |
| 12 Library Street **G8** | 4 Longlands Avenue **G14** | 19 Malone Heights **E2** | 12 Matilda Gardens **G7(43)** |
| 14 Lichfield Avenue **K7** | 4 Longlands Bridge **G14** | 25 Malone Hill Park **F4** | 16 Mawhinney Park **Q7** |
| 8 Liffey Court **F9(8)** | 4 Longlands Court **G14(8)** | 25 Malone Meadows **F3** | 12 Maxwell Street **G7(39)** |
| 8 Ligoniel Road **D11** | 4 Longlands Park **G14** | 25 Malone Park **F4** | 12 Maxwell's Place **G7(40)** |
| 24 Lille Park **D3(1)** | 4 Longlands Road **G14** | 19 Malone Pk. Central **F4(16)** | 2 May Street **H7** |
| 9 Lilliput Court **H9(1)** | 4 Longlands Walk **G14(3)** | 12 Malone Place **G7(55)** | 2 May's Meadow **H7(3)** |
| 8 Lilliput Street **G10(12)** | 4 Longwood Road **H14** | 19 Malone Road **F5** | 21 Mayfair Avenue **K6** |
| 12 Lime Court **G8** | 21 Loopland Crescent **K6** | 24 Malone View Avenue **E2** | 8 Mayfair Court **F9(39)** |
| 6 Limegrove **G13(9)** | 21 Loopland Drive **K6** | 24 Malone View Cres **E3(4)** | 19 Mayfield Street **F5(20)** |
| 7 Limehill Grove **D11(1)** | 21 Loopland Gardens **K6** | 24 Malone View Park **E2** | 13 Mayflower Street **K7** |
| 7 Limehill Street **D11(2)** | 21 Loopland Grove **K6(4)** | 24 Malone View Road **E2** | 13 Maymount Street **J7(67)** |
| 7 Limepark Mews **D10(8)** | 21 Loopland Parade **K6(2)** | 24 Malton Court **E3(19)** | 11 Mayo Court **E8(16)** |
| 8 Limestone Road **G10** | 21 Loopland Park **K6** | 11 Malton Fold **E13(16)** | 11 Mayo Link **E8(7)** |
| 15 Limewood Grove **M8(15)** | 21 Loopland Road **K6** | 5 Malton Rise **E3(20)** | 11 Mayo Street **E8** |
| 8 Lincoln Avenue **G9** | 13 Lord Street **J7** | 24 Malton Vale **E3(18)** | 12 McAdam Gardens **G7(64)** |
| 12 Lincoln Place **G8** | 19 Lorne Street **F6** | 8 Malvern Close **F9(21)** | 12 McAdam Park **G7(24)** |
| 1 Lincoln Square **F7(7)** | 16 Lothain Avenue **P7** | 8 Malvern Street **F9(47)** | 14 McAllister Court **K8(22)** |
| 8 Linden Gardens **F10** | 8 Lothair Avenue **G10** | 8 Malvern Way **F9(20)** | 13 McArthur Court **J8** |
| 1 Linden Street **F8(93)** | 8 Louden Street **G8(58)** | 24 Malwood Close **E3(9)** | 2 McAuley Street **H7** |
| 12 Lindsay Court **G7(101)** | 13 Lough Lea **J8** | 24 Malwood Park **E3** | 8 McCandless Street **F9** |
| 12 Lindsay Street **G7** | 4 Loughmoney Park **H16(8)** | 14 Manderson Street **K8(11)** | 21 McCaughan Park **K5** |
| 2 Lindsay Street **H7(19)** | 8 Loughrey Court **G10(18)** | 21 Manna Grove **K6** | 9 McCaughey Road **J10** |
| 7 Lindsay Way **G7(91)** | 20 Loughview Drive **J4** | 8 Manor Court **F9(38)** | 12 McCavana's Place **G7(21)** |
| 7 Linen Grove **D11(15)** | 7 Loughview Street **D10(1)** | 8 Manor Drive **F9(19)** | 8 McCleery Street **G9(41)** |
| 7 Linenhall Street **G7** | 9 Loughview Terrace **H10** | 23 Manor Mews **C3(4)** | 12 McClintock Street **G7** |
| 12 Linenhall Street W. **G7(18)** | 8 Lovatt Street **K7(3)** | 8 Manor Street **F9** | 2 McClure Street **H7** |
| 12 Linfield Avenue **G7(63)** | 22 Lower Braniel Road **M6** | 21 Manse Road **L4** | 1 McDonnell Court **F7(34)** |
| 12 Linfield Drive **G7(65)** | 1 Lower Clonard St **F8(105)** | 1 Mansfield Street **F8(40)** | 1 McDonnell Street **F7(36)** |
| 12 Linfield Gardens **G7(62)** | 12 Lower Crescent **G7** | 23 Maple Crescent **C1(2)** | 12 McIvors Place **G8(40)** |
| 12 Linfield Road **G7** | 12 Lower Garfield St **G8(23)** | 19 Maralin Place **G9(32)** | 12 McKibbenn's Court **G8(17)** |
| 12 Linfield Street **G7(25)** | 1 Lower Kilburn Street **F7(5)** | 19 Marborough Park **F5(4)** | 13 McMaster Street **J8** |
| 4 Linford Green **H16** | 12 Lower Regent Street **G8(3)** | 19 Marborough Park **F5(8)** | 13 McMullan's Lane **J7(20)** |
| 4 Linford Place **H16(17)** | 1 Lower Rockview Street **F7** | 11 March Street **E8** | 1 McQuillan Street **F7(2)** |
| 24 Linkview Park **E3(7)** | 19 Lower Windsor Avenue **F6** | 1 Marchioness Gn. **F7(32)** | 19 Meadowbank Place **F6** |
| 1 Linview Court **F7(1)** | 16 Lowland Avenue **P7(22)** | 1 Marchioness St **F7(30)** | 19 Meadowbank Street **F6** |
| 14 Lisavon Court **K8(51)** | 16 Lowland Gardens **P7(11)** | 12 Marcus Ward St **G7(30)** | 13 Medway Court **J8(5)** |
| 14 Lisavon Drive **K9** | 16 Lowland Walk **P7(10)** | 23 Margaretta Court **B4(1)** | 13 Medway Street **J8** |
| 14 Lisavon Parade **K8(3)** | 15 Lowland Walk **N7** | 23 Margaretta Park **B4(11)** | 14 Meekon Street **K8** |
| 14 Lisavon Street **K8** | 20 Lowry Court **H4(3)** | 23 Marguerite Park **D4(6)** | 12 Melbourne Street **G8(43)** |
| 13 Lisbon Street **J8(68)** | 6 Lowwood Gdns **G12(11)** | 21 Marina Park **L6** | 15 Melfort Drive **N7** |
| 19 Lisburn Avenue **F5** | 6 Lowwood Park **G12** | 9 Marine Street **H9** | 14 Melrose Avenue **K7(23)** |
| 19 Lisburn Road **F6** | 19 Lucerne Parade **G5** | 3 Mark Royal Court **G14(7)** | 19 Melrose Street **F6** |
| 5 Lisdarragh Park **F12** | 11 Lucknow Street **E8** | 2 Market Street **H7(24)** | 1 Meridi Street **F7(29)** |
| 12 Lisfaddan Drive **G8(71)** | 8 Ludlow Square **G9(15)** | 19 Marlborough Av **F5(2)** | 11 Merkland Place **E8(5)** |
| 12 Lisfaddan Place **G8(73)** | 7 Lupus Grove **D11(20)** | 19 Marlborough Court **F5(18)** | 21 Merok Crescent **K5** |
| 18 Lislea Avenue **E5(2)** | 14 Luxor Gardens **K7** | 19 Marlborough Gdns **F5(10)** | 21 Merok Drive **K5** |
| 18 Lislea Drive **E5** | 8 Lyle Street **F9(71)** | 21 Marlborough Hts. **L5(10)** | 21 Merok Gardens **K5** |
| 22 Lisleen Road **N4** | 20 Lynden Court **J6(16)** | 19 Marlborough Pk Cent **F5** | 21 Merok Park **K5** |
| 20 Lismain Street **J6** | 20 Lynden Gate **J5(12)** | 19 Marlborough Park Cross | 17 Merrion Park **B4** |
| 13 Lismore Street **J7** | 7 Lyndhurst Close **D9(4)** | Avenue **F5(7)** | 5 Merryfield Drive **F12(2)** |
| 5 Lismoyne Park **F12** | 7 Lyndhurst Drive **D9** | 19 Marlborough Park N. **F5** | 14 Mersey Street **K8** |
| 21 Lisnabreeny Road **L4** | 7 Lyndhurst Gardens **D9** | 19 Marlborough Park S. **F5** | 6 Merston Gardens **G14(5)** |
| 21 Lisnabreeny Road E. **L4(1)** | 7 Lyndhurst Grove **D9(3)** | 2 Marlborough St **H8(23)** | 27 Mertoun Park **M10** |
| 21 Lisnasharragh Park **L5** | 7 Lyndhurst Link **D9(1)** | 22 Marlfield Drive **N6** | 4 Merville Gdn. Village **H14** |
| 21 Lisnasharragh Terr. **L5(9)** | 7 Lyndhurst Parade **D9** | 22 Marlfield Rise **N6(7)** | 4 Merville Mews **H14(4)** |
| 20 Lissan Close **J5** | 7 Lyndhurst Park **D9** | 27 Marmont Crescent **M9** | 8 Mervue Court **G9(4)** |
| 20 Lissan Link **J5** | 7 Lyndhurst Rise **D9(5)** | 27 Marmont Drive **M9(10)** | 8 Mervue Street **G9** |
| 1 Lisvarna Heights **F8(71)** | 7 Lyndhurst Way **D9(2)** | 27 Marmont Park **M9** | 5 Meyrick Park **E11** |
| 1 Lisvarna Place **F7** | 2 Mabel Court **G7(42)** | 7 Marmount Gardens **E11** | 11 Mica Drive **E7** |
| 2 Little Charlotte St **H7(12)** | 8 Macart Road **H8** | 8 Marquis Street **G8** | 11 Mica Street **E7** |
| 9 Little Corporation St **H9(5)** | 8 Mackey Street **G10(17)** | 8 Marsden Gardens **G10** | 22 Middle Braniel Road **N5** |
| 12 Little Donegall St **G8** | 8 Madison Avenue **F11** | 8 Marsden Gdns Flats | 8 Middlepath Street **H8** |
| 2 Little Edward Street **H8(1)** | 14 Madison Avenue E. **K8(9)** | **G10(26)** | 9 Midland Close **H9(10)** |
| 8 Little George's St **G9(25)** | 4 Madras Street **F9** | 25 Marsden Terrace **G10(25)** | 9 Midland Crescent **H9(15)** |
| 2 Little May Street **H7** | 13 Madrid Court **J8(23)** | 21 Marshalls Road **L6(5)** | 9 Midland Terrace **H9(16)** |
| 7 Little Patrick Street **H8** | 13 Madrid Street **J8** | 13 Martin Park **J15(6)** | 9 Mileriver Street **G10** |
| 12 Little Victoria t **G7(99)** | 19 Magdala Street **G6** | 13 Martin Street **J8** | 9 Milewater Road **H10** |
| 9 Little York Street **H9** | 13 Magee's Lane **J9(36)** | 14 Martinez Avenue **L7** | 10 Milewater Street **H10(4)** |
| 11 Locan Street **E7** | 13 Maghies Place **J7(41)** | 23 Martinville Park **J2** | 12 Milford Rise **G8(72)** |
| 16 Lochinver Drive **P7** | 25 Mahee Close **G2(2)** | 25 Marylebone Park **G4** | 12 Milford Street **G8(53)** |
| 19 Lockside Court **G5(15)** | 12 Majestic Drive **G7** | 19 Maryville Avenue **F5(21)** | 23 Milfort Avenue **C2** |
| 24 Locksley Drive **D4(5)** | 13 Major Street **J8** | 19 Maryville Court **G7(95)** | 23 Milfort Terrace **C2(6)** |
| 24 Locksley Gardens **D3** | 1 Malcolmson Street **F8(98)** | 19 Maryville Park **F4** | 4 Mill Road **H14** |
| 24 Locksley Grange **D4(9)** | 1 Maldon Street **F7** | 12 Maryville Street **G7** | 8 Mill Street West **F9(26)** |

20 Millar Street **J6**
7 Millbank Park **D11(19)**
25 Millburn Court **G2(8)**
12 Millfield **G8**
25 Milltown Hill **G2**
25 Milltown Road **F2**
18 Milltown Row **E6**
7 Millview Court **D11(18)**
1 Milner Street **F7**
9 Mineral Street **H10**
25 Minnowburn Drive **G2(6)**
25 Minnowburn Gdns **G2(7)**
25 Minnowburn Terr. **G2(9)**
17 Mizen Gardens **B5(18)**
16 Moatview Crescent **Q7**
16 Moatview Park **Q7**
8 Moffatt Street **G9(7)**
13 Moira Court **J8(54)**
13 Moira Street **J8(70)**
19 Moltke Street **F6**
7 Molyneaux Street **H9(6)**
17 Monagh By-Pass **C6**
17 Monagh Crescent **C6(4)**
17 Monagh Grove **C6(1)**
17 Monagh Link **C6**
1 Monarch Parade **F7**
1 Monarch Street **F7**
13 Moneyrea Street **J7**
21 Montgomery Court **K5(8)**
21 Montgomery Road **K5**
2 Montgomery Street **H8**
7 Montreal Street **E9**
13 Montrose Street **J8(47)**
13 Montrose Street S. **J8(24)**
13 Montrose Walk **J8(25)**
19 Moonstone Street **F5**
23 Moor Park Ave. **C4(13)**
23 Moor Park Dr. **C4(14)**
23 Moor Park Gdns. **C4(15)**
17 Moor Park Mews **C4(16)**
12 Moore's Place **G7(47)**
14 Moorfield Street **K7**
14 Moorgate Street **K7**
3 Moreland Avenue **F15**
18 Moreland Cres. **D5(12)**
18 Moreland Drive **D5(8)**
18 Moreland Park **D5**
20 Mornington **H4(1)**
20 Mornington Mews **H4(2)**
1 Morpeth Street **F8(22)**
1 Moscow Street **F8(75)**
7 Mossvale Street **E9(21)**
27 Motelands **M9**
23 Motorway M1 **C4**
3 Motorway M2 **G14**
4 Motorway M5 **J14**
24 Mount Aboo Park **D3**
19 Mount Charles **G6**
5 Mount Coole Park **F12**
25 Mount Eden Park **F4**
20 Mount Merrion Av **J5**
20 Mount Merrion Cr. **J5(10)**
20 Mount Merrion Drive **J5**
20 Mount Merrion Gdns **J5**
20 Mount Merrion Park **J5**
26 Mount Michael Dr. **J4(2)**
26 Mount Michael Park **J3**
26 Mount Oriel **J3(11)**
19 Mount Pleasant **G5**
19 Mount Prospect Park **F6**
6 Mount Street **H13**
13 Mount Street **J7(45)**
13 Mount Street S. **J7(12)**
6 Mount Vernon Ct . **G11(24)**
6 Mount Vernon Drive **G12**
6 Mount Vernon Gdns **G12**
6 Mount Vernon Gve **G11(1)**
6 Mount Vernon Park **H12**
6 Mount Vernon Pass **H11(1)**
6 Mount Vernon Rd **H11**
6 Mount Vernon Wk **H11(5)**
6 Mount Vernon Walk **H12(5)**
16 Mount-Regan Av **Q8**
7 Mountainhill Lane **D11(5)**
7 Mountainhill Road **D11**

7 Mountainhill Walk **D11(7)**
7 Mountainview Drive **E9**
7 Mountainview Gdns **E9**
7 Mountainview Pde. **E9**
7 Mountainview Pk **E9(18)**
7 Mountainview Place **E9(1)**
11 Mountcashel Street **E8**
9 Mountcollyer Av **H10**
8 Mountcollyer Cl. **G10(9)**
8 Mountcollyer Rd **H10(11)**
8 Mountcollyer Street **G10**
8 Mountcoole Gardens **F12**
13 Mountforde Court **J8(34)**
13 Mountforde Drive **J8**
13 Mountforde Gdns **J8(35)**
13 Mountforde Park **J8(27)**
13 Mountforde Road **J8**
24 Mountview Court **F9(31)**
4 Mountview Pass **J15(2)**
4 Mountview Place **J15(3)**
8 Mountview Street **F9**
13 Mourne Street **K8(32)**
4 Mournebeg Drive **H16**
4 Mournebeg Way **H16(16)**
24 Moveen House **D3(24)**
14 Movilla Park **H16(13)**
19 Mowhan Street **F5(19)**
11 Moyard Crescent **D8**
11 Moyard Parade **D8**
11 Moyard Park **D8**
25 Moyle Walk **G2(13)**
24 Moylena House **D3(25)**
16 Moyne Park **P6**
6 Moyola Park **E16(6)**
8 Moyola Street **G9**
4 Mulderg Drive **G14**
7 Mulhouse Road **F7**
17 Mulroy Park **B5(7)**
12 Murray Street **G7(34)**
9 Musgrave Channel Rd **J9**
18 Musgrave Park Ct. **E4(6)**
2 Musgrave Street **H8**
2 Music Hall Court **H8(21)**
2 Music Hall Lane **H8(21)**
13 My Lady's Road **J7**
26 Myrtledene Drive **J2(8)**
26 Myrtledene Road **J2**
19 Myrtlefield Park **F4**
11 Nansen Street **E7**
12 Napier Street **G7(80)**
17 Naroon Park **B5(15)**
17 Navan Green **C5**
6 Navarra Place **G14(6)**
14 Neill's Hill Park **L7**
1 Nelson Square **F8(17)**
14 Nendrum Gardens **K7**
4 Nendrum Gdns **H16(10)**
23 Netherlands Drive **B3**
23 Netherlands Park **B3**
15 Netherleigh Mews **N8(1)**
15 Netherleigh Park **N8**
14 Nevis Avenue **K8**
11 New Barnsley Drive **D7**
11 New Narnsley Gdns **D7(1)**
11 New Barnsley Green **D7(2)**
11 New Barnsley Grove **D7(3)**
11 New Barnsley Parade **D7**
11 New Barnsley Park **D7**
2 New Bond Street **H7(20)**
7 New Farm Lane **D11(23)**
25 New Forge Dale **F4(15)**
25 New Forge Grange **F4(12)**
25 New Forge Lane **F4**
8 New Lodge Place **G9(17)**
8 New Lodge Road **G9**
13 Newcastle Manor **J8(64)**
13 Newcastle Street **J8**
25 Newforge Dale **F4(6)**
8 Newington Avenue **G10**
8 Newington St **G10(21)**
8 Newport Court **F9(40)**
13 Newry Street **J7**

6 Newton Gardens **H14**
26 Newton Park **J3**
13 Newtownards Road **J8**
26 Newtownbreda Rd **H3**
1 Ninth Street **F8(49)**
14 Norbloom Gdns **K7(11)**
18 Norbury Street **D6(13)**
18 Norfolk Drive **D6**
18 Norfolk Gardens **D6**
18 Norfolk Grove **D6**
18 Norfolk Parade **D6**
18 Norfolk Road **D6**
18 Norfolk Way **D6(1)**
18 Norglen Crescent **D6**
18 Norglen Drive **D6**
17 Norglen Gardens **D6**
17 Norglen Road **C6**
20 North Bank **J5**
12 North Boundary St **G8**
5 North Circular Rd **F12**
9 North Derby St **H10**
14 North Gardens **L7**
17 North Green **C5**
9 North Hill St **G9(30)**
1 North Howard Ct **F8(57)**
1 North Howard Link **F8(72)**
1 North Howard St **F8**
1 North Howard Wk **F8(62)**
12 North King St **G8(25)**
18 North Link **D5**
8 North Parade **H6**
8 North Queen Street **H9**
14 North Road **L7**
15 North Sperrin **P7** .
15 North Sperrin **N7**
17 North Street **G8**
12 North Street Arc. **G8(22)**
19 Northbrook Gdns **F6(2)**
19 Northbrook Street **F6**
4 Northern Road **H10**
22 Northfield Rise **M6(15)**
1 Northland Court **F8(54)**
1 Northland Street **F8**
17 Northlands Park **C4(7)**
1 Northumberland St **F8**
10 Northwick Drive **E10**
9 Northwood Cres **H11**
9 Northwood Drive **H11**
9 Northwood Parade **H11**
9 Northwood Road **H11**
25 Norton Drive **F4**
10 Norwood Avenue **L8**
10 Norwood Court **L9**
14 Norwood Crescent **L8**
14 Norwood Drive **L8**
15 Norwood Gardens **M8**
14 Norwood Grove **L8(2)**
15 Norwood Park **M8**
12 Norwood Street **G7**
19 Notting Hill **G5**
19 Notting Hill Court **G5**
19 Notting Hill Manor **F5(17)**
1 Nubia Street **F7**
12 O'Dempsey St **H10(2)**
12 Oak Street **G7(50)**
12 Oak Way **G7**
14 Oakdale Street **K8(27)**
14 Oakdene Drive **K8(4)**
14 Oakdene Parade **K8**
23 Oakhurst Ave **C3**
18 Oakland Avenue **L8**
23 Oakland Way **B1(5)**
23 Oakley Street **D10**
11 Oakman Street **E7**
9 Oakmount Drive **H11**
23 Oakvale Gdns **B3**
25 Oakwood Court **F4(7)**
25 Oakwood Grove **F4(8)**
25 Oakwood Mews **F4(5)**
25 Oakwood Park **F4**
20 Oberon Street **J6**
8 Oceanic Avenue **G10**
13 Odessa Street **F8**
13 Ogilvie Street **J7**
7 Ohio Street **E9**

5 Old Cavehill Road **G12**
2 Old Channel Road **H8**
4 Old Church Road **H14**
24 Old Coach Gardens **E2**
24 Old Coach Lane **E2**
24 Old Coach Road **E2**
17 Old Colin **B4(13)**
16 Old Dundonald Rd **Q7**
24 Old Forge Manor **D2**
23 Old Golf Course Rd **C3**
27 Old Holywood Rd **N11**
6 Old Irish Highway **H16**
8 Old Lodge Road **F9(9)**
4 Old Mill Drive **H14(7)**
7 Old Mill Road **D11**
7 Old Mill Way **D11(14)**
25 Old Milltown Road **G2**
17 Old Suffolk Road **B5(21)**
8 Old Westland Road **F11**
8 Oldpark Avenue **F10**
8 Oldpark Road **F10**
8 Oldpark Square **F10(2)**
8 Oldpark Terrace **F10**
7 Olive Street **E9**
19 Olympia Drive **F6**
19 Olympia Parade **F6**
19 Olympia Street **F6**
13 Omeath Street **J7**
4 O'Neill Road **G16**
1 O'Neill Street **F8(99)**
20 Onslow Gardens **J6**
20 Onslow Parade **J6**
20 Onslow Park **J6(19)**
5 Ophir Gardens **F11**
14 Orangefield Av **L7**
21 Orangefield Cres **K6**
14 Orangefield Drive **L7**
14 Orangefield Drive S. **L7**
14 Orangefield Gdns **L7**
14 Orangefield Green **L7(10)**
14 Orangefield Gve **L7(14)**
14 Orangefield Lane **L7**
14 Orangefield Parade **L7**
14 Orangefield Park **L7**
14 Orangefield Road **L7**
17 Oranmore Drive **B4**
1 Oranmore Street **F8**
21 Orby Drive **K6**
21 Orby Drive **L6**
14 Orby Gardens **K7**
21 Orby Green **K6(1)**
21 Orby Grove **K6**
14 Orby Link **K7**
14 Orby Mews **K7(16)**
21 Orby Parade **K6**
21 Orby Park **K6**
21 Orby Place **K6**
14 Orby Road **K7**
21 Orby Street **L6**
15 Orchard Close **N6(8)**
26 Orchard Rise **J3**
9 Orchard Street **H9(11)**
18 Orchardville Avenue **D4**
18 Orchardville Cres **D4**
18 Orchardville Gdns **D4**
7 Oregon Gardens **E9(24)**
8 Orient Gardens **F10**
8 Orkney Street **F9**
24 Orlock Square **D3**
12 Ormeau Avenue **G7**
20 Ormeau Bridge **H6**
2 Ormeau Embankment **H7**
20 Ormeau Road **H6**
2 Ormeau Street **H7**
15 Ormiston Crescent **M8**
15 Ormiston Drive **M8**
15 Ormiston Gardens **M7**
15 Ormiston Parade **M8**
15 Ormiston Park **M8**
1 Ormond Place **F8(31)**
24 Ormonde Av **D3(2)**
21 Ormonde Gardens **K6**
23 Ormonde Park **C3**
24 Orpen Avenue **D3**
24 Orpen Drive **D3**

# ALPHABETICAL STREET INDEX

24 Orpen Park **D3**
24 Orpen Road **D3**
19 Osborne Drive **F5**
19 Osborne Gardens **F5**
19 Osborne Park **F4**
1 Osman Street **F8**
3 Osterley Park **F16**
12 Oswald Park **G7(41)**
7 Ottawa Street **E9**
14 Oval Street **K8**
4 Owenreagh Cl. **H15(6)**
4 Owenreagh Drive **H15**
18 Owenvarragh Gdns **D5(9)**
18 Owenvarragh Park **D5**
2 Oxford Street **H8**
8 Pacific Avenue **G10**
12 Packenham Street **G7**
27 Palace Grove **N11**
5 Palace Gdns **G11(12)**
20 Palestine Street **H6**
7 Palmer Court **E9(15)**
7 Palmer Street **E9**
10 Palmerston Park **L9(5)**
10 Palmerston Road **L9**
1 Pandora Street **F7(50)**
13 Pansy Street **K8**
1 Panton Street **F8(29)**
23 Pantridge Road **B4**
1 Paris Street **F9**
16 Park Avenue **Q7**
14 Park Avenue **K8**
16 Park Drive **Q7**
14 Park Grange **K8(31)**
19 Park Lane **G6(7)**
26 Park Lodge **H3(10)**
13 Park Place **J7(39)**
20 Park Road **H6**
23 Parkdale House **B1(12)**
8 Parkend Street **G10**
13 Parker Street **J8**
14 Parkgate Avenue **K8**
14 Parkgate Cres **K8(36)**
14 Parkgate Drive **K8(35)**
14 Parkgate Gdns **K8(38)**
14 Parkgate Parade **K8(37)**
27 Parklands Close **M9(13)**
20 Parkmore Street **H5(1)**
4 Parkmore Terr **G14(4)**
9 Parkmount Cl. **H10(6)**
6 Parkmount Gdns **H12**
6 Parkmount Lane **H12(3)**
6 Parkmount Parade **G12**
6 Parkmount Pass **H12(1)**
6 Parkmount Pl. **H12(4)**
6 Parkmount Road **G12**
9 Parkmount St **H10(8)**
6 Parkmount Terrace **H12**
6 Parkmount Way **H12(2)**
8 Parkside Gardens **G10**
8 Parkview Court **F9(41)**
7 Parkview Terr. **E9(10)**
15 Pasedena Gdns **M7**
12 Patterson's Pl. **G8(33)**
13 Paulett Avenue **H7(2)**
13 Paxton Street **J7**
13 Pearl Street **J7**
14 Pembroke Mews **L7(17)**
1 Pembroke St. **F7(48)**
19 Penge Gardens **G5(12)**
26 Pennington Park **J2**
20 Penrose Street **H6**
1 Percy Place **F8**
1 Percy Street **F8**
1 Pernau Street **F8(78)**
13 Perry Court **J7(38)**
12 Peter's Hill **G8**
24 Phennick Drive **D3**
21 Picardy Avenue **K5**
9 Pilot Place **H9(9)**
9 Pilot Street **H9**
8 Pim Street **G9**
14 Pim's Avenue **L8**
23 Pine Cross **B1**
2 Pine Street **H7(23)**
2 Pine Way **H7**

3 Pineview Drive **G14**
3 Pineview Gardens **G14(2)**
3 Pineview Park **G14**
3 Pineview Road **G14**
25 Piney Hills **F4**
25 Piney Lane **F3**
25 Piney Park **F4**
25 Piney Walk **F3**
25 Piney Way **F3**
8 Pinkerton Walk **G9(18)**
20 Pirrie Park Gdns **J6(12)**
15 Pirrie Road **M8(2)**
13 Pitt Place **J8(20)**
9 Pittsburgh Street **H10**
1 Plevna Park **F8(19)**
12 Plunkett Court **G8(11)**
11 Pollard Close **E8(4)**
11 Pollard Street **E8(22)**
9 Pollock Road **H9**
21 Pommern Parade **K6**
14 Pommona Avenue **K8**
8 Ponsonby Avenue **G10**
13 Portallo Street **J7**
24 Porter Park **D3**
3 Portland Avenue **E16**
4 Portmore Hill **G14**
17 Portnamona Ct. **C6(13)**
4 Portrosse Park **H15(14)**
12 Posnett Court **G7(31)**
12 Posnett Street **G7**
13 Pottinger Street **J7(69)**
2 Pottinger's Entry **H8(10)**
13 Powerscourt Place **H6**
20 Powerscourt Street **H6(1)**
7 Premier Drive **G11**
8 Premier Grove **G11(8)**
7 Prestwick Drive **E11(3)**
7 Prestwick Park **E11**
19 Pretoria Street **G6**
20 Primrose Street **H5(13)**
7 Primrose Street **D10(4)**
1 Prince Andrew Gdns **F7(41)**
1 Prince Andrew Pk. **F7(38)**
3 Prince Charles Way **F16**
19 Prince Edward Dr. **G5**
19 Prince Edward Gdns **G5(2)**
19 Prince Edward Park **G5**
21 Prince Regent Road **L6**
15 Prince of Wales Av. **N8**
4 Prince's Avenue **H16**
2 Prince's Court **H8(14)**
9 Prince's Dock Street **H9**
2 Prince's Street **H8**
2 Prince's Street Ct. **H8(13)**
27 Prior's Lea **N11(1)**
24 Priory Gardens **D4(10)**
24 Priory Park **D4**
16 Private Avenue **Q7(1)**
10 Purdy's Lane **J4**
25 Purdysburn **G1**
26 Purdysburn Road **H2**
12 Quadrant Place **G8(31)**
16 Quarry Cottages **Q7(8)**
16 Quarry Lane **Q7**
27 Quarry Road **N9**
4 Quay Road **H14**
2 Queen Elizabeth Bridge **H8**
12 Queen Street **G8**
8 Queen Victoria Gdns **G11(21)**
14 Queen Victoria St. **K8(17)**
12 Queen's Arcade **G8(38)**
2 Queen's Bridge **H8**
8 Queen's Parade **G9**
2 Queen's Quay **H8**
2 Queen's Quay Road **H8**
9 Queen's Road **J9**
2 Queen's Square **H8**
20 Queensberry Park **J5**
8 Queensland Street **F9**
14 Quinton Street **K7**
20 Raby Street **H5**
13 Radnor Street **J7(24)**
23 Railway Street **B1(1)**
23 Railway Street **C2(1)**

12 Railway Street **G7(105)**
23 Railway View **B1(2)**
12 Rainey Way **G7(81)**
8 Raleigh Street **F9**
17 Ramoan Drive **C5(17)**
17 Ramoan Gardens **C5**
24 Ramore Park **E3**
4 Randal Park **F5**
20 Ranelagh Street **J6**
14 Ranfurly Drive **L8(7)**
2 Raphael Street **H7**
12 Ratcliffe Street **G7(103)**
2 Rathbone Street **H7(1)**
19 Rathcool Street **F5**
4 Rathcoole Close **H14(5)**
4 Rathcoole Drive **H15**
4 Rathcoole Gardens **H14(6)**
4 Rathdrum Park **H15(7)**
4 Rathdrum Street **F5**
19 Rathgar Street **F5**
7 Rathlin Street **E9**
24 Rathmore Avenue **D3**
4 Rathmore Drive **H15**
4 Rathmore Gardens **D3(17)**
24 Rathmore Park **D3(14)**
4 Rathmore Way **G15**
23 Rathmoyne House **B2(12)**
4 Rathmullan Drive **H15**
14 Ravencroft Avenue **K8**
13 Ravenhill Avenue **J6**
20 Ravenhill Court **J6(15)**
13 Ravenhill Crescent **J7(35)**
20 Ravenhill Gardens **J6**
20 Ravenhill Parade **J6**
20 Ravenhill Park **J6**
20 Ravenhill Park Gdns **J5**
20 Ravenhill Road **J6**
13 Ravenhill Street **J7**
14 Ravenscroft Street **K8(16)**
13 Ravensdale Cres. **J7(69)**
13 Ravensdale Street **J7(70)**
20 Ravensdene Crescent **J6**
20 Ravensdene Mews **J6(18)**
20 Ravensdene Park **J6**
20 Ravenswood Crescent **M6**
22 Ravenswood Park **M6**
13 Redcar Street **J7**
14 Redcliffe Drive **K8**
14 Redcliffe Parade **K8**
14 Redcliffe Street **K8(47)**
24 Redhill Manor **D3(23)**
23 Regent Street **G9**
20 Reid Street **J6**
12 Renagh Park **H16(4)**
12 Renfrew House **G7(96)**
12 Renfrew Walk **G7(60)**
12 Renwick Street **G7(52)**
13 Riada Close **J8(65)**
14 Ribble Street **K8**
13 Richardson Ct. **J7(48)**
13 Richardson Street **J7**
15 Richhill Crescent **M7**
16 Richhill Park **M7**
18 Richmond Mews **D4(11)**
18 Richmond Park **D4**
19 Richmond Park **G5**
8 Richmond Sq. **G10(3)**
1 Richview Street **F7**
19 Ridgeway Street **G5**
2 Riga Street **F8**
17 Ringford Crescent **B4**
17 Ringford Park **B4(7)**
17 Rinnalea Close **B5(27)**
17 Rinnalea Gdns **B5(28)**
17 Rinnalea Grove **B5(29)**
17 Rinnalea Walk **B5(30)**
17 Rinnalea Way **B5(31)**
9 Ritchie Street **H10**
17 River Close **C4(9)**
2 River Terrace **H7**
18 Riverdale Close **D5(11)**
18 Riverdale Gardens **D5**
18 Riverdale Park E. **D5**
17 Riverdale Park N. **C5**

18 Riverdale Park S. **D4**
17 Riverdale Park W. **C5**
17 Riverdale Pk. Av. **C5(14)**
17 Riverdale Park Drive **C5**
18 Riverdale Place **D5(10)**
1 Riverside Sq. **F7(19)**
1 Riverside Way **F7(23)**
19 Riverview Street **G5(8)**
8 Robina Court **G10(7)**
8 Robina Street **G10**
21 Rochester Avenue **K5**
21 Rochester Drive **K5**
21 Rochester Road **K5**
21 Rochester Street **J7(64)**
11 Rock Grove **D7(10)**
11 Rockdale Street **E7**
11 Rockland Street **E7**
11 Rockmore Road **E7**
16 Rockmount **Q7(3)**
11 Rockmount Street **E7**
3 Rockview Lane **G16**
12 Rockview Street **F6**
10 Rockville Court **L9(9)**
11 Rockville Street **E7**
21 Rocky Road **K4**
15 Rocky Road **N6**
21 Roddens Crescent **L6**
21 Roddens Gdns **L6(4)**
21 Roddens Park **L6**
1 Roden Pass **F7(10)**
1 Roden Square **F7(15)**
1 Roden Street **F7**
1 Roden Way **F7(11)**
18 Rodney Drive **E6**
18 Rodney Parade **E6**
8 Roe Street **F9**
26 Rogers Park **J3**
26 Rogers Place **J3(13)**
1 Roosevelt Rise **F7(44)**
1 Roosevelt Sq. **F7(43)**
1 Roosevelt Street **F7(25)**
9 Rosapenna Court **F9(5)**
8 Rosapenna Drive **F10**
8 Rosapenna Parade **F10**
17 Rosapenna Sq. **B5(11)**
8 Rosapenna Street **F9**
8 Rosapenna Wk. **F10(27)**
4 Roscor Square **H15(5)**
7 Rosebank Street **E9**
13 Rosebery Gardens **J7**
13 Rosebery Road **J7**
14 Rosebery Street **K7**
12 Roseland Place **G7(27)**
8 Roseleigh Street **F10**
25 Rosemary Park **F3**
12 Rosemary Street **G8**
16 Rosemount Av. **P7(1)**
8 Rosemount Gdns. **G10**
21 Rosemount Park **L5**
16 Rosepark **P7**
16 Rosepark Central **P7**
16 Rosepark Meadows **P7(27)**
16 Rosepark East **P7**
16 Rosepark South **P7**
16 Rosepark West **P7**
20 Rosetta Avenue **H5**
20 Rosetta Court **H5(11)**
20 Rosetta Drive **H5**
20 Rosetta Parade **H5**
20 Rosetta Park **H5**
20 Rosetta Road **J5**
20 Rosetta Road East **J5**
20 Rosetta Way **J5(4)**
8 Rosevale Street **F9**
8 Rosewood Court **F9(30)**
21 Rosewood Park **L5**
8 Rosewood Street **F9**
17 Rosgoill Drive **B5**
17 Rosgoill Gardens **B5**
17 Rosgoill Park **C5**
16 Roslin Gardens **P7(19)**
13 Roslyn Street **J7**
1 Ross Cottages **F8(20)**
1 Ross Court **F8(88)**
1 Ross Rise **F8(21)**

| | | | |
|---|---|---|---|
| 1 Ross Road **F8** | 17 St. Patrick's Grove **C6** | 6 Serpentine Road **G13** | 17 Slieveban Drive **C5** |
| 1 Ross Street **F8** | 13 St. Patrick's Walk **J8(30)** | 1 Servia Street **F7(31)** | 5 Slievecoole Park **F12** |
| 5 Rosscoole Park **F12** | 9 St. Paul's Fold **H9(13)** | 1 Sevastopol St. **F8(100)** | 5 Slievedarragh Park **F12** |
| 4 Rosslea Way **H15** | 9 St. Paul's Street **H9(18)** | 1 Seventh Street **F8** | 17 Slievegallion Drive **C5** |
| 20 Rossmore Avenue **H5** | 1 St. Peter's Court **F8(34)** | 14 Severn Street **K8** | 5 Slievegoland Park **G13(1)** |
| 20 Rossmore Cres **H5(17)** | 12 St. Peter's Place **G8(64)** | 23 Seymour Hill House **C2(14)** | 5 Slievemoyne Park **G12** |
| 20 Rossmore Drive **H5(16)** | 1 St. Peter's Sq. E. **F8(90)** | 23 Seymour Hill Mews **C2(13)** | 5 Slievetoye Park **F12** |
| 17 Rossnareen Avenue **C5** | 1 St. Peter's Sq. N. **F8(91)** | 2 Seymour Lane **H8(23)** | 19 Sloan Court **F6(4)** |
| 17 Rossnareen Grove **C5(24)** | 1 St. Peter's Sq. S. **F8(92)** | 8 Seymour Row **H8(22)** | 12 Smithfield Sq. N. **G8(50)** |
| 17 Rossnareen Park **B5(17)** | 12 St. Peter's Walk **G8(64)** | 2 Seymour Street **H8(25)** | 4 Snakey Path **G14** |
| 17 Rossnareen Road **C5(1)** | 3 St. Quentin Avenue **F16** | 8 Shaftesbury Av. **H7** | 8 Snugville Street **F9** |
| 8 Rothsay Square **F9(1)** | 3 St. Quentin Pk . **E16(16)** | 2 Shaftesbury Square **G7** | 13 Solway Street **J8** |
| 2 Rotterdam Court **H8(15)** | 12 St. Stephens Ct. **G8(49)** | 21 Shalom Park **L5(2)** | 7 Somerdale Gardens **E10(6)** |
| 2 Rotterdam Street **H8(28)** | 9 St. Vincent Street **H11** | 13 Shamrock Court **J7(28)** | 7 Somerdale Park **E10** |
| 1 Roumania Rise **F8(45)** | 12 Sackville Court **G8(41)** | 13 Shamrock Place **J7(40)** | 20 Somerset Street **H5(14)** |
| 13 Rounhill Street **J8** | 14 Sagimor Gardens **K7** | 13 Shamrock Street **J7(54)** | 5 Somerton Close **G11(14)** |
| 23 Rowan Drive **B1** | 26 Saintfield Road **J3** | 5 Shancoole Park **F12** | 8 Somerton Court **G11** |
| 12 Rowland Way **G7** | 5 Salisbury Avenue **F11** | 12 Shandarragh Park **F12** | 8 Somerton Drive **G11(6)** |
| 12 Royal Lodge Ave. **J2(11)** | 12 Salisbury Court **G7(78)** | 22 Shandon Court **M6(21)** | 8 Somerton Gardens **G11** |
| 26 Royal Lodge Ct. **J2(12)** | 5 Salisbury Gardens **F11** | 22 Shandon Hts. **M5(5)** | 6 Somerton Park **G11** |
| 26 Royal Lodge Gdns. **J2(13)** | 12 Salisbury Place **C2(3)** | 22 Shandon Park **M6** | 6 Somerton Road **G11** |
| 26 Royal Lodge Mews **J2(14)** | 12 Salisbury Street **G7** | 5 Shaneen Park **F12** | 21 Somme Drive **K5** |
| 26 Royal Lodge Park **J2(15)** | 12 Samuel Street **G8** | 5 Shangarry Park **F12** | 1 Sorella Street **F7** |
| 26 Royal Lodge Road **J2** | 4 Sanda Road **H14** | 12 Shankhill Parade **G8** | 12 Soudan Street **F6** |
| 23 Royal Mews **C3(3)** | 14 Sandbrook Gdns. **K9(2)** | 8 Shankhill Road **F8** | 20 South Bank **J5** |
| 20 Rugby Avenue **H6** | 14 Sandbrook Grove **K9(1)** | 12 Shankhill Terrace **G8(42)** | 25 South Crescent **G2** |
| 20 Rugby Court **H6(11)** | 14 Sandbrook Park **K9** | 5 Shanlieve Park **F12** | 17 South Green **C5** |
| 19 Rugby Mews **G6(10)** | 8 Sandcroft Street **F9(25)** | 14 Shanlieve Road **D5** | 18 South Link **D5** |
| 19 Rugby Parade **G6(15)** | 14 Sandford Avenue **L7** | 8 Shannon Court **F9(10)** | 20 South Parade **H6** |
| 19 Rugby Road **G6** | 14 Sandhill Drive **L7** | 8 Shannon Street **F9** | 16 South Sperrin **P7** |
| 19 Rugby Street **G6(16)** | 14 Sandhill Gardens **L7** | 19 Sharman Close **G4(6)** | 15 South Sperrin **N7** |
| 1 Rumford Street **F8** | 14 Sandhill Green **L7(7)** | 19 Sharman Drive **G4** | 22 Southland Dale **M6** |
| 19 Runnymede Dr. **F6(6)** | 14 Sandhill Parade **L7** | 19 Sharman Gardens **G4(8)** | 8 Southport Court **F9(42)** |
| 19 Runnymede Pde. **F6(7)** | 14 Sandhill Park **L7** | 19 Sharman Park **G4** | 20 Southview Cotts **H6(13)** |
| 3 Rural Gardens **E16(4)** | 19 Sandhurst Ct. **G6(12)** | 19 Sharman Road **G5** | 20 Southview Street **H6(12)** |
| 4 Rusheen Gdns. **H15(4)** | 19 Sandhurst Drive **G6** | 19 Sharman Way **G4(7)** | 8 Southwell Street **G9(26)** |
| 20 Rushfield Avenue **H5** | 19 Sandhurst Gardens **G6** | 14 Shaw Street **L8** | 8 Spamount Street **G9** |
| 19 Rusholme Street **F9(52)** | 20 Sandhurst Road **H6(3)** | 17 Shaw's Avenue **C5(28)** | 16 Sperrin Drive **P7(9)** |
| 22 Russell Park **N6** | 14 Sandown Drive **L7** | 17 Shaw's Close **B5(20)** | 16 Sperrin Park **P7(8)** |
| 1 Russell Place **H7(18)** | 15 Sandown Park **M7** | 17 Shaw's Court **C5(26)** | 1 Spier's Place **F8(14)** |
| 2 Russell Street **H7(22)** | 11 Sandown Park S. **E7(6)** | 17 Shaw's Park **C5(25)** | 1 Spinner Square **F8(94)** |
| 8 Ruth Street **G9** | 15 Sandown Road **M7** | 17 Shaw's Place **C5(27)** | 7 Spinnershill Lane **D11(10)** |
| 7 Rutherglen Street **E9** | 15 Sandringham Mews **M7(6)** | 17 Shaw's Road **C5** | 13 Spring Place **J7(43)** |
| 22 Rutland Street **H6** | 19 Sandringham St. **F6** | 20 Shelbourne Road **J6** | 13 Spring Street **J7(17)** |
| 22 Ryan Park **M4** | 12 Sandy Row **G7** | 12 Sherbrook Close **G8(9)** | 11 Springdale Gdns. **E8(8)** |
| 1 Rydalmere Street **F7** | 19 Sandymount Street **G5** | 8 Sherbrook Terrace **G9** | 11 Springfield Avenue **E8** |
| 17 St. Agnes Drive **D5** | 19 Sans Souci Park **G5** | 20 Sheridan Court **G9(14)** | 11 Springfield Cl. **D8(15)** |
| 17 St. Agnes Place **C5(23)** | 5 Sarajac Crescent **F11** | 8 Sheridan Street **G9** | 11 Springfield Court **F8(25)** |
| 19 St. Albans Gdns. **G5(13)** | 13 Sark Street **J8(12)** | 13 Sheriff Street **J8(51)** | 11 Springfield Cres. **E8(10)** |
| 12 St. Andrew's Sq. E. **G7(19)** | 13 Saunders Close **J8(27)** | 12 Sheringhurst Park **H12** | 11 Springfield Drive **E8** |
| 12 St. Andrew's Sq. N. **G7(20)** | 8 Saunderson Court **F9(2)** | 13 Sherwood Street **J7(62)** | 11 Springfield Hts. **D8(16)** |
| 12 St. Andrew's Sq. W. **G7(26)** | 15 Sawel Hill **C5** | 11 Sheskin Way **J5** | 11 Springfield Parade **E8** |
| 9 St. Aubyn Street **H11** | 12 Schomberg Av. **M8** | 20 Shimna Close **J5** | 11 Springfield Park **D8** |
| 8 St. Colman's Ct. **F9(60)** | 15 Schomberg Drive **G7(38)** | 9 Ship Street **H9** | 11 Springhill Avenue **D7** |
| 16 St. Elizabeth Ct. **Q8(2)** | 15 Schomberg Park **M8** | 9 Shipbuoy Street **H9(19)** | 11 Springhill Close **D7(14)** |
| 8 St. Gemmas Ct. **F9(3)** | 12 Schomberg Street **G7(85)** | 8 Shore Crescent **H12** | 11 Springhill Crescent **D7(33)** |
| 12 St. George's Gdns **G7(90)** | 22 School Road **N4** | 6 Shore Road **H12** | 11 Springhill Drive **D7(34)** |
| 19 St. Ives Gardens **G8** | 26 School Road **J3** | 2 Short Strand **H8** | 11 Springhill Gdns. **D7(24)** |
| 11 St. James's Av. **E7(8)** | 13 Scotch Row **J8(18)** | 9 Short Street **H9(20)** | 11 Springhill Heights **D7(32)** |
| 11 St. James's Cres. **E6** | 12 Scott Street **G7** | 6 Shrewsbury Drive **F4(13)** | 11 Springhill Rise **D7(35)** |
| 11 St. James's Drive **E7** | 2 Scrabo Street **H8(30)** | 18 Shrewsbury Gardens **E4** | 11 Springmadden.Ct. **D8(14)** |
| 11 St. James's Gardens **E7** | 8 Seabank Parade **H11** | 19 Shrewsbury Park **F4** | 11 Springmartin Road **D8** |
| 11 St. James's Pde. **E7(20)** | 8 Seabourne Parade **G11** | 24 Sicily Park **E3** | 7 Springvale Drive **D11** |
| 11 St. James's Park **E7** | 13 Seaforde Court **J8(36)** | 1 Silver Birch Courts **F8(65)** | 7 Springvale Fold **D11(34)** |
| 11 St. James's Place **E7** | 13 Seaforde Gardens **J8(37)** | 8 Silverstream Avenue **E11** | 11 Springvale Gdns. **D11** |
| 11 St. James's Road **E6** | 13 Seaforde Street **J8** | 7 Silverstream Crescent **E11** | 11 Springvale Parade **D11** |
| 8 St. James's St. **G9(12)** | 9 Seagrove Parade **H11** | 7 Silverstream Drive **E11** | 7 Springvale Pk. **D11(29)** |
| 11 St. John's Avenue **H5** | 8 Seagrove Place **G11(7)** | 7 Silverstream Gardens **E11** | 7 Springview Walk **F7(33)** |
| 20 St. John's Court **H5(10)** | 8 Seaholm Parade **G11** | 7 Silverstream Parade **E11** | 11 Squire's Hill Cres. **D11** |
| 20 St. John's Park **H4** | 8 Seal Road **J11** | 7 Silverstream Park **E11** | 11 Squire's Hill Park **D11** |
| 16 St. John's Wood Pk. **Q8(1)** | 8 Sealands Parade **G11** | 7 Silverstream Road **E11** | 11 Squire's Hill Road **D11** |
| 20 St. Jude's Avenue **H5** | 9 Seamount **H11(3)** | 7 Silverstream Terr. **D11(26)** | 2 Stanfield Place **H7(14)** |
| 20 St. Jude's Crescent **H5** | 8 Seamount Parade **G11** | 8 Silvio Street **F9** | 2 Stanfield Row **H7(13)** |
| 20 St. Jude's Parade **H5** | 8 Seapark Drive **G11** | 9 Simpson's Villas **J16(11)** | 12 Stanhope Drive **G8** |
| 8 St. Katherine Road **E6** | 8 Seascape Pde. **G11(22)** | 9 Sinclair Road **J10** | 8 Stanhope St. **G9(40)** |
| 2 St. Kilda Court **H7(10)** | 8 Seaview Close **G10(16)** | 7 Sinclair Street **L7(4)** | 12 Stanley Court **G8(46)** |
| 2 St. Kilda Street **H7(16)** | 9 Seaview Drive **G11** | 14 Sintonville Avenue **K8(46)** | 7 Stanley Street **G7** |
| 13 St. Leonard's Cr. **J8(28)** | 9 Seaview Gardens **H11(2)** | 17 Siulnamona Court **C6(12)** | 10 Station Road **L9** |
| 13 St. Leonard's St. **J8(49)** | 9 Seaview Street **H10(7)** | 8 Skegoneill Avenue **G11** | 4 Station Road **J16** |
| 13 St. Luke's Close **F8(3)** | 14 Sefton Drive **L8** | 8 Skegoneill Drive **G10** | 2 Station Street **H8** |
| 1 St. Luke's Walk **F8(18)** | 1 Selby Court **F7(14)** | 8 Skegoneill Street **H10(1)** | 8 Station St. Flyover **H8** |
| 8 St. Mary's Street **F9(24)** | 8 Selby Walk **F7(20)** | 2 Skipper Street **H8(26)** | 23 Station View **C3(1)** |
| 13 St. Matthew's Ct. **J8(60)** | 16 Selkirk Row **P7(7)** | 14 Skipton Street **K8** | 8 Steam Mill Lane **H8** |
| 18 St. Meryl Park **D6** | 6 Serpentine Gdns. **G14** | 18 Slemish Way **D5** | 14 Steen's Row **K7(8)** |
| | 6 Serpentine Pde. **G13(5)** | | 12 Stephen Street **G8(62)** |

2 Stewart Street H7
17 Stewartstown Av. B5
17 Stewartstown Gdns B5(19)
17 Stewartstown House B2(17)
17 Stewartstown Park B5
17 Stewartstown Road B4
21 Stirling Avenue K5
21 Stirling Gardens K5
21 Stirling Road K5
18 Stockman's Av. D5
18 Stockman's Ct. D5(13)
18 Stockman's Cres. D5
18 Stockman's Drive D5
18 Stockman's Gdns. D5(7)
18 Stockman's Lane D5
18 Stockman's Lane E5
18 Stockman's Park D5
18 Stockman's Way D5
16 Stoney Road P8
7 Stoneycairn Ct. D11(6)
14 Stonyford Street K8(28)
15 Stormont Court N7(10)
15 Stormont Park N8
9 Stormont Road J10
15 Stormont Villas N8(2)
13 Stormount Cres. J7(6)
13 Stormount Lane J7(9)
13 Stormount St. J7(53)
16 Stornaway Row P7(7)
21 Stracam Corner K5
13 Strand Close J8(57)
13 Srand Court L8(27)
13 Strand Mews J8(56)
13 Strand Walk J8(52)
14 Strandburn Ct. K8(23)
14 Strandburn Cres. L8(1)
14 Strandburn Drive L8
14 Strandburn Gdns. K8(1)
10 Strandburn Pde. L9(1)
14 Strandburn Park L8(38)
14 Strandburn Street K8
19 Strandview St. G5(9)
18 Strangford Avenue E4
19 Stranmillis Ct. G5(4)
19 Stranmillis Embank. G6
19 Stranmillis Gdns. G6
19 Stranmillis Mews G5(5)
19 Stranmillis Park G6
19 Stranmillis Road G5
19 Stranmillis Street G5
7 Stratford Gardens E10
24 Strathallen Park D2
14 Strathearn Mews L8(17)
27 Strathearn Park M9
8 Stratheden Street G9
8 Stratheden St. G9(51)
5 Strathmore Pk. G12(12)
5 Strathmore Park N. G12
5 Strathmore Park S. G12
7 Strathroy Park E10
24 Strathyre Park D2
12 Stroud Street G7
12 Sturgeon Street G7(23)
17 Suffolk Avenue B4
17 Suffolk Cres. C4
17 Suffolk Drive B4
17 Suffolk Parade B4(10)
17 Suffolk Road B4
1 Sugarfield Street F8
1 Sultan Square F8(43)
1 Sultan Way F8(38)
8 Summer Street F9
15 Summerhill Avenue N7
8 Summerhill Court F9(7)
23 Summerhill Drive B2
23 Summerhill Gdns. B2(6)
15 Summerhill Pde. N7(3)
23 Summerhill Park B2(4)
15 Summerhill Park N7
23 Summerhill Place B2(5)
23 Summerhill Road B3
14 Sunbury Avenue L7(13)
21 Sunderland Road K5
5 Sunningdale Drive F11
5 Sunningdale Gdns. E11

5 Sunningdale Gn. E11(2)
8 Sunningdale Gve. E11(1)
5 Sunningdale Park F11
5 Sunningdale Pk. N. F11
5 Sunninghill Drive F11
5 Sunninghill Gdns. E11
5 Sunninghill Park E11
20 Sunninghill Park H5
23 Sunnymede Av. B2(7)
23 Sunnymede Park B2
20 Sunnyside Cres. H5
20 Sunnyside Drive H5
23 Sunnyside Park B2
20 Sunnyside Park H5
20 Sunnyside Street H5
13 Sunwich Street J7(36)
19 Surrey Street F6
13 Susan Street J8
2 Sussex Place H7(31)
13 Swift Place J7(8)
13 Swift Street J7(46)
14 Sycamore Grove L8(28)
14 Sydenham Avenue L8
14 Sydenham By-Pass K9
14 Sydenham Cres. L8
14 Sydenham Drive L8(35)
14 Sydenham Gardens L8
14 Sydenham Park L8
13 Sydenham Road J8
8 Sydney Street West F9
8 Sylvan Street F10
1 Symons Street F7
3 Syringa Street G9(1)
2 Talbot Street H8
14 Tamar Court K8(52)
14 Tamar Street K8
13 Tamery Pass J7(14)
18 Tardree Park D5(1)
8 Tasmania Street F9(64)
8 Tate's Avenue F6
19 Tate's Mews F6(11)
6 Taunton Avenue G12
19 Tavanagh Street F6
25 Taylor Court G2(19)
12 Taylor Street G7(28)
7 Tedburn Park D10
7 Telfair Street H8(16)
13 Temple Street J7(57)
13 Templemore Av. J8
13 Templemore Cl. J7(13)
13 Templemore Pl. J7(22)
13 Templemore Street J7
8 Tennent Street F9
13 Tern Street J8(14)
12 Teutonic Gdns. G7(69)
1 Thalia Street F7
11 Thames Court E7(21)
11 Thames Street E7(5)
20 The Beeches H4(3)
24 The Close D3(15)
24 The Crescent D2
23 The Cutts B1
4 The Diamond H15
19 The Drive G4(2)
14 The Earls Court L8(18)
26 The Gables J2(10)
8 The Glen G10
27 The Grange N9(2)
23 The Green C3
15 The Hamlets M8(23)
23 The Hawthorns C3
13 The Hill D3
24 The Hollies L7(12)
24 The Laurels D3(13)
24 The Manor C3
26 The Mews H2(9)
4 The Mount J7
8 The Oaks H15(16)
13 The Park B3
25 The Plateau Piney Hills f4
27 The Stables M9(12)
13 The Straight K5
21 The Village Green K6(9)
24 The Vines D3
21 The Willows K4(3)

1 Theodore Street F7(37)
21 Thiepval Street K5
1 Third Street F8
5 Thirlmere Gardens F11
13 Thistle Court J8(40)
8 Thomas Street G9(50)
13 Thompson Street J8(69)
9 Thompson Wharf Rd J10(1)
4 Thorburn Road G14
8 Thorndale Avenue G9
13 Thorndyke Street J7
23 Thornhill Court B2(3)
23 Thornhill Cres. B2(2)
15 Thornhill Cres. N7(1)
15 Thornhill Drive N7
19 Thornhill Gdns. F5(9)
15 Thornhill Grove N7(7)
23 Thornhill House B2(16)
7 Thornhill Malone F5(11)
15 Thornhill Parade N7
15 Thornhill Park N7
23 Thornhill Road B2
18 Thone Terrace G14(1)
12 Tierney Gdns. G7(79)
17 Tildarg Avenue B4
13 Tildarg Street J6
27 Tillysburn Dr. M10(1)
27 Tillysburn Gve. M9(11)
27 Tillysburn Park M10
20 Timbey Park H5
20 Titania Street J6
5 Tivoli Gardens F11
3 Tobarcooran Av. F16
12 Tobergill Street F9(17)
5 Tokio Gardens F11
17 Tollnamona Ct. C6(11)
2 Tomb Street H8
13 Toronto Street J7
24 Torr Way D3
8 Torrens Avenue F10
8 Torrens Court F10(28)
8 Torrens Crescent F10
8 Torrens Drive F10
8 Torrens Gdns. F10(32)
8 Torrens Parade F10
8 Torrens Road F10
5 Tory Lane West F15(4)
13 Tower Court J8(38)
13 Tower Street J8
2 Townhall Street H8(32)
12 Townsend Street G8
12 Townsley Street K8(12)
9 Trafalgar Street H9(3)
9 Trainfield Street G9(3)
11 Tralee Street E8(18)
10 Tramway Street G10(8)
20 Trassey Close J5
17 Trench Avenue C4
17 Trench Park C4
17 Trenchard B4(8)
21 Trigo Parade K6
13 Trillick Court J7(47)
13 Trillick Street J7
12 Trinity Street G7(33)
24 Trossachs Drive D2
24 Trossachs Gardens D2
24 Trossachs Park D2(1)
18 Trostan Gardens D5(14)
18 Trostan Way D5(6)
21 Tudor Avenue K5
10 Tudor Dale L9(11)
21 Tudor Drive K5
5 Tudor Place F9
17 Tullagh Park C5
4 Tulleevin Drive H16
4 Tulleevin Walk H16(3)
21 Tullyard Way L5
17 Tullymore Drive C5(2)
17 Tullymore Gardens C5
17 Tullymore Walk C5(3)
1 Turin Street F7(53)
7 Twaddell Avenue E9
13 Tweskard Lodge N9(6)
27 Tweskard Park N9
5 Tyndale Crescent E11

5 Tyndale Drive E11(4)
5 Tyndale Gardens E11
5 Tyndale Green E11
5 Tyndale Grove E11
1 Tyne Street F8(103)
12 Tyrone Street G8(65)
2 Ulster Avenue C2
14 Ulsterdale St. K7(18)
19 Ulsterville Avenue F6
19 Ulsterville Drive F6
19 Ulsterville Gardens F6
19 Ulsterville Place F6(1)
12 Union Street G8
14 Uniondale St. K7(17)
12 Unity Walk G8(16)
20 University Avenue H6
19 University Road G6
19 University Square G6
19 University Sq. Mews G6(5)
19 University Street G6
19 University Terr. G6(6)
12 Upper Arthur Street G8
5 Upper Castle Pk. F12(5)
5 Upper Cavehill Rd. F12
8 Upper Charleville St. F9
2 Upper Church Lane H8
19 Upper Crescent G6
19 Uper Cres. Lane G6(2)
23 Upper Dunmurry Lane B3
13 Upper Frank Street J7
20 Upper Galwally J4
8 Upper Glenfarne St. F9(65)
23 Upper Green C3
21 Upper Knockbreda Rd. K5
24 Upper Lisburn Road D4
24 Upper Malone Cl. E3(21)
24 Upper Malone Cres E3(22)
24 Upper Malone Gdns E3(23)
24 Upper Malone Pk. E3(24)
24 Upper Malone Road E2
8 Uper Meadow Street G9
8 Upper Mervue Street G10
15 Upper Newtownards Rd M7
16 Upper Newtownards Rd Q8
12 Upper Queen St. G8(63)
1 Upper Riga Street F8
17 Upper Springfield Rd. C6
2 Upper Stanfield St. H7(29)
12 Up. Townsend Terr G8(52)
16 Upperlands Walk P7(5)
23 Upton Avenue D3
18 Upton Cottages D6(5)
18 Upton Court D6(23)
24 Upton Park D3
12 Utility Street G7(74)
12 Utility Walk G7(7)
3 Vaddegan Avenue F15
3 Vaddegan Drive F15
3 Vaddegan Gardens F15(2)
3 Vaddegan Park F15
11 Valleyside Close E8(21)
3 Vaddegan Road F15
8 Vancouver Drive G11
6 Vandyck Crescent G13
6 Vandyck Drive G13(3)
6 Vandyck Gardens G13
11 Vara Drive E8
19 Vauxhall Park G4
7 Velsheda Park E10
7 Velsheda Park E10
7 Velsheda Way E10
12 Ventry Lane G7(107)
12 Ventry Street G7(106)
11 Vere Foster Walk D8(18)
2 Verner Street H7(33)
12 Vernon Court G7(89)
12 Vernon Street G7
6 Veryan Gardens G13
13 Vicarage Street J8(41)
8 Vicinage Park G9
8 Vicinage Place G9(47)
13 Victor Place J7(10)

10 Victoria Avenue **L9**
10 Victoria Court **L9(12)**
10 Victoria Drive **L9**
23 Victoria Gardens **C2(2)**
5 Victoria Gardens **F11**
8 Victoria Parade **G9**
10 Victoria Road **L9**
9 Victoria Road **J9**
2 Victoria Square **H8**
2 Victoria Street **H8**
10 Vidor Court **L9(13)**
10 Vidor Gardens **L9(16)**
24 Viewfort Park **D2**
26 Village Court **H3(9)**
1 Violet Street **F7**
16 Vionville Close **P6(6)**
16 Vionville Court **P7(14)**
16 Vionville Green **P7(13)**
16 Vionville Heights **P6(5)**
16 Vionville Place **P7(16)**
16 Vionville Park **P7(17)**
16 Vionville Rise **P7**
16 Vionville View **P7(15)**
16 Vionville Way **P6(4)**
12 Virginia Street **G7(87)**
12 Virginia Way **G7(88)**
8 Vistula Street **F9**
6 Voltaire Gdns. **G13(6)**
13 Vulcan Court **J8(58)**
13 Vulcan Gardens **J8(59)**
13 Vulcan Link **J8(67)**
13 Vulcan Street **J8**
12 Wall Street **G8(66)**
7 Wallasey Park **E11**
20 Walmer Street **H5**
2 Walnut Court **H7(26)**
2 Walnut Street **H7**
15 Wandsworth Ct. **M8(22)**
15 Wandsworth Cres. **M8(4)**
15 Wandsworth Drive **M8**
15 Wandsworth Gdns. **M8**
15 Wandsworth Road **M8**
19 Wansbeck St. **G5(10)**
16 Wanstead Avenue **Q6**
16 Wanstead Gdns. **Q6(1)**
2 Waring Street **H8**
22 Warren Grove **M6**
1 Waterford Gdns. **F8(73)**
1 Waterford Street **F8**
1 Waterford Way **F8(33)**
6 Waterloo Gardens **G12**
5 Waterloo Park **G12**
5 Waterloo Park N. **G12**
5 Waterloo Park S. **G12**
11 Watermouth Cres. **E8(17)**
1 Waterville Street **F8**
9 Watkin's Road **H10**
12 Watson Street **G7(22)**
13 Watt Street **J7**
1 Wauchope Court **F7(17)**
6 Waveney Avenue **G12**
6 Waveney Drive **G12(5)**
6 Waveney Grove **G12(6)**
6 Waveney Hts. **H12(6)**
6 Waveney Park **G12**
14 Wayland Street **K7(15)**
22 Wayside Close **M6(13)**
7 Weavershill Lane **D11(12)**
7 Weavershill Walk **D11(11)**
24 Wedderburn Av. **D3**
24 Wedderburn Gdns. **D3**
13 Well Place **J7(44)**
14 Welland Street **K8(21)**
19 Wellesley Avenue **G6**
12 Wellington Court **G7(8)**
19 Wellington Park **G6**
19 Wellington Pk. Av. **G6(17)**
19 Wellington Pk Terr **G6(18)**
12 Wellington Place **G8**
12 Wellington Street **G7**
10 Wellwood Av. **K9(3)**
10 Wellwood Close **K9(5)**
12 Wellwood Street **G7**
2 Welsh Street **H7**
1 Wesley Court **G7(49)**

1 Wesley Street **G7(83)**
11 West Circular Cres. **D8**
11 West Circular Rd. **D8**
4 West Crescent **G15**
13 Westbourne St. **J8**
14 Westcott Street **K8(29)**
11 Westhill Way **D7(8)**
8 Westland Drive **F11**
8 Westland Gardens **F11**
8 Westland Road **F11**
8 Westland Way **F11(1)**
14 Westminster Av. **K8(10)**
14 Westminster Av. N. **K8(20)**
20 Westminster St. **H6(21)**
18 Weston Drive **E4**
11 Westrock Court **D7(18)**
11 Westrock Cres. **D7(17)**
11 Westrock Drive **D7**
11 Westrock Gdns. **D7**
11 Westrock Green **D7(21)**
11 Westrock Grove **E7(9)**
11 Westrock Pde. **D7(27)**
11 Westrock Park **D7(20)**
11 Westrock Place **D7(22)**
11 Westrock Sq. **E7(16)**
11 Westrock Way **E7(17)**
11 Westview Pass **D7(9)**
7 Westway Crescent **D9**
7 Westway Drive **D9**
7 Westway Gardens **D9**
7 Westway Grove **D9**
7 Westway Parade **D9**
7 Westway Park **D9**
7 Wheatfield Cres. **E10**
7 Wheatfield Drive **E10**
7 Wheatfield Gdns. **E10**
22 Whincroft Road **M6**
22 Whincroft Way **M6**
26 Whinney Heights **J3(2)**
25 Whinneyhill Dr. **G2(17)**
11 Whitecliff Cres. **D7**
11 Whitecliff Drive **D7(7)**
11 Whitecliff Parade **D7**
20 Whitehall Gardens **H5**
20 Whitehall Mews **H5(15)**
20 Whitehall Parade **H5**
4 Whitehouse Gdns. **J14(1)**
4 Whitehouse Park **J15**
11 Whiterock Close **D7(30)**
11 Whiterock Crescent **D7**
11 Whiterock Drive **D7**
11 Whiterock Gardens **D7**
11 Whiterock Pde. **D7(13)**
11 Whiterock Road **D7**
6 Whitewell Cres. **H13**
6 Whitewell Drive **H13**
6 Whitewell Parade **H13**
4 Whitewell Road **G14**
9 Whitla Street **H9(17)**
1 Wigton Street **F8(25)**
19 Wildflower Way **F6**
14 Wilgar Close **L8(29)**
14 Wilgar Street **L8**
19 Willesden Park **G4**
23 William Alexander Pk. **C3**
2 William Street **G8(56)**
2 William Street S. **H8(18)**
24 Willisfield Avenue **D3**
24 Willisfield Gdns. **D3(10)**
24 Willisfield Park **D3(16)**
4 Willow Park **H15(8)**
12 Willow Street **G7(110)**
21 Willowbank Cres. **K4(1)**
21 Willowbank Drive **K4**
8 Willowbank Gdns. **G10**
20 Willowbank Park **J5**
20 Willowbrook House **K6(17)**
13 Willowfield Avenue **J7**
13 Willowfield Cres. **J7(61)**
13 Willowfield Drive **J7**
13 Willowfield Gdns. **J7**
13 Willowfield Parade **J7**
13 Willowfield Street **J7**
13 Willowfield Walk **J7(26)**
20 Willowholme Cres. **J6(1)**

20 Willowholme Drive **J6**
20 Willowholme Pde. **J6(2)**
20 Willowholme St. **J6(20)**
17 Willowvale Avenue **C4**
17 Willowvale Gardens **C4**
17 Willowvale Mews **C4(11)**
24 Wilmont Park **D2**
27 Wilshere Drive **M9**
12 Wilson Street **G8(10)**
11 Wilson's Court **H8(7)**
1 Wilton Court **F8(105)**
1 Wilton Square N. **F8(58)**
1 Wilton Street **F8(61)**
8 Wimbledon Street **F9(67)**
8 Winchester Street **F9(68)**
11 Windermere Gardens **F11**
19 Windsor Avenue **F5**
19 Windsor Avenue N. **G6**
19 Windsor Close **F5(14)**
19 Windsor Court **F5(12)**
19 Windsor Drive **F6**
19 Windsor Mews **F5(16)**
19 Windsor Park **F5**
19 Windsor Road **F6**
12 Windsor Street **G7(108)**
12 Winecellar Entry **G8(47)**
12 Winetavern Street **G8**
14 Wingrove Gardens **K7**
15 Winston Gardens **M7**
14 Witham Street **K8**
7 Wolfend Drive **D11**
7 Wolfend Way **D11(4)**
13 Wolff Close **J8(21)**
10 Wolff Road **K10**
9 Wolseley Street **G6**
23 Wood Side **B1(6)**
23 Woodbourne Cres. **B4(6)**
26 Woodbreda Avenue **J3**
26 Woodbreda Crescent **J3(3)**
26 Woodbreda Drive **J3**
26 Woodbreda Gardens **J3(4)**
26 Woodbreda Park **J3**
5 Woodburn Drive **F11(4)**
14 Woodcot Avenue **K7**
22 Woodcroft Heights **M5(3)**
22 Woodcroft Rise **M5(4)**
26 Woodford Green **J2(4)**
8 Woodland Avenue **G10(20)**
4 Woodland Close **J15(1)**
4 Woodland Crescent **J15**
4 Woodland Drive **J15**
17 Woodland Grange **C4**
4 Woodland Place **J15**
4 Woodland Terrace **J15(4)**
15 Woodlands Court **M8(16)**
14 Woodlee Street **K7(21)**
21 Woodstock House **K6(8)**
13 Woodstock Link **J7**
13 Woodstock Place **J7(19)**
13 Woodstock Road **J7**
11 Woodvale Avenue **E8**
7 Woodvale Drive **E9**
7 Woodvale Gardens **E9**
7 Woodvale Parade **E9**
11 Woodvale Pass **E8**
7 Woodvale Road **E9**
7 Woodvale Street **E9**
22 Woodview Drive **N6**
22 Woodview Place **N6(3)**
22 Woodview Terrace **N6(2)**
11 Workman Avenue **E8**
10 Workman Road **K10**
7 Wye Street **J8(16)**
15 Wynard Park **M7**
20 Wynchurch Avenue **J4**
20 Wynchurch Close **J4(9)**
20 Wynchurch Gardens **J4(1)**
20 Wynchurch Park **J5**
20 Wynchurch Road **J4**
20 Wynchurch Terrace **J4**
20 Wynchurch Walk **J4**
8 Wyndham Drive **F10(29)**
8 Wyndham Street **F10(20)**
14 Wynfield Court **L8(23)**
14 Wynford Street **K7(2)**

4 Wynthorp Grove **J15(5)**
8 Yarrow Street **F9**
7 Yew Street **E9**
9 York Crescent **H11**
9 York Drive **H11**
12 York Lane **G8**
9 York Link **H9(14)**
9 York Parade **H11**
9 York Park **H11**
9 York Road **H10**
9 York Street **H9**
4 Ypres Park **J16**
14 Yukon Street **K8**

# NUMERICAL STREET INDEX

To find the map reference of the square in which the numbered street lies, refer to the letters in red on the horizontal edge of the map page and the figures in red on the vertical edge of the map page.

## B1

| | |
|---|---|
| 1 | Railway Street |
| 2 | Railway View |
| 3 | Colinview |
| 5 | Oakland Way |
| 6 | Wood Side |
| 12 | Parkdale House |
| 13 | Ferndale House |

## B2

| | |
|---|---|
| 1 | Laburnum Row |
| 2 | Thornhill Crescent |
| 3 | Thornhill Court |
| 4 | Summerhill Park |
| 5 | Summerhill Place |
| 6 | Summerhill Gardens |
| 7 | Sunnymede Avenue |
| 8 | Hawthorn Park |
| 9 | Harris Crescent |
| 10 | Alina Gardens |
| 11 | Coolmoyne House |
| 12 | Rathmoyne House |
| 13 | Aghery Walk |
| 14 | Beechtree Court |
| 15 | Kingscourt |
| 16 | Thornhill House |
| 17 | Stewartstown House |

## B3

| | |
|---|---|
| 1 | Laburnum Park |
| 2 | Glasvey Crescent |
| 3 | Cherry Park |
| 4 | Cherry Court |
| 5 | Cherry Walk |
| 6 | Cherry Close |
| 7 | Laburnum Way |
| 8 | Aspen Walk |
| 9 | Areema Court |
| 10 | Harcourt Terrace |
| 11 | Cotlands Green |

## B4

| | |
|---|---|
| 1 | Margaretta Court |
| 2 | Old Colin |
| 3 | Kilbourne Park |
| 4 | Caranmore Gardens |
| 5 | Glenview Terrace |
| 6 | Woodbourne Crescent |
| 7 | Ringford Park |
| 8 | Trenchard |
| 9 | Leestone Terrace |
| 10 | Suffolk Parade |
| 11 | Brooklands |
| 12 | Lenadoon Walk |
| 13 | Horn Walk |
| 14 | Doon Cottages |

## B5

| | |
|---|---|
| 1 | Glencolin Heights |
| 2 | Glencolin Park |
| 3 | Glencolin Close |
| 4 | Glencolin Walk |
| 5 | Glencolin Avenue |
| 6 | Glencolin Way |
| 7 | Mulroy Park |
| 8 | Glenveagh Park |
| 9 | Bunbeg Park |
| 10 | Gweedore Gardens |
| 11 | Rosapenna Square |
| 12 | Buncrana Gardens |
| 13 | Creeslough Walk |
| 14 | Creeslough Gardens |
| 15 | Naroon Park |
| 16 | Culmore Gardens |
| 17 | Rossnareen Park |
| 18 | Mizen Gardens |
| 19 | Stewartstown Gardens |

| | |
|---|---|
| 20 | Shaw's Close |
| 21 | Old Suffolk Road |
| 22 | Glencolin Court |
| 23 | Glencolin Grove |
| 24 | Glencolin Rise |
| 25 | Creeslough Park |
| 26 | Gweedore Crescent |
| 27 | Rinnalea Close |
| 28 | Rinnalea Gardens |
| 29 | Rinnalea Grove |
| 30 | Rinnalea Walk |
| 31 | Rinnalea Way |
| 32 | Falcarragh Drive |

## C1

| | |
|---|---|
| 1 | Larch Hill |
| 2 | Maple Crescent |

## C2

| | |
|---|---|
| 1 | Railway Street |
| 2 | Victoria Gardens |
| 3 | Salisbury Place |
| 4 | Auburn Street |
| 5 | Malone Gardens |
| 6 | Milfort Terrace |
| 7 | Beattie Park Terrace |
| 8 | Beattie Park North |
| 9 | Glenburn Court |
| 10 | Beattie Park South |
| 11 | Auburn Place |
| 12 | Lenwood Drive |
| 13 | Seymour Hill Mews |
| 14 | Seymour Hill House |

## C3

| | |
|---|---|
| 1 | Station View |
| 2 | Grange Avenue |
| 3 | Royal Mews |
| 4 | Manor Mews |
| 5 | Edenvale Meadows |

## C4

| | |
|---|---|
| 1 | Ladybrook Parade |
| 2 | Ladybrook Grove |
| 3 | Ladybrook Gardens |
| 4 | Drenia |
| 5 | Arlington Park |
| 6 | Farmhill |
| 7 | Northlands Park |
| 8 | Brooke Close |
| 9 | River Close |
| 10 | Ladybrook Cross |
| 11 | Willowvale Mews |
| 12 | Greenane Drive |
| 13 | Moor Park Avenue |
| 14 | Moor Park Drive |
| 15 | Moor Park Gardens |
| 16 | Moor Park Mews |

## C5

| | |
|---|---|
| 1 | Rossnareen Road |
| 2 | Tullymore Drive |
| 3 | Tullymore Walk |
| 4 | Ramoan Gardens |
| 5 | Tullymore Gardens |
| 6 | Killeen Park |
| 7 | Errigal Park |
| 8 | Brenda Park |
| 9 | Glenshane Gardens |
| 10 | Bingnian Way |
| 11 | Collin Gardens |
| 12 | Croaghan Gardens |
| 13 | Benbradagh Gardens |
| 14 | Riverdale Park Avenue |
| 15 | Coolnasilla Close |
| 16 | Hillhead Court |
| 17 | Ramoan Drive |

| | |
|---|---|
| 18 | Greenan |
| 19 | Hillhead Cottages |
| 20 | Cois Cluana |
| 21 | Hillhead Heights |
| 22 | Glen Road Cottages |
| 23 | St. Agnes Place |
| 24 | Rosnareen Grove |
| 25 | Shaw's Park |
| 26 | shaw's Court |
| 27 | Shaw's Place |
| 28 | Shaw's Avenue |

## C6

| | |
|---|---|
| 1 | Monagh Grove |
| 2 | Downfine Gardens |
| 3 | Ballaghbeg |
| 4 | Monagh Crescent |
| 5 | Gortnamona Rise |
| 6 | Gortnamona Heights |
| 7 | Gortnamona Court |
| 8 | Gortnamona View |
| 9 | Gortnamona Place |
| 10 | Carnnamona Court |
| 11 | Tollnamona Court |
| 12 | Siulnamona Court |
| 13 | Portnamona Court |
| 14 | Fodnamona Court |
| 15 | Closnamona Court |
| 16 | Coolnasilla Park |

## D2

| | |
|---|---|
| 1 | Trossachs Park |
| 2 | Aberfoyle Gardens |

## D3

| | |
|---|---|
| 1 | Lille Park |
| 2 | Ormande Avenue |
| 3 | Kirklowe Drive |
| 4 | Doon End |
| 5 | Killard Place |
| 6 | Locksley Park |
| 7 | Cranfield Gardens |
| 8 | Hillmount Court |
| 9 | Benmore Walk |
| 10 | Willisfield Gardens |
| 11 | Erinvale Park |
| 12 | Erinvale Gardens |
| 13 | The Laurels |
| 14 | Rathmore Park |
| 15 | The Close |
| 16 | Willisfield Park |
| 17 | Rathmore Gardens |
| 18 | Chippendale Court |
| 19 | Chippendale Gardens |
| 20 | Hollymount Court |
| 21 | Benmore Court |
| 22 | De Bere Court |
| 23 | Redhill Manor |
| 24 | Moveen House |
| 25 | Moylena House |

## D4

| | |
|---|---|
| 1 | Ardmore Park South |
| 2 | Diamond Avenue |
| 3 | Grangeville Drive |
| 4 | Aboo Court |
| 5 | Locksley Drive |
| 6 | Marguerite Park |
| 7 | Beechmount Park |
| 8 | Ardmore Court |
| 9 | Locksley Grange |
| 10 | Priory Gardens |
| 11 | Richmond Mews |

## D5

| | |
|---|---|
| 1 | Tardree Park |
| 2 | Derrin Pass |

| | |
|---|---|
| 3 | Benraw Terrace |
| 4 | Benraw Gardens |
| 5 | Dunmisk Terrace |
| 6 | Trostan Way |
| 7 | Stockman's Gardens |
| 8 | Mooreland Drive |
| 9 | Owenvarragh Gardens |
| 10 | Riverdale Place |
| 11 | Riverdale Close |
| 12 | Mooreland Crescent |
| 13 | Stockman's Court |
| 14 | Trostan Gardens |
| 15 | Benraw Green |

## D6

| | |
|---|---|
| 1 | Norfolk Way |
| 2 | Downfine Walk |
| 3 | Gransha Rise |
| 4 | Downfine Park |
| 5 | Upton Cottages |
| 6 | Gransha Grove |
| 7 | Denewood Drive |
| 8 | Andersonstown Parade |
| 9 | Andersonstown Drive |
| 10 | Andersonstown Gardens |
| 11 | Andersonstown Park |
| 12 | Andersonstown Grove |
| 13 | Norbury Street |
| 14 | Gransha Way |
| 15 | Bearnagh Glen |
| 16 | Glencourt |
| 17 | Lake Glen Crescent |
| 18 | Lake Glen Park |
| 19 | Lake Glen Parade |
| 20 | Lake Glen Close |
| 21 | Lake Glen Green |
| 22 | Glenmurry Court |
| 23 | Upton Court |

## D7

| | |
|---|---|
| 1 | New Barnsley Gardens |
| 2 | New Barnsley Green |
| 3 | New Barnsley Grove |
| 4 | Divismore Way |
| 5 | Glenalina Pass |
| 6 | Glenalina Gardens |
| 7 | Whitecliff Drive |
| 8 | Westhill Way |
| 9 | Westview Pass |
| 10 | Rock Grove |
| 11 | Ardmonagh Way |
| 13 | Whiterock Parade |
| 14 | Springhill Close |
| 15 | Ballymurphy Crescent |
| 16 | Ballymurphy Parade |
| 17 | Westrock Crescent |
| 18 | Westrock Court |
| 20 | Westrock Park |
| 21 | Westrock Green |
| 22 | Westrock Place |
| 23 | Carnmore Place |
| 24 | Springhill Gardens |
| 25 | Bleach Green Court |
| 26 | Bleach Green Terrace |
| 27 | Westrock Parade |
| 28 | Daisyhill Court |
| 29 | Altigarron Court |
| 30 | Whiterock Close |
| 31 | Westrock Drive |
| 32 | Springhill Heights |
| 33 | Springhill Crescent |
| 34 | Springhill Drive |
| 35 | Springhill Rise |

## D8

| | |
|---|---|
| 1 | Black Mountain Walk |
| 2 | Black Mountain Way |
| 3 | Highburn Gardens |
| 4 | Black Mountain Grove |

42

5 High Way
6 Black Mountain Park
7 Black Mountain Place
8 Highpark Cross
9 High Link
10 High Pass
11 High Side
12 High Gate
13 High Gate Terrace
14 Springmadden Court
15 Springfield Close
16 Springfield Heights
17 Britton's Lane
18 Vere Foster Walk
19 Black Mountain Parade

## D9

1 Lyndhurst Link
2 Lyndhurst Way
3 Lyndhurst Grove
4 Lyndhurst Close
5 Lyndhurst Rise
6 Forthriver Pass
7 Forthriver Fold
8 Forthbrook Court

## D10

1 Loughview Street
2 Glenside Drive
3 Forthriver Close
4 Primrose Street
5 Glenbank Parade
6 Legmail Street
7 Forthriver Crescent
8 Limepark Mews
11 Legaan Street
12 Harmony court
13 Cairndale

## D11

1 Limehill Grove
2 Limehill Street
4 Wolfend Way
5 Mountainhill Lane
6 Stoneycairn Court
7 Mountainhill Walk
8 Boodles Lane
9 Boodles Hill
10 Spinnershill Lane
11 Weavershill Walk
12 Weavershill Lane
13 Flaxton Place
14 Old Mill Way
15 Linen Grove
16 Greenhill Grove
17 Greenhill Lane
18 Millview Court
19 Millbank Park
20 Lupus Grove
21 Bleach Green
22 Leginn Street
23 New Farm Lane
24 Leggagh Court
26 Silverstream Terrace
27 Brae Hill Way
28 Brae Hill Link
29 Springvale Park
30 Brookmill Way
32 Legnavea Place
34 Springvale Fold

## E3

1 Locksley Place
2 Cloghan Gardens
3 Greystown Close
4 Malone View Crescent
5 Fairway Crescent
6 Fairway Drive
7 Linkview Park
8 Malfin Court
9 Malwood Close
10 Finch Close

11 Findon Place
12 Drummond Park
13 Finch Way
14 Finnis Close
15 Finbank Court
16 Malton Fold
17 Finwood Court
18 Malton Vale
19 Malton Court
20 Malton Rise
21 Upper Malone Close
22 Upper Malone Crescent
23 Upper Malone Gardens
24 Upper Malone Park
25 Findon Grove
26 Finch Court
27 Finch Place
28 Malone Cottages

## E4

1 Drummond Park
2 Balmoral Court
3 Kings Court
4 Balmoral Gardens
5 Balmoral Drive
6 Musgrave Park Court

## E5

1 Larkstone Street
2 Lislea Avenue

## E6

1 Glenmachan Place
2 Clondara Street
3 Clondara Parade

## E7

1 Dairy Street
2 Brighton Street
3 Islandbawn Drive
4 Braemar Street
5 Thames Street
6 Fallswater Drive
7 La Salle Gardens
8 St. James Avenue
9 Westrock Grove
10 Broadway Court
11 Britton's Court
12 Iris Court
13 Iris Grove
14 Iris Mews
15 Irwell Court
16 Westrock Square
17 Westrock Way
18 La Salle Mews
19 Beechmount Crescent
20 St. Jame's Parade
21 Thames Court

## E8

1 Dunmoyle Street
2 Forth Parade
3 Brookmount Gardens
4 Pollard Close
5 Merkland Place
6 Centurion Street
7 Mayo Link
8 Springdale Gardens
9 Esmond Street
10 Springfield Crescent
11 Cavendish Court
12 Benares Street
13 Caledon Court
14 Clovelly Street
15 Iris Walk
16 Mayo Court
17 Watermouth Crescent
18 Tralee Street
19 Ceylon Street
20 Belair Street
21 Valleyside Close

22 Pollard Street
23 Colinpark Street
24 Elswick Street
25 Springfield Court

## E9

1 Mountainview Place
2 Ballygomartin Park
3 Glenvale Street
4 Ainsworth Parade
5 Brookfield Place
6 Brookfield Walk
7 Butler Place
8 Butler Walk
9 Brookfield Street
10 Parkview Terrace
11 Disraeli Court
12 Disraeli Walk
13 Bray Court
14 Kerrera Street
15 Kerrera Court
16 Kerrera Mews
17 Palmer Court
18 Mountainview Park
19 Enfield Parade
20 Enfield Drive
21 Mossvale Street
22 Fingal Street
23 Lawnview Street
24 Oregon Gardens
25 Leopold Place
26 Mount Eden Court

## E10

1 Deerpark Parade
2 Farringdon Court
3 Farringdon Gardens
4 Cranbrook Gardens
5 Cranbrook Court
6 Somerdale Gardens
7 Hesketh Gardens

## E11

1 Sunningdale Grove
2 Sunningdale Green
3 Prestwick Drive
4 Tyndale Drive

## E15

1 Glenwell Drive
2 Hightown Crescent
3 Hightown Drive
4 Hightown Park
5 Collinbridge Close
6 Collinbridge Court
7 Farmley Mews

## E16

3 Harmin Parade
4 Rural Gardens
5 Glenbourne Avenue
6 Moyola Park
11 Braemar Court
12 Elm Court
13 Farrier Court
14 Hightown Court
15 Glencoole Park
16 St. Quentin Park
17 Lauren Court

## F4

1 Broomhill Close
2 Broomhill Court
3 Malone Grange
4 Malone Court Mews
5 Oakwood Mews
6 Newforge Dale
7 Oakwood Court
8 Oakwood Grove
9 Malone Beeches

10 Forest Hill
11 Balmoral Mews
12 New Forge Grange
13 Shrewsbury Drive
14 Broomhill Manor
15 New Forge Dale
16 Malone Park Central

## F5

1 Eileen Gardens
2 Marlborough Avenue
3 Ferndale Place
4 Marlborough Park
5 Charleville Avenue
6 Capstone Street
7 Marlborough Park Cross Avenue
8 Marlborough Park
9 Thornhill Gardens
10 Marlborough Gardens
11 Thornhill Malone
12 Windsor Drive
13 Bawnmore Court
14 Windsor Close
15 Kerrington Court
16 Windsor Mews
17 Notting Hill Manor
18 Marlborough Court
19 Mowhan Street
20 Mayfield Street
21 Maryville Avenue

## F6

1 Ulsterville Place
2 Northbrook Gardens
3 Eglantine Place
4 Sloan Court
5 Ashleigh Manor
6 Runnymede Drive
7 Runnymede Parade
8 Donegall Parade
9 Belgravia Avenue
10 Berkley Court
11 Tate's Mews

## F7

1 Linview Court
2 McQuillan Street
3 Grove Tree South
4 Granville Place
5 Lower Kilburn Street
6 Burnaby Way
7 Lincoln Square
8 Burnaby Walk
9 Grosvenor Court
10 Roden Pass
11 Roden Way
12 Burnaby Place
13 Burnaby Court
14 Selby Court
15 Roden Square
16 Brassey Street
17 Wauchope Court
18 Blackwater Way
19 Riverside Square
20 Selby Walk
21 Distillery Court
22 Distillery Way
23 Riverside Way
24 Excise Walk
25 Roosevelt Street
26 Abyssinia Walk
27 Barrington Gardens
28 Colchester Park
29 Meridi Street
30 Marchioness Street
31 Abercorn Walk
32 Marchioness Green
33 Springview Walk
34 McDonnell Court
35 Burnaby Park
36 McDonnell Street
37 Theodore Street

# NUMERICAL STREET INDEX

38 Prince Andrew Park
39 Abyssinia Street
40 Abercorn Street North
41 Prince Andrew Gardens
42 Iverna Street
43 Roosevelt Square
44 Roosevelt Rise
45 Arundel Courts
46 Arundel Walk
47 Genoa Street
48 Pembroke Street
49 Euterpe Street
50 Pandora Street
51 Empire Parade
52 Cavendish Square
53 Turin Street

## F8

1 Albany Place
2 Huss Row
3 St. Luke's Close
4 Huss Court
5 Canning's Court
6 Crossland Street
7 Canmore Court
8 Craven Street
9 Crossland Court
10 Dunlewey Walk
11 Cairns Street
12 Kendal Street
13 Craig's Terrace
14 Spier's Place
15 Cumberland Walk
16 Annsboro' Street
17 Nelson Square
18 St. Luke's Walk
19 Plevna Park
20 Ross Cottages
21 Ross Rise
22 Morpeth Street
23 Balkan Court
24 Cumberland Street
25 Wigton Street
26 Glenwood Court
27 North Howard Street
28 Haddow Street
29 Panton Street
30 Ashmore Place
31 Ormond Place
32 Albert Terrace
33 Waterford Way
34 St. Peter's Court
35 Christian Place
36 Ladymar Court
36 Ladymar Grove
36 Ladymar Park
36 Ladymar Walk
36 Ladymar Way
37 Albany Square
38 Sultan Way
39 Bread Street
40 Mansfield Street
41 Downing Street
42 Derby Terrace
43 Sultan Square
44 Carolina Street
45 Roumania Rise
46 Falls Court
47 Conway Link
48 Clonard Crescent
49 Ninth Street
50 Clonard Heights
51 Clonard Place
52 Clonard Court
53 Belgrave Street
54 Northland Court
55 Conway Court
56 Argyle Court
57 North Howard Court
58 Wilton Square North
59 Conway Walk
60 Argyle Street
61 Wilton Street
62 North Howard Walk
63 Conway Walk

64 St. Peter's Place
65 Silver Birch Courts
66 Ardmoulin Close
67 Crimea Court
68 Devenish Court
69 Kilmore Close
70 Kilmore Square
71 Lisvarna Heights
72 North Howard Link
73 Waterford Gardens
74 Jude Street
75 Moscow Street
76 Dundee Street
77 Aberdeen Street
78 Pernau Street
79 Ardmoulin Avenue
80 Grove Tree North
81 Kane Street
82 Clonard Rise
83 Centurion Way
84 Conway Square
85 Edwina Street
86 Lawnbrook Drive
87 Lawnbrook Square
88 Ross Court
89 Bombay Street
90 St. Peter's Square East
91 St. Peter's Square North
92 St. Peter's Square South
93 Linden Street
94 Spinner Square
95 Glenwood Street
96 Ardmoulin Street
97 Ardmoulin Terrace
98 Malcolmson Street
99 O'Neill Street
100 Sevastopol Street
101 Dunlewey Street
102 Sugarfield Street
103 Tyne Street
104 Lower Clonard Street
105 Wilton Court

## F9

1 Rothsay Square
2 Saunderson's Court
3 St. Gemmas Court
4 Ballymena Court
5 Rosapenna Court
6 Landscape Terrace
7 Summerhill Court
8 Liffey Court
9 Old Lodge Road
10 Shannon Court
11 Ariel Street
12 Forster Street
13 Crimea Close
14 Blaney Street
15 Agnes Court
16 Klondyke Street
17 Tobergill Street
18 Bann Court
19 Manor Drive
20 Malvern Way
21 Malvern Close
22 Glenfarne Street
23 Charleville Street
24 St. Mary's Street
25 Sancroft Street
26 Mill Street West
27 Edenderry Street
28 Churchview Court
29 Fairfax Court
30 Rosewood Court
31 Mountview Court
32 Hillview Court
33 Bandon Court
34 Glenview Court
35 Gracehill Court
36 Groomsport Court
37 Groomsport Street
38 Manor Court
39 Mayfair Court
40 Newport Court
41 Parkview Court

42 Southport Court
43 Harrison Walk
44 Beechnut Place
45 Beechpark Street
46 Courtrai Street
47 Malvern Street
48 Annalee Court
49 Avonbeg Close
50 Langley Street
51 Daisyfield Street
52 Rusholme Street
53 Hazelfield Street
54 Bell Close
55 Vistula Street
56 Brussels Street
57 Glenpark Court
58 Glenhill Court
59 Antigua Court
60 St. Colman's Court
61 Bromley Street
62 Century Street
63 Glentilt Street
64 Tasmania Street
65 Upper Glenfarne Street
66 Geoffrey Street
67 Wimbledon Street
68 Winchester Street
69 Coniston Close
70 Ghent Place
71 Lyle Street

## F10

1 Deerpark Grove
2 Cliftonville Drive
3 Cliftonville Parade
4 Cliftonville Street
5 Bennett Drive
6 Brookvale Parade
7 Ballyclare Street
7 Ballyclare Way
7 Ballynure Way
8 Brookvale Fold
9 Arbour Street
10 Heathfield Court
11 Elimgrove Street
12 Ardilea Drive
13 Ardoyne Walk
14 Havana Court
15 Havana Way
16 Havana Walk
17 Havana Gardens
18 Jamaica Way
19 Kingston Court
20 Wyndham Street
21 Jamaica Court
22 Oldpark Square
23 Ardoyne Court
24 Ardoyne Place
25 Ardilea Court
26 Ballycastle Court
27 Rosapenna Walk
28 Torrens Court
29 Wyndham Drive
30 Jamaica Street
31 Ballycarry Street
32 Torrens Gardens
33 Easton Avenue
34 Cliftonville Bowling Club
35 Brookvale Court

## F11

1 Westland Way
2 Chichester Mews
3 Cooldarragh Park North
4 Woodburn Drive

## F12

1 Carncoole Park
2 Merryfield Drive
3 Henderson Avenue Flats
4 Henderson Court
5 Upper Castle Park
6 Old Cavehill Road

## F14

1 Bellevue Drive

## F15

1 Fairyknowe Drive
2 Vaddegan Gardens
3 Glenelm Park
4 Collinward Park

## F16

1 Glebe Villas
2 Collinward Drive
3 Glebecoole Drive

## G2

1 Belvoir Close
2 Mahee Close
3 Downhill Walk
4 Drumart Walk
5 Gray's Park Gardens
6 Minnowburn Drive
7 Minnowburn Gardens
8 Millburn Court
9 Minnowburn Terrace
10 Altnacreeva Close
11 Gray's Park Drive
12 Kilwarlin Walk
13 Moyle Walk
14 Killynether Gardens
15 Killynether Walk
16 Kirkistown Walk
17 Whinnyhill Drive
18 Belvoir House
19 Taylor Court

## G4

1 Broomhill Park Central
2 The Drive
3 Cricklewood Crescent
4 Deramore Court
5 Knightsbridge Mews
6 Sharman Close
7 Sharman Way
8 Sharman Gardens

## G5

1 Annadale Terrace
2 Prince Edward Gardens
3 Hampton Grove
4 Stranmillis Court
5 Stranmillis Mews
6 Cleaver Court
7 Cherryhill
8 Riverview Street
9 Strandview Street
10 Wansbeck Street
11 Geneva Gardens
12 Penge Gardens
13 St. Albans Gardens
15 Lockside Court

## G6

1 Crescent Gardens
2 Upper Crescent Lane
3 Abercorn Street
4 Claremont Mews
5 University Square Mews
6 University Terrace
7 Park Lane
8 Eglantine Gardens
9 Cloreen Park
10 Rugby Mews
11 Colenso Court
12 Sandhurst Court
13 College Park
14 Fountainville Avenue
15 Rugby Parade
16 Rugby Street

17 Wellington Park Avenue
18 Wellington Park Terrace
19 Ceara Court
20 College Park East
21 College Park Avenue
22 Botanic Court
23 Canterbury Street
24 Claremont Court

**G7**

1 Devonshire Place
2 Devonshire Close
3 Devonshire Way
4 Hutchinson Street
5 Egmont Gardens
6 Athol Street Lane
7 Fisherwick Place
8 Wellington Court
9 Clarence Place Mews
10 Donegall Square Mews
11 Franklin Street Place
12 Keyland's Place
13 Glengall Lane
14 Glengall Mews
15 Bain's Place
16 Clarence Street West
17 Utility Walk
18 Linen Hall Street West
19 St. Andrew's Square East
20 St. Andrew's Square North
21 McCavanna's Place
22 Watson Street
23 Sturgeon Street
24 McAdam Park
25 Linfield Street
26 St. Andrew's Square West
27 Roseland Place
28 Taylor Street
29 Holmes Street
30 Marcus Ward Street
31 Posnett Court
32 Harmony Street
33 Downshire Place
34 Murray Street
35 Blakeley Terrace
36 Glenburn Alley
37 Howard Street South
38 Schomberg Drive
39 Maxwell Street
40 Maxwell's Place
41 Oswald Park
42 Mabel Court
43 Matilda Gardens
44 Britannic Park
45 City Walk
46 Innes Place
47 Moore's Place
48 Craigmore Way
49 Wesley Court
50 Oak Street
51 Albion Lane
52 Renwick Street
53 Blondin Street
54 Bankmore Square
55 Malone Place
56 Crescent Lane
57 Elm Court
58 Britannic Drive
59 Boyne Court
60 Renfrew Walk
61 Lawyer Gardens
62 Linfield Gardens
63 Linfield Avenue
64 McAdam Gardens
65 Linfield Drive
66 Kenmare Park
67 Clementine Park
68 Clementine Drive
69 Teutonic Gardens
70 City Way
71 Britannic Terrace
72 Clementine Gardens
73 Hurst Park
74 Utility Street
75 Hunter Park

76 Matilda Avenue
77 Matilda Drive
78 Salisbury Court
79 TierneyGardens
80 Napier Street
81 Rainey Way
82 Kensington Street
83 Wesley Street
84 Combermere Street
85 Schomberg Street
86 Aughrim Park
87 Virginia Street
88 Virginia Way
89 Vernon Court
90 St. George's Gardens
91 Lindsay Way
92 Erin Way
93 Ashburne Mews
94 Ashburne Place
95 Maryville Court
96 Renfrew House
97 Albion Street
98 Fulton Street
99 Little Victoria Street
100 Hartington Street
101 Lindsay Court
102 Chambers Street
103 Ratcliffe Street
104 Beggs Street
105 Railway Street
106 Ventry Street
107 Ventry Lane
108 Windsor Street
109 Blackstaff Square
110 Willow Street

**G8**

1 Arnon Street
2 Kildare Place
3 Lower Regent Street
4 Donegall Lane
5 Clarke's Lane
6 Coar's Lane
7 Brown's Row
8 Alton Court
9 Sherbrook Close
10 Wilson Street
11 Plunkett Court
12 Boundary Way
13 Boundary Walk
14 California Close
15 Finglass Court
16 Unity Walk
17 McKibbens Court
18 Exchange Street West
19 Exchange Place
20 Commercial Court
21 Donegall Street Place
22 North Street Arcade
23 Lower Garfield Street
24 Law's Court
25 North King Street
26 Brady's Lane
27 Dover Walk
28 Crosby Street
29 Dover Court
30 Dayton Street
31 Quadrant Place
32 Durham Court
33 Trinity Street
34 Haymarket
35 Killen Street
36 College Place North
37 College Street Mews
38 Queen's Arcade
39 Finn Square
40 McIvors Place
41 Sackville Court
42 Shankhill Terrace
43 Melbourne Street
43 Southwell Street
44 Fountain Lane
45 Castle Arcade
46 Stanley Court
47 Winecellar Entry

48 Crown Entry
49 St. Stephens Court
50 Smithfield Square North
51 Albert Court
52 Upper Townsend Terrace
53 Milford Street
54 Clonfaddan Street
55 Clonfaddan Crescent
56 William Street
57 Donegal Arcade
58 Louden Street
59 Ardmoulin Place
60 Lombard Street
61 Galway Street
62 Stephen Street
63 Upper Queen Street
64 Kildare Street
65 Tyrone Street
66 Wall Street
67 Alton Street
68 Institution Place
69 Berry Street
70 Church Street
71 Lisfaddan Drive
72 Milford Rise
73 Lisfaddan Place
74 Divis Court
75 College Avenue
76 Chapel Lane

**G9**

1 Syringa Street
2 Glenrosa Street South
3 Trainfield Street
4 Mervue Court
5 Cosgrave Street
6 Hartwell Place
7 Moffatt Street
8 Donore Place
9 Kinnaird Terrace
10 Kinnaird Place
11 Kinnaird Street
12 St. James's Street
13 Glenrosa Link
14 Sheridan Court
15 Ludlow Square
16 Hardinge Place
17 New Lodge Place
18 Pinkerton Way
19 Bruslee Way
20 Carlisle Walk
21 Cranburn Street
22 Adela Place
23 Donore Court
24 Florence Walk
25 Little George's Street
26 Southwell Street
27 Fairview Street
28 Annesley Street
29 Carlisle Square
30 North Hill Street
31 Edlingham Street
32 Maralin Street
33 Trinity Street
34 Earl Close
35 Hopewell Place
36 Magee's Lane
37 Glenravel Street
38 Hopewell Square
39 Halliday's Road
40 Stanhope Street
41 McCleery Street
42 Adela Street
43 Greenmount Street
44 Florence Square
45 Kinnaird Close
46 Brucevale Court
47 Vicinage Place
48 Florence Court
49 Greenmount Place
50 Thomas Street
51 Fleetwood Place
52 Thorndale Centre

**G10**

1 Ashfield Crescent
2 Glandore Parade
3 Richmond Square
4 Brantwood Street
5 Clanchattan Street
6 Lawther Court
7 Robina Court
8 Tramway Street
9 Mountcollyer Close
10 Ashfield Court
11 Cosgrave Court
12 Lilliput Street
13 Alexandra Avenue
14 Crosscollyer Street
15 Ashdene Drive
16 Seaview Close
17 Mackey Street
18 Loughrey Court
19 Atlantic Avenue
20 Woodland Avenue
21 Newington Street
22 Dunmore Crescent
23 Jubilee Avenue
24 Brookvale House
25 Marsden Terrace
26 Marsden Garden Flats
27 Imperial Court

**G11**

1 Mount Vernon Grove
2 Chichester Court
3 Kenbella Parade
4 Kansas Avenue Flats
5 Evewilliam Park
6 Somerton Drive
7 Seagrove Place
8 Premier Grove
9 Jellicoe Park
10 Jellicoe Parade
11 Chichester Close
12 Palace Gardens
13 Chichester Park Central
14 Somerton Close
15 Chichester Gardens
16 Fortwilliam Court
17 Hopefield Court
18 James Court
19 Fortwilliam Gardens
20 Glantrasna Drive
21 Queen Victoria Gardens
22 Seascape Parade
23 Chester Manor
24 Mount Vernon Court
25 Ardmillan
26 Fortwiliam Fold

**G12**

1 Innisfayle Pass
2 Innisfayle Drive
3 Fairhill Gardens
4 Fairhill Way
5 Waveney Drive
6 Waveney Grove
7 Landsowne Park North
8 Alexander Court
9 Downview Park West
10 Lansdowne Drive
11 Lowwood Gardens
12 Strathmore Park

**G13**

1 Slievegoland Park
2 Glenhurst Parade
3 Vandyck Drive
4 Graymount Gardens
5 Serpentine Parade
6 Voltaire Gardens
7 Glenhurst Gardens
8 Downview Lodge
9 Limegrove
10 Farringdon House

## G14

1 Throne Terrace
2 Pinewood Gardens
3 Longlands Walk
4 Parkmore Terrace
5 Merston Gardens
6 Navarra Place
7 Mark Royal Court
8 Longlands Court
9 Bresk Hill
10 Ben Madigan Heights
11 Ballyroney Hill
12 Laragh Court

## G15

1 Drumcor Green
2 Carlan Close
3 Carnreagh Gardens
4 Clonmore Walk
5 Fairyknowe Gardens
6 Drumcor Court

## G16

1 Glynn Park
2 Gransha Grove
3 Dunowen Pass
4 Grainon Way

## H2

1 Castlehume Gardens
2 Drumart Gardens
3 Drumart Square
4 Drumart Green
5 Cedarhurst Rise
6 Brerton Grove
7 Breda House
8 The Beeches
9 The Mews

## H3

1 Coleshill Gardens
2 Crevenish Walk
3 Castleward Park
4 Castlecoole Walk
5 Belvoir View Park
6 Beaufort Gardens
7 Beaufort Grove
8 Berkley Court
9 Village Court
10 Park Lodge

## H4

1 Mornington
2 Mornington Mews
3 Lowry Court
4 Laurel Wood
5 Hampton Manor Drive
6 Laganvale Court
7 Laganvale Manor

## H5

1 Parkmore Street
2 Annadale Grove
3 Annadale Gardens
4 Annadale Drive
5 Annadale Green
6 Hampton Strand
7 Hampton Place
8 Hampton Gardens
9 Hampton Parade
10 St. John's Court
11 Rosetta Court
12 Deramore Street
13 Primrose Street
14 Somerset Street
15 Whitehall Mews
16 Rossmore Drive
17 Rossmore Crescent

## H6

1 Powerscourt Street
2 Belmore Street
3 Sandhurst Road
4 Kinallen Street
5 Cadogan Street
6 Curzon Street
7 Collingwood Avenue
8 Fitzroy Court
9 Baroda Drive
10 Baroda Parade
11 Rugby Court
12 Southview Street
13 Southview Cottages
14 Kinallen Court
15 Elmwood
16 Harrow Street
17 Dromara Street
18 Artana Street
19 Agincourt Street
20 Derlett Street
21 Westminster Street
22 Collingwood Road

## H7

1 Rathbone Street
2 Holmes Court
3 May's Meadow
4 Eliza Street Close
5 Friendly Row
6 Catherine Street North
7 Friendly Way
8 Cooke Place
9 Havelock Street
10 St. Kilda Court
11 Eliza Street Terrace
12 Little Charlotte Street
13 Stanfield Row
14 Stanfield Place
15 Jame's Pass
16 St. Kilda Street
17 Howard Street South
18 Russell Place
19 Lindsay Street
20 New Bond Street
21 Coyle Street
22 Russell Street
23 Pine Street
24 Market Street
25 Friendly Place
26 Walnut Court
27 Coyle's Place
28 Lower Stanfield Street
29 Upper Stanfield Street
30 Henrietta Street
31 Sussex Place
32 Catherine Street
33 Verner Street

## H8

1 Little Edward Street
2 Exchange Street
3 Bradford Square
4 Seymour Lane
5 High Street Court
6 Custom House Square
7 Wilson's Court
8 Joy's Entry
9 Pottinger's Court
10 Pottinger's Entry
11 Hamilton's Court
12 Cole's Alley
13 Prince's Street Court
14 Prince's Court
15 Rotterdam Court
16 Telfair Street
17 Arthur Square
18 William Street South
19 Arthur Place
20 Arthur Lane
21 Music Hall Court
21 Music Hall Lane

22 Seymour Row
23 Marlborough Street
24 Ulster Street
25 Seymour Street
26 Skipper Street
27 Laganview Court
28 Rotterdam Street
29 Laganview Mews
30 Scrabo Street
31 Central Arcade
32 Townhall Street
33 Dalton Street
34 Gamble Street
35 Steam Mill Lane
36 Corporation Square

## H9

1 Lilliput Court
2 Cultra Street
3 Trafalgar Street
4 Carnalea Place
5 Little Corporation Street
6 Molyneaux Street
7 Canning Place
8 Cambridge Street
9 Pilot Place
10 Midland Close
11 Orchard Street
12 Bentinck Street
13 St. Paul's Fold
14 York Link
15 Midland Crescent
16 Midland Terrace
17 Whitla Street
18 St. Paul's Street
19 Shipbuoy Street
20 Short Street
21 Barnett Dock Road

## H10

1 Skegoneill Street
2 O'Dempsey Street
3 Castleton Avenue
4 Milewater Street
5 Grove Place
6 Parkmount Close
7 Seaview Street
8 Parkmount Street
10 Keadyville Avenue
11 Mountcollyer Road

## H11

1 Mount Vernon Pass
2 Seaview Gardens
3 Seamount
4 Fortwilliam Grange
5 Mount Vernon Walk

## H12

1 Parkmount Pass
2 Parkmount Way
3 Parkmount Lane
4 Parkmount Place
5 Mount Vernon Walk
6 Waveney Heights

## H13

1 Graymount Grove
2 Graymount Terrace
3 Catherine Row
4 High Street
5 Greencastle Close
6 Greencastle Place
7 Finlay Park

## H14

1 Bawnmore Grove
2 Bawnmore Place
3 Bawnmore Terrace

4 Merville Mews
5 Rathcoole Close
6 Rathcoole Gardens
7 Old Mill Drive

## H15

1 Innishrush Gardens
2 Iona Park
3 Inveresk Park
4 Rusheen Gardens
5 Roscor Square
6 Owenreagh Close
7 Rathdrum Park
8 Willow Park
9 Green Side
10 Clare Gardens
11 Belmore Gardens
12 Ardmillan Gardens
13 Ardfarn Close
14 Portrosse Park
15 Bracken Way
16 The Oaks
17 Ardeen Gardens

## H16

1 Knockenagh Walk
3 Tullevin Walk
4 Renagh Park
5 Gortmore Terrace
6 Knockreagh Gardens
7 Killowen Terrace
8 Loughmoney Park
9 Lenadery Terrace
10 Nendrum Gardens
11 Heather Drive
12 Foyle Hill
13 Movilla Park
14 Derrycoole Park
15 Mournebeg Drive
16 Mournebeg Way
17 Linford Place
18 Derrycoole Walk
19 Glanroy Terrace

## J2

1 Glenhugh Crescent
2 Hill Green
3 Cairnshill Avenue
4 Woodford Green
5 Finsbury Park
6 Cairnshill Crescent
7 Beechill Court
8 Myrtledene Drive
9 Cairnshill Court
10 The Gables
11 Royal Lodge Avenue
12 Royal Lodge Court
13 Royal Lodge Gardens
14 Royal Lodge Mews
15 Royal Lodge Park
16 Cedarhurst Court

## J3

1 Glendale Avenue West
2 Whinney Heights
3 Woodbreda Crescent
4 Woodbreda Gardens
5 Lenaghan Gardens
6 Cairnshill Green
7 Cairnshill Gardens
8 Cairnshill Drive
9 Breda Crescent
10 Lenaghan Court
11 Mount Oriel
12 Beechill Park
13 Rogers Place

## J4

1 Wynchurch Gardens
2 Mount Michael Drive
3 Glencreagh Court

4 Long Acre
5 Drumkeen Court
6 Knockbreda Drive
7 Drumkeen Manor
8 Bradford Place
9 Wynchurch Close

## J5

1 Knock Eden Grove
2 Drumragh End
3 Cappagh Gardens
4 Rosetta Way
5 Flush Drive
6 Cheltenham Gardens
7 Lissan Link
8 Flush Gardens
9 Knock Eden Drive
10 Mount Merrion Crescent
11 Dennet End
12 Lynden Gate

## J6

1 Willowholme Crescent
2 Willowholme Parade
3 Chesham Grove
4 Chesham Crescent
5 Earl Haig Crescent
6 Gibson Park Drive
7 Chesham Drive
8 Chesham Gardens
9 Chesham Terrace
10 Gibson Park Avenue
11 Earl Haig Gardens
12 Pirrie Park Gardens
13 Finsbury Street
14 Ravensdene Park Gardens
15 Ravenhill Court
16 Lyndon Court
17 Willowbrook House
18 Ravensdene Mews
19 Onslow Park
20 Willowholme Street

## J7

1 Constance Street
2 Paulett Avenue
3 Belle Bashford Court
4 Glenwherry Place
5 Kenbaan Street
6 Stormont Crescent
7 Grovefield Place
8 Swift Place
9 Stormont Lane
10 Victor Place
11 Back Mount Street
12 Mount Street South
13 Templemore Close
14 Tamery Pass
15 Frank Place
16 Crossley Street
17 Spring Street
18 Dann's Row
19 Woodstock Place
20 McMullan's Lane
21 Canada Street
22 Templemore Place
23 Grovefield Street
24 Radnor Street
25 Canton Court
26 Willowfield Walk
27 Kenbaan Court
28 Shamrock Court
29 Bryansford Place
30 Edith Street
31 Isthmus Street
32 Eversleigh Street
33 Dublin Street
34 Gotha Street
35 Ravenhill Crescent
36 Sunwich Street
37 Ampere Street
38 Perry Court
39 Park Place

40 Shamrock Place
41 Maghies Place
42 Glentoran Place
43 Spring Place
44 Well Place
45 Mount Street
46 Swift Street
47 Trillick Court
48 Richardson Court
49 Templemore Street
50 Cluan Place
51 Coburg Street
52 Frank Street
53 Stormont Street
54 Shamrock Street
55 Ballarat Court
56 Clandeboye Street
57 Temple Street
58 Pottinger Street
59 Trillick Street
60 Ledley Hall Close
61 Willowfield Crescent
62 Cappy Street
63 Halcombe Street
64 Rochester Street
65 Florida Street
66 Lawnmount Street
67 Maymount Street
68 Park Parade
69 Ravensdale Crescent
70 Ravensdale Street
71 Jocelyn Gardens
72 Mashona Court

## J8

1 Kenilworth Place
2 Lackagh Court
3 Arran Court
4 Fraser Street
5 Medway Court
6 Harvey Court
7 Frazer Pass
8 Harland Walk
9 Convention Walk
10 Cuba Walk
11 Finmore Court
12 Sark Street
13 Baskin Street
14 Tern Street
15 Fern Street
16 Wye Street
17 Saunders Close
18 Scotch Row
19 Cable Close
20 Pitt Place
21 Wolff Close
22 Kathleen Court
23 Madrid Court
24 Montrose Street South
25 Montrose Walk
26 Carnforth Street
27 Mountforde Park
28 St. Leonard's Crescent
29 Clyde Court
30 St. Patrick's Walk
31 Humber Court
32 Comber Gardens
33 Tower Street
34 Mountforde Court
35 Mountforde Gardens
36 Seaforde Court
37 Seaforde Gardens
38 Tower Court
39 Beechfield Court
40 Thistle Court
41 Vicarage Street
42 Convention Court
43 Bryson Court
44 Bryson Gardens
45 Comber Court
46 Bright Street
47 Mountrose Street
48 Newcastle Street
49 St. Leonard's Street
50 Duke Street

51 Sheriff Street
52 Strand Walk
53 Anderson Court
54 Moira Court
55 Arran Street
56 Strand Mews
57 Strand Close
58 Vulcan Court
59 Vulcan Gardens
60 St. Matthew's Court
61 Hornby Parade
62 Clandeboye Drive
64 Newcastle Manor
65 Riada Close
66 Chadolly Street
67 Vulcan Link
68 Lisbon Street
69 Thompson Street
70 Moira Street

## J14

1 Whitehouse Gardens

## J15

1 Woodland Close
2 Mountview Pass
3 Mountview Place
4 Woodland Terrace
5 Wynthorp Grove
6 Martin Park

## J16

2 Cambrai Park
4 Abbey Court
11 Simpson's Villas

## K4

1 Willowbank Crescent
2 Beechgrove Crescent
3 The Willows

## K5

1 Greenway
2 Downshire Parade
3 Carnamena Gardens
4 Carnamena Park
5 Glensharragh Park
6 Glen Side
7 Hindsdale Park
8 Montgomery Court
9 Kibroney House

## K6

1 Orby Green
2 Loopland Parade
3 Elesington Court
4 Loopland Grove
5 Ladas Walk
6 Cregagh Court
7 Graham Gardens
8 Woodstock House
9 The Village Green

## K7

1 Factory Street
2 Wynford Street
3 Lovatt Street
4 Bloomfield Crescent
5 Greenville Avenue
6 Clara Crescent Lower
7 Clara Crescent Upper
8 Steen's Row
9 Foxglove Street
10 Ardgowan Drive
11 Bloomfield Park West
12 Jonesboro Park
13 Abetta Parade
14 Glenhoy Drive
15 Wayland Street

16 Orby Mews
17 Uniondale Street
18 Ulsterdale Street
19 Avoniel Parade
20 Lecumpher Street
21 Woodlee Street
22 Hillsborough Parade
23 Melrose Avenue
24 Heatherbell Street
25 Bloomfield Street
26 Bloomfield Court
27 Dunraven Street
28 Avonorr Drive

## K8

1 Strandburn Gardens
2 Devon Drive
3 Lisavon Parade
4 Oakdene Drive
5 Brandon Terrace
6 Brandra Street
7 Ballymacarrett Walkway
8 Chater Street
9 Madison Avenue East
10 Westminster Avenue
11 Manderson Street
12 Townsley Street
13 Hemp Street
14 Hart Street
15 Laburnum Lane
16 Ravenscroft Street
17 Queen Victoria Street
18 Chobham Street
19 Beechwood Street
20 Westminster Avenue North
21 Welland Street
22 McAllister Court
23 Strandburn Court
24 Humber Street
25 Armitage Close
26 Glendale Court
27 Oakdale Street
28 Stonyford Street
29 Westcott Street
30 Bloomdale Street
31 Lena Street
32 Mourne Street
33 Hornby Crescent
34 Laburnum Street
35 Parkgate Drive
36 Parkgate Crescent
37 Parkgate Parade
38 Parkgate Gardens
39 Kimona Drive
40 Hynd Street
41 Lelia Street
42 Lomond Street
43 Cheviot Street
44 Banbury Street
45 Downpatrick Street
46 Sintonville Avenue
47 Redcliffe Street
48 Laburnum Court
49 Connswater Grove
50 Connswater Mews
51 Lisavon Court
52 Tamar Court

## K9

1 Sandbrook Grove
2 Sandbrook Gardens
3 Wellwood Avenue
4 Larkfield Manor
5 Wellwood Close

## L4

1 Lisnabreeny Road East

## L5

1 Camlough Place
2 Shalom Park
3 Crawford Park

4 Casaeldona Drive
5 Castle Court
6 Castle Mews
7 Ardkeen Crescent
8 Leadhill View
9 Lisnasharragh Terrace
10 Marlborough Heights

### L6

1 Clarawood Grove
2 Clarawood Drive
3 Killarn Close
4 Roddens Gardens
5 Marshalls Road

### L7

1 Kerrsland Drive
2 Kerrsland Parade
3 Kerrsland Crescent
4 Sinclair Street
5 Hillcrest Gardens
6 Sandown Park South
7 Sandhill Green
8 Clara Way
9 Clarawood Walk
10 Orangefield Green
11 Norbloom Gardens
12 The Hollies
13 Sunbury Avenue
14 Orangefield Grove
15 Dean Crooks Fold
16 Houston Court
17 Pembridge Mews

### L8

1 Strandburn Crescent
2 Norwood Grove
3 Edgecumbe Drive
4 Dehra Grove
5 Edenvale Gardens
6 Edenvale Park
7 Ranfurly Drive
8 Belmont Court
9 Belmont Avenue West
10 Dundela View
11 Dundela Drive
12 Dundela Flats
13 Earlswood Park
14 Castleview Terrace
15 Bethany Street
16 Douglas Court
17 Strathearn Mews
18 The Earls Court
19 Earlswood Court
20 Dundela Court
21 Belmont Grange
22 Belmont Close
23 Wynfield Court
24 Belmont Mews
25 Edenvale Court
26 Edenvale Grove
27 Strand Court
28 Sycamore Grove
29 Wilgar Close
30 Earlswood Grove
31 Dundela Manor
32 Kingsley Court
33 Bathgate Drive
34 Ferguson Court
35 Sydenham Drive
36 Edgecumbe View
37 Edgecumbe Park
38 Strandburn Park
39 Dundela Close
40 Hopedene Mews
41 Hopedene Court
42 Library Court
43 Clonallon Court

### L9

1 Strandburn Parade

2 Inverwood Court
3 Ashbrook Crescent
4 Ashbrook Drive
5 Palmerston Park
6 Larkfield Grove
7 Helgor Park Mews
8 Larkfield Court
9 Rockville Court
10 Inglewood Court
11 Tudor Dale
12 Victoria Court
13 Vidor Court
14 Clonaver Crescent North
15 Clonaver Crescent South
16 Vidor Gardens
17 Fernvale Street

### M5

1 Glenview Drive
2 Cormorant Park
3 Woodcroft Heights
4 Woodcroft Rise
5 Shandon Heights

### M6

1 Knockwood Grove
2 Knockwood Drive
3 Knock Link
4 Knock Way
5 Knock Green
6 Knockmount Gardens
7 Knockmount Park
8 Kingsden Park
9 Kensington Gardens West
10 Kimscourt
11 Cherryvalley Park West
12 Creevy Way
13 Wayside Close
14 Braniel Way
15 Northfield Rise
16 Glen Rise
17 Braniel Park
18 Green Mount
19 Greenlea Gardens
20 Castleview Court
21 Shandon Court
22 Ascot Mews

### M7

1 Astoria Gardens
2 Cherryvalley Green
3 Astoria Gardens
4 Kensington Court
5 Hawthornden Court
6 Sandringham Mews
7 Cabin Hill Court
8 Cherry Tree Walk
9 Kensington Gate
10 Johnston Court

### M8

1 Hawthornden Gardens
2 Pirrie Road
3 Hawthornden Park
4 Wandsworth Crescent
5 Wandsworth Place
6 Ardgreenan Mount
7 Ardgreenan Place
8 Aston Gardens
9 Ardgreenan Gardens
10 Ardgreenan Crescent
12 Laurelvale
13 Campbell Court
14 Eastleigh Dale
15 Limewood Grove
16 Woodlands Court
18 Ashbourne Court
19 Greenwood Manor
20 Hawthornden Mews
21 Knocklofty Court
22 Wandsworth Court
23 The Hamlets

24 Belmont Drive

### M9

1 Ardvarna Crescent
2 Ashford Green
3 Ashmount Grove
4 Ashburn Green
5 Ashmount Place
6 Cairnburn Dell
7 Finchley Drive
8 Finchley Gardens
9 Glenmillan Park
10 Glenmachan Grove
11 Tillysburn Grove
12 The Stables
13 Parklands Close
14 Garranard Manor
15 Kennel Bridge

### M10

1 Tillysburn Drive
2 Garnerville Grove
3 Glenluce Green
4 Glenlea Grove
5 Knocknagoney Grove
6 Knocknagoney Green
7 Knocknagoney Way
8 Knocknagoney Gardens
9 Glenloch Gardens
10 Glendhu Grove
11 Henderson Court

### N6

1 Alder Close
2 Woodview Terrace
3 Woodview Place
4 Farmhurst Way
5 Gortland Avenue
6 Charters Avenue
7 Marlfield Rise
8 Orchard Close
9 Church Wynd
10 Cherrytree
11 Helen's Lea
12 Kensington Manor
13 Brook Meadow

### N7

1 Thornhill Crescent
2 Knockland Park
3 Summerhill Parade
4 Kingsland Drive
5 Barnett's Crescent
6 Kingsway Close
7 Thornhill Grove
8 Kings Manor
9 Cabin Hill Mews
10 Stormont Court

### N8

1 Netherleigh Mews
2 Stormont Villas
3 Castlehill Park West
4 Castleorr Manor
5 Castlekaria Manor

### N9

1 Knockmarloch Park
2 The Grange
3 Glenmachan Avenue
4 Massey Green
5 Glenmachan Mews
6 Tweskard Lodge

### N10

1 Glenmachan Park
2 Glen Ebor Heights
3 Glenmachen Tower
Nursing Home

### N11

1 Prior's Lea
4 Holywood Private
Nursing Home

### P6

1 Leven Place
2 Leven Close
3 Leven Crescent
4 Vionville Way
5 Vionville Heights
6 Vionville Close

### P7

1 Rosemount Avenue
2 Cloghan Gardens
3 Ardcarn Park
4 Ardcarn Green
5 Upperlands Walk
6 Dairy Park
7 Langholm Row
7 Selkirk Row
7 Stornaway Row
8 Sperrin Park
9 Sperrin Drive
10 Lowland Walk
11 Lowland Gardens
12 Kirn Park
13 Vionville Green
14 Vionville Court
15 Vionville View
16 Vionville Place
17 Vionville Park
18 Kilmory Gardens
19 Roslin Gardens
20 Kincraig Avenue
21 Govan Drive
22 Lowland Avenue
23 Alford Park
25 Cloghan Crescent
26 Abbey Court
27 Rosepark Meadows
28 Crofthouse Court
29 Abbey Gardens

### Q6

1 Wanstead Gardens

### Q7

1 Private Avenue
2 Cumberland Avenue
3 Rockmount
4 Ardara Avenue
5 Gransha Walk
6 Hanwood Avenue
7 Dundonald Heights
8 Quarry Cottages
9 Cumberland Close
10 Galway Court
11 Galway Mews
12 Hanwood Farm
13 Beechwood Manor

### Q8

1 St. John's Wood Park
2 St. Elizabeth's Court
3 Grangewood terrace
4 Grangewood Heights

### R8

4 Cherryhill Gardens
13 Grangewood Park

Belfast, like so many other cities, grew up on the banks of a river - its Irish name, Béal Feirste, means 'the mouth of the ford'. It enjoys a setting of natural beauty in the valley of the River Lagan, sheltered on one side by the mountains of Antrim and on the other by the green hills of County Down.

The Industrial Revolution saw Belfast grow from a small town into one of the world's major commercial ports. Queen Victoria gave it city status in 1888 when the population was approximately 300,000, and Belfast thrived on the development of its ship building and textile industries. The post-war decline of these major industries is best illustrated by the experience of Harland & Wolff who employ approximately 2,000 workers today compared to the 60,000 men who worked for the company in its heyday, building famous ships such as the Titanic.

Industrial decline combined with twenty five years of the 'Troubles' have had a profound effect on the urban landscape and its population. The last decade, however, has been one of regeneration and the heartbeat of Belfast is strong and vibrant once again. The paramilitary ceasefires of 1994 have brought the city to another historic crossroads. Lasting peace will surely enhance the prosperity which is already returning to the city, but the road to political settlement will doubtless be a long and difficult one.

As we approach our first year of peace for a generation, the atmosphere of hope and optimism which now pervades the city and its people is almost tangible. A stroll through the city centre will reveal a shopping environment which would be the envy of many other UK provincial cities. Pedestrianisation was originally introduced largely for security reasons but it looks set to remain now that the city centre security cordon and civilian searches have been phased out. The CastleCourt shopping complex has brought retailing in Belfast into the 21st century, and success has bred success as other major retailers have flocked to take advantage of the relatively high disposable incomes which

are a feature of the Northern Ireland economy. Shops now stay open late on Friday nights as well as on Thursdays.

The city's 'Golden Mile', based around Great Victoria Street and the Dublin Road area, continues to flourish. This is the entertainment hub of the city, bursting with theatres, cinemas, pubs and restaurants. Belfast, above all else, is a city that knows how to enjoy itself, where 'good crack' flows freely from our love of banter, rather than being sold on the streets as it is in some other cities.

Belfast will probably never turn its back on the past, but it now seems to be looking more than ever towards the future. One only has to stand on the Queen's Bridge to get a glimpse of what lies ahead. This one vantage point lets you view some of the key projects which will shape the city for many years to come : the recently completed Lagan Weir, the Belfast Waterfront Hall which is currently under construction, and the new Lagan Bridges. These projects alone, which are outlined in more detail below, account for investment of several hundred million pounds and are indicative of a far-sighted vision which aims to make Belfast an even better place to live, work and visit.

### Lagan Weir

The Laganside Corporation was formed in 1989 to implement the Laganside concept which aims to completely transform Belfast's neglected waterfront areas with a series of inter-connecting developments stretching from the Abbercorn Basin, in the inner docks, to the Ormeau Bridge. The Lagan Weir, the Corporation's major infrastructure project, was completed in 1994 and has already made a huge difference to water quality, with salmon returning to the river for the first time in many years.

The Laganside Civic Trail incorporates the new public walkways which have been installed along the river banks, and a number of riverside housing projects are under construction. Perhaps for the first time in the city's history, the river is

being viewed as a major recreational resource and, as we go to press, a new watersports centre has opened close to the Albert Bridge.

### Waterfront Hall

The current focus of public interest, however, is Laganbank, the site for the Belfast Waterfront Hall which is due for completion in late 1996. Described as the most significant civic building to be erected in Northern Ireland's history, the £29 million Conference and Concert Centre is being funded by Belfast City Council with support from Laganside Corporation and the European Union. This project offers concrete evidence of Belfast's renewed self-confidence and will be a major contribution to the cultural life of the city.

Unlike many new facilities around the world, the Belfast Waterfront Hall is being constructed in a city centre location, five minutes walk from the City Hall and close to the vibrant nightlife of the city's 'Golden Mile'.

Its state-of-the-art facilities will accommodate major leisure, arts and entertainment events. The main auditorium will have a fully seated capacity of 2,235, and the minor hall will accommodate up to 500. Many bookings have already been taken but the opening two weeks have been allocated to a festival of special events featuring a showcase of local and national talent. A gala opening will follow later in 1997 and a performer of world renown has been booked, although his or her identity is being kept a closely guarded secret!

The Waterfront Hall is the cornerstone of the Laganbank development but the site will also include a 187 bedroomed four star Hilton International hotel, 450,000 square feet of offices, specialist retailing space and multi-storey car parking.

### The Lagan Bridges

Landmark projects can do much for city pride but, when it comes to every day living, timely investment in transport infrastructure can have

Photograph Courtesy of Northern Ireland Tourist Board

**Belfast City Hall**

an even greater impact on the quality of life in any city. The 1995 opening of the £89 million Lagan Bridges has provided much needed relief for Belfast's increasingly congested roads. The bridges link the M2 with the Sydenham Bypass and connect the Larne railway line to Central Station and through to Dublin.

By Autumn 1996, traffic will flow uninterrupted between the bridge and the Sydenham Bypass. This will facilitate the final phase of the scheme, the rebuilding of the Ballymacarrett viaduct ,which will become a one way system carrying traffic bound for the city centre when work is completed in autumn 1997.

This book will help you to find your way around the city's streets and will hopefully point you in the direction of some of the many attractions which are on offer. Belfast looks forward to sharing these attractions with the thousands of visitors that are certain to arrive as long as peace holds.

The bus system in Belfast and Northern Ireland comes under the umbrella of one company, but for practical purposes, you will find yourself boarding either a Citybus or an Ulsterbus. Citybus services tend to start or finish close to the City Hall, right in the heart of the city centre, with routes covering all parts of the greater Belfast area. More information is provided below under the Citybus heading.

The Ulsterbus network, on the other hand, connects all the major towns and cities in Northern Ireland and extends to destinations in the Republic of Ireland, the UK mainland, and even on to mainland Europe. The network is operated under different service names and each is outlined on pages 52 & 53 under the Ulsterbus heading. Both Ulsterbus and Citybus operate a no smoking policy.

## CITYBUS

As mentioned above, the focal point for Citybus services is Belfast City Hall which is situated in Donegall Square. Buses leave from different points, all within the vicinity of the City Hall, and tickets and information for all routes are available from the Citybus Kiosk which is situated on Donegall Square West. Citybus routes are extensive, but all are highlighted in grey on the face of the street maps on pages 1 to 27, and all the route numbers are shown in red.

### FARES AND TICKETS

Fares can be paid in cash to the driver when boarding a Citybus, but a range of multi-journey tickets and travel cards can be purchased from the Citybus Kiosk in Donegall Square West or from the large number of ticket agents located in newsagents, sweet shops and post offices throughout the city.

### TIMETABLE INFORMATION

Once again, the hub of activity is the Citybus Kiosk in Donegall Square West. A 24-hour service is available by telephoning (01232) 246485. For lost property inquiries, telephone (01232) 458356.

### RAIL - LINK

Rail-Link runs a frequent service between Central Railway Station and Donegall Square in the city centre.

### CITYBUS TOURS

Citybus Tours operate mainly during the summer months, starting in early June and finishing in early September. The original Belfast City Tour, which has been operating since 1985, lets you see and enjoy many of the interesting features which Belfast has to offer. The tour departs from Castle Place every Wednesday at 1.30 p.m.

A new tour for 1995 is "Belfast : A living History", which takes in many of Belfast's historical places, leaving from Castle Place every Tuesday, Thursday & Sunday at 9.30 a.m. and 2.00 p.m.

Other tours include a scenic tour of North Down, a Parks and Gardens tour, and even a mystery tour! These tours are not all operated on a weekly basis so it is best to check details beforehand.

Advance booking is adviseable and can be made at the Citybus Kiosk, Donegall Square West. Credit card bookings can be made by phone on (01232) 458484.

### LATE NIGHT SERVICES

Citybus operates its Nightline service on five citywide routes, departing from Shaftesbury Square at midnight, 1 a.m., and 2 a.m. every Friday and Saturday night. Tickets are £2 and must be bought in advance from the ticket office in Shaftesbury Square between 9.00 p.m. and 1.50 a.m. - they are not available from the drivers. For further information, telephone (01232) 246485.

**CITYBUS INQUIRIES**
**(24 HOUR SERVICE)**
Telephone (01232) 246485

## ULSTERBUS

As mentioned earlier, Ulsterbus operates a comprehensive network of services which connects all the major towns in Northern Ireland. Services extend to destinations in the Republic of Ireland, the UK mainland, and even on to mainland Europe. The network is operated under different service names and each is outlined below.

### GOLDLINE EXPRESS SERVICES

The Ulsterbus Goldline Express services link all the major towns within Northern Ireland, and include the Maiden City Flyer which operates every hour between Belfast and Londonderry (journey time 1 hour 40 minutes), and a Belfast to Dublin service with up to seven departures every day (journey time approximately three hours).

Belfast services operate out of either Oxford Street Bus Station or the Europa Buscentre in Glengall Street. The Oxford Street station is due to be replaced by a new station which is currently being built on the nearby McCausland site, and is due to open in 1996. The Europa Buscentre is a state of the art station, built recently behind the Europa Hotel on Great Victoria Street. Waiting is done in comfort, food and refreshments are on hand, and the complex includes the Travel Centre which will handle any inquiries or booking requirements. Most Goldline Express services go to the Europa Buscentre for inter-town connections.

As with Citybus, Ulsterbus routes which go through Belfast are highlighted in grey on the face of the street maps on pages 1-27, but the route numbers are shown in blue as opposed to red.

### BUSYBUS

Ulsterbus uses a fleet of small coaches, or Busybuses, to operate a large number of locally based services throughout Northern Ireland.

### AIRBUS

An excellent airport shuttle service operates between Belfast International Airport and Belfast city centre. Coaches leave half hourly from the Europa Buscentre between 6 a.m. and 9.30 p.m (Monday to Saturday), with a slightly less frequent service operating between 6.30 a.m. and 9.30 p.m. on Sundays.

The return service leaves every half hour from in front of the main terminal building between 6.40 a.m. and 10.50 p.m. (Monday to Staurday). Sunday departures, once again, are slightly less frequent, operating between 7.10 a.m. and 10.50 p.m. A special timetable operates on Public Holidays.

Fares at the time of writing are £3.50 single and £6.40 return and journey time is approximately 20 minutes. Wheelchair space on the Airbus may be booked in advance by telephoning (01232) 337008.

### FLEXIBUS

Flexibus operates a fleet of 19 seat mini-coaches for private hire, with drivers, for varied travel requirements in and outside Ireland. Wheelchair facilities are provided for the disabled.

Flexibus also operates a number of late night services to and from Belfast on Fridays and Saturdays, and a shuttle service linking the Seacat terminal with Belfast City Centre. Information on the Nightrider service and other Flexibus services is available from the Europa Buscentre or by telephoning (01232) 233933.

### USEFUL TELEPHONE NUMBERS

Oxford Street Station (01232) 232356
Europa Buscentre (01232) 320011
Flexibus Inquiries (01232) 233933

## FREEDOM OF NORTHERN IRELAND TICKETS

The Freedom of Northern Ireland Ticket offers 7 days unlimited travel within Northern Ireland on all Ulsterbus and Citybus scheduled services (including Busybus & Airbus). Cost at the time of writing is £28. These tickets can be bought at all Ulsterbus depots and at the Travel Centre in the Europa Buscentre, but they are not available from drivers.

## ULSTERBUS DAYTOURS

Ulsterbus DayTours operate mainly during the summer months, but a progamme of tours is also available for Easter and the May Public Holiday. Destinations are too numerous to mention but include most of the province's resorts and beauty spots. Variety even extends to a tour which visits Daniel O'Donnell at his home in Donegal during his annual open day (Daniel, with the help of his mammy, managed to serve tea to 7,000 fans in a single day last year!).

DayTours depart from the Europa Buscentre, Glengall Street and bookings can be made there in person at the Travel Centre. Telephone inquiries can be made on (01232) 337004. Day Tours also operate from Ulsterbus depots outside Belfast.

## ULSTERBUS CROSS CHANNEL EXPRESS SERVICES

Services leave from Europa Buscentre in Glengall Street and connect to all major cities and towns across the UK. The services extend to some European destinations including Paris and Amsterdam. Tickets can be obtained at the Travel Centre in the Europa Buscentre (01232) 337003, and at any Ulsterbus station or Travel Agent in Northern Ireland.

## ULSTERBUS TOURS

Ulsterbus Tours offer a wide choice of luxury coach holidays in Ireland, north and south, as well as the UK mainland and Europe. For further information, phone (01232) 337004.

## TIMETABLE AND OTHER INFORMATION

For any travel information or other type of inquiry, look no further than the Travel Centre in the Europa Buscentre. Full address and telephone numbers are given below.

**The Travel Centre**
**Europa Buscentre**
**Glengall Street**
**Belfast**
**BT12 5AH**

Normal Opening hours:
Monday - Friday 0845 until 1730, Saturday 0900 - 1200, Sunday closed. The Travel Centre stays open for an extra half hour during the summer months, and opens for tour departures on Sundays during these months. Opening hours are restricted, however, on certain public holidays.

### TELEPHONE NUMBERS

General Inquiries : (01232) 320011
Cross Channel Express :
(01232) 337002 / 337003
Ulsterbus Tours : (01232) 337004
Private Hire : (01232) 337006

Fax : (01232) 246926

Northern Ireland Railways operate services within Northern Ireland as well as providing rail links to the Republic of Ireland, Britain and Europe.

Central Station in East Bridge Street stands at the hub of the rail network. The completion of the Cross Harbour Rail Line in November 1994 joined the Larne line to the rest of the network. Central Station is a ten minute walk from the city centre but a frequent Rail-Link bus service operates throughout the day bringing passengers into the centre of Belfast. If you are travelling by train into Belfast for a night out, it may be more convenient to get off at Botanic Station or, from September 1995, Great Victoria Street Station, as both are closer to Belfast's "Golden Mile", the city's main area for restaurants, pubs and clubs.

**MAIN ROUTES FROM CENTRAL STATION**

**1. North west to Londonderry via Ballymena and Coleraine.** Journey time between Central and Londonderry is approximately 2 hours 20 minutes.

**2. North east to Larne via Carrickfergus.** There is a regular service to Larne Harbour for passengers wishing to connect with the ferry crossings to Stranraer and Cairnryan. The journey time from Central Station is approximately 50 minutes.

**3. East to Bangor along the shore of Belfast Lough.** Journey time is approximately half an hour.

**4. South to Dublin via Lisburn, Portadown and Newry.** Several trains per day leave Central Station for Dublin's Connolly Station. Journey times vary, the shortest being approximately two hours. The line between Belfast and Dublin is currently being upgraded and this will help to reduce journey times when the work is completed late in 1996.

**NEW STATION AT GREAT VICTORIA STREET**

In September 1995, a new station will be opening in Great Victoria Street which is close to the commercial heart of the city centre and forms part of the "Golden Mile" referred to above. The station will be located next to the Europa Buscentre, providing Belfast with a fully integrated transport centre, combining rail, bus and car-parking facilities. In addition to its four platforms, the new station will have a Sales and Information Centre, concourse and waiting area. All commuter routes will have frequent access to the new station.

**TICKET TYPES**

There is a wide range of tickets available from NIR which includes :

**7 Day Weekly Ticket :** Offers seven days of unlimited travel between any two designated stations (valid Monday to Sunday).

**Monthly Moneysavers :** Offer unlimited travel between any two designated stations for a full calendar month.

**Rail Travel / Contract Tickets :** books of multiple tickets which offer reduced fares on some journeys within Northern Ireland and on cross-border services. Tickets can be used as and when it suits and are valid for six months.

**7 Day Rail Runabout Ticket :** only available from April to October, this ticket offers unlimited travel within Northern Ireland for any seven consecutive days, and also permits travel over the border to Dundalk.

**PASSENGER INQUIRIES**

N. Ireland & Cross Border Services :
Belfast Central (01232) 899411

**NIR TRAVEL OFFICES**

Wellington Place, Belfast (01232) 230671
Gt. Northern Mall, Belfast (01232) 315110
Larne Harbour (01574) 270517
British Rail Passenger Inquiries :
NIR Travel (01232) 230671

**TAXIS**

There are taxi ranks at Central Station, the two main bus stations and the City Hall. Consult the Yellow Pages if you wish to book one in advance, or try **City Cab** on 242000 or **Fon-A-Cab** on 233333.

## BELFAST CITY AIRPORT p10 L9

**B**elfast City Airport is situated on the main Belfast to Bangor Road, the A2, less than 10 minutes drive from the city centre. The airport offers good access to an excellent road network linking Belfast with the rest of Northern Ireland. Bus and rail links are about 5 minutes walk from the terminal building.

The airport has benefited from an ongoing programme of investment since it started providing scheduled services in 1983. Facilities have been upgraded to cope with the rapid growth in passenger numbers which now exceed one million per year.

Ownership of the airport looks set to change, however, and the consequences for future growth seem uncertain, but speculation includes the possibility of a new terminal building.

The information desk, which is situated inside the terminal entrance, provides tourist information and a booking service for accommodation anywhere in Ireland. A 10% deposit and a booking fee of up to £2 are payable at the time of booking.

### CAR PARKS

Car parks are situated close to the airport entrance and a courtesy bus is provided to take passengers the short distance to the terminal building.The Long Stay Car Park costs £2 per day and prices for the Short Stay Car Park start at £1 for the first hour, rising to a maximum of £5 per day. Payment is made by machine in the terminal building, so remember to keep your ticket with you.

### TAXIS, TRAINS & BUSES

There is a taxi rank in front of the terminal building and the journey into the city centre is quick and inexpensive. Alternatively, Sydenham railway station is about five minutes walk from the terminal building via the footbridge at the airport entrance, and the train journey to Belfast Central Station takes only a few minutes (see "Northern Ireland Railways" on page 55). A frequent Citybus service operates into the city centre from Station Road which is opposite the train station. The service number is 21 and the journey time is about 20 minutes (see "Bus Services" on pages 51-54).

### CAR HIRE

The car hire companies which operate from the airport are listed below. Their offices are located in the arrivals area.

| | |
|---|---|
| Avis | (01232) 240404 |
| Cosmo Eurodollar | (01232) 739400 |
| Hertz | (01232) 732451 |
| Budget | (01232) 451111 |
| Europcar | (01232) 450904 |
| McCauseland | (01232) 333777 |

### AIRLINES & DESTINATIONS

#### BRITISH AIRWAYS EXPRESS

Services to Aberdeen, Blackpool, Cardiff, Edinburgh, Glasgow, Isle of Man, Jersey, Liverpool, Luton, Manchester, and Southampton. Telephone 0345 222111 for reservations.

#### JERSEY EUROPEAN

Services to Birmingham, Blackpool, Bristol, Dublin, Exeter, Guernsey, Isle of Man, Jersey, Leeds/Bradford, London Gatwick, London Stanstead, and Londonderry. Telephone (01232) 457200 for reservations.

#### GILL AIR

Services to Newcastle-Upon-Tyne and Prestwick. Telephone (0191) 2862222 for reservations.

**FOR AIRPORT INFORMATION :
TELEPHONE (01232) 457745**

## BELFAST INTERNATIONAL AIRPORT

Belfast International Airport is located about 18 miles north-west of Belfast and is served by an excellent road network which links it to all parts of Northern Ireland. Passenger facilities, which include a new 108 room Airport Hotel, put Belfast International among the most modern regional airports in Europe and allow it to cope comfortably with the 2.5 million passengers who use it annually. The Information Desk in the arrivals area will deal with queries regarding onward travel and accommodation.

### CAR PARKS

There is a choice of Short Stay, Main Stay, and Holiday Car Parks. Prices start at £1 for half an hour in the Short Stay, and alternative tariffs include one week in the Holiday Car Park for £10. Off-airport parking is available just outside the airport entrance and a courtesy coach service is provided to convey passengers to the terminal building.

### BUSES, TRAINS & TAXIS

An excellent bus service to Belfast leaves every half hour from in front of the terminal building (full details are given on page 52). Buses stop at Belfast's main rail and bus stations for onward journeys to other parts of the province and to the Republic of Ireland (see pages 51-55). The airport's taxi rank is also in front of the terminal building and the journey time to the centre of Belfast is about twenty minutes.

### CAR HIRE

Several car hire companies have reception desks in the arrivals area. Their phone numbers are listed below.

| | |
|---|---|
| Avis | (01849) 422333 |
| Europcar | (01849) 423444 |
| Hertz | (01849) 422533 |
| McCausland | (01849) 422022 |

## AIRLINES & DESTINATIONS

### AIR BELFAST
Services to London Stanstead. Telephone (0345) 464748 for reservations.

### BRITISH AIRWAYS
Services to Birmingham, Glasgow, London Heathrow and Manchester. Telephone (0345) 222111 for reservations.

### BRITISH MIDLAND
Services to East Midlands, Jersey and London Heathrow. Telephone (0345) 554554 for reservations.

### BUSINESS AIR
Services to Manchester. Telephone (0500) 340146 for reservations.

### EMERALD EUROPEAN
Services to Luton. Telephone (0345) 585572 for reservations.

### KLM CITYHOPPER
Services to Amsterdam. Telephone (0181) 7509000 for reservations.

### KNIGHT AIR
Services to Leeds/Bradford. Telephone (0345) 626489 for reservations.

**Many other destinations in Europe and North America are served by direct charter flights.**

**FOR AIRPORT INFORMATION: TELEPHONE (01849) 422888**

## N. IRELAND SEA ROUTES

**Belfast to Stranraer :** Crossing by Seacat, 1 hour 30 minutes. Phone (0141) 2042266.
**Belfast to Liverpool :** Crossing by Norse Irish Ferries, 11 hours. Phone (01232) 779090.
**Larne to Stranraer :** Crossing Stena Sealink 2 hours 30 minutes. Phone (01776) 702262.
**Larne to Cairnryan :** Crossing by P&O European Ferries, 2 hours 15 minutes. Phone (01581) 200276.
**Belfast to Douglas :** Crossing by Isle of Man Steam Packet, 4 hours 30 minutes. (01624) 661661.

## BELFAST CITY HALL   `p2 G8`

Arguably the finest piece of architecture in Belfast, the City Hall is situated in Donegall Square on the site of the former White Linen Hall. It was designed by Sir Brumwell Thomas and completed in 1906. The building was constructed in Portland stone in a style somewhat reminiscent of Wren's Saint Paul's Cathedral, with a central copper dome rising 173 feet to dominate the city skyline. A guided tour of the City Hall will reveal its impressive marbled interior which houses many items of interest, including a mural by Belfast artist, John Luke, symbolising the foundation of the city and its principle industries, and the Charter of Belfast granted by James I on 27th April, 1613.

## BELFAST CASTLE   `p5 F13`

Baronial style castle set high up on Cave Hill giving spectacular views of Belfast and beyond. Facilities include a fine restaurant and a Heritage Centre.

## BELFAST PARKS

See pages 61 & 62.

## BELFAST WATERFRONT HALL   `p2 H8`

See page 50.

## BELFAST PUBLIC LIBRARY   `p2 G8`

Houses some of the oldest books printed in Belfast as well as old photographs of the city.

## BELFAST ZOO   `p3 F14`

Antrim Road. Award-winning Zoo nestling on the slopes of Cave Hill. Spectacular views of the city below.

## CUSTOM HOUSE   `p2 H8`

Queen's Square. Designed by Charles Lanyon, and currently undergoing major refurbishment, its most striking feature is the sculptured pediment portraying Britannia, Neptune and Mercury.

## GRAND OPERA HOUSE   `p1 G7`

See pages 63 & 66.

## CROWN LIQUOR SALOON   `p1 G7`

See pubs section.

## THE GIANT'S RING   `p25 F1`

Neolithic site featuring a stone dolmen which stands at the centre of an earth rampart 600 feet in diameter.

## HARBOUR OFFICE   `p2 H8`

Corporation Square. Built for the Harbour Commission in 1854, its interior is noted for its stained glass and many paintings and sculptures depicting the city's seafaring history. Guided tours.

## LAGAN LOOKOUT   `p2 H8`

Visitor centre, located on Donegall Quay beside the Lagan Weir, housing an nterpretive exhibition which explains the workings of the Weir and reveals the industrial and folk history of the River Lagan. River and harbour boat trips depart from here.

## LINEN HALL LIBRARY   `p2 G8`

Donegall Square North. Belfast's oldest library, it was established in 1788 and houses many important collections, including a comprehensive archive on the 'Troubles'.

## ORMEAU BATHS GALLERY   `p2 H7`

Ormeau Avenue. What do you do when a city has more swimming pools than it knows what

to do with? You convert one into a gallery for contemporary art, of course!

## PUBLIC RECORDS OFFICE `p19 F4`
68 Balmoral Avenue. The Public Search Room is the place to start tracing your Ulster family tree.

## QUEEN'S UNIVERSITY `p19 G6`
University Road. One of Charles Lanyon's finest buildings, the main college was modelled on Magdalen College Oxford and was completed in 1849.

## ROYAL COURTS OF JUSTICE `p2 H7`
The building was a gift to the city from the Westminster Parliament in 1933. Built from Portland stone, it houses four courts with rich interiors of polished marble and woodwork.

## ST. ANNE'S CATHEDRAL `p2 G8`
Donegall Street. Begun in 1899 and consecrated in 1904, the style is Romanesque and the building contains stone from every county in Ireland. Mosaic depicting the arrival of Saint Patrick in Ireland in 432 A.D.

## ST. MALACHY'S CHURCH `p2 H7`
Alfred Street. Best known for its fine vaulted ceiling which is similar to the one in Henry VII's chapel in Westminster Abbey.

## SINCLAIR SEAMAN'S CHURCH `p2 H8`
Corporation Square. Designed by Charles Lanyon in the Venetian style and consecrated in 1853 for seamen visiting the port of Belfast, this church has become something of a maritime museum. The pulpit is a ship's prow, and the organ has the port and starboard lights of a Guinness boat from the Liffey and a bell from HMS Hood.

## STORMONT `p16 P9`
Situated on the Upper Newtownards Road, about three miles from the city centre, Stormont was home to the Northern Ireland Parliament until 1972 when Direct Rule from Westminster was introduced. Both the building and the setting are impressive : the Portland stone construction has a floor space of 5 acres and it stands on an elevated position in 300 acres of parkland. The debating chamber was recently destroyed by fire but there are plans to restore it. Government departments are housed in Stormont Castle, which is next door, and access to both buildings is restricted for security reasons.

## ULSTER MUSEUM `p19 G6`
Situated in Botanic Gardens, just a mile from the city centre, the museum holds and exhibits diverse and fascinating collections of art, antiquities, botany and zoology, geology and local history. Other attractions include temporary exhibitions, Sunday afternoon events, lectures and films. The museum is open Monday to Friday from 10am to 5pm; Saturday from 1pm to 5pm; Sunday from 2pm to 5pm. Admission is free. Citybus numbers 69 & 71.

## ULSTER FOLK & TRANSPORT MUSEUM
Situated on the Belfast to Bangor road at Cultra, this is a museum of two complimentary halves. The Folk Museum gives a unique insight into Ulster life, past and present, by reconstructing an ever-increasing number of houses, workshops, mills, shops, schools, churches and other public buildings which have been gathered from across the province. The end result is a living and working museum. The Transport Museum, across the road, exhibits most forms of transport and has recently added a purpose-built gallery to house its 'Irish Railway Collection'. Catch a bus or train heading for Bangor and get off at Cultra.

# *BELFAST CITY COUNCIL*
## *CITY HALL TOURS*

**Public tours of the City Hall
are held Monday to Friday
at 10.30 a.m. & 2.30 p.m.
July, August and September**

*AND*

**every Wednesday at 10.30 a.m.
October to June**

*Each Tour Lasts Approx 1 Hour
Admission Free*

**To Book Please Telephone**

**Belfast (01232) 320202 Ext. 2618**

Belfast City Council's Parks and Amenities Section has properties, staff and responsibilities spread throughout what is a fairly large city. There are, at present, over 52 parks under its control, along with a Zoological Garden, seven cemeteries and historical graveyards, and numerous open spaces scattered throughout the city.

Ever since the first public park was opened at Ormeau on Easter Saturday 1871, the commitment to providing public open space has been on the increase. By the turn of the century, another five parks were open, and by the mid-1930's a further eight had been added, including the major property of Belfast Castle Estate. Many properties, once private demesnes, have been generously donated to the City Council - none more beautifully situated than the riverside Barnett Demesne and Sir Thomas and Lady Dixon Park, both named after their benefactors.

Today there is much within Belfast to attract visitors and citizens alike, such as the magnificent early 19th century Palm House within Botanic Gardens. Its foundation stone was laid in 1839 and the dome was finally finished in 1852. Extensively renovated in the 1980's and reopened in 1983, one of the first examples of a curvilinear glasshouse now stands as a reminder of bygone eras in Belfast's history. The nearby 100 year old Tropical Ravine is a unique example of 'Victoriana', where visitors view tropical and temperate plants from a peripheral railed balcony. Its valuable plant collection provides a captivating and educational experience for many local school children.

The rose gardens at Sir Thomas and Lady Dixon Park are world famous for the International Rose Trials held annually. Roses are sent from many different countries and are judged over a two year period. Up to 20,000 blooms can be enjoyed in this splendid park setting. Sir Thomas and Lady Dixon Park is one of four riverside parks that provide ample opportunity for those who enjoy walking. Clement Wilson Park, Barnett Demesne and Lagan Meadows are rich in seasonal colour and interest, with the last being managed primarily for wildlife and education. In these parks, guided walks nature trails and school tours help to increase awareness of the value and variety of wildlife within the city.

The Zoological Gardens are currently being re-developed into one of the most modern in Europe, and now attract more visitors than ever before. Sited on the hillsides to the north west of the city, the Gardens together with Hazelwood, Bellevue and Belfast Castle Estates form the Cave Hill Country Park, ideal for walking, orienteering, and nature study. Belfast Castle, with its panoramic views over the city and Belfast Lough, has undergone major refurbishment and has become a busy conference and function centre. Similar use has been made of the late Georgian mansion, Malone House. Set in the heart of the Lagan Valley Regional Park, this house provides the parks' main information centre. A meal in the restaurant of either of these fine buildings is a great way to complete a day out.

There is good provision for all manner of recreation. The range includes activities such as tennis and BMX racing, and family recreation such as putting, boating and over 50 children's playgrounds. Specialist facilities include an International Junior Soccer pitch, a popular par 3 golf course and the Mary Peters Athletics Track, the last having been recently taken over from Queen's University Belfast.

Horticultural standards are high throughout the city, with many bedding schemes, floral features, and bulb and shrub planting, etc. They reach perfection (or as near as possible) at Grovelands, Musgrave Park. Certain features are carried out on a large scale. Literally tens of thousands of crocus and daffodil bulbs brighten the spring months throughout the city, while in the summertime hanging baskets bring a splash of colour to the city centre streets. They compliment the plant tubs and tree planting that is also a feature of Belfast.

Belfast City Council believes that it is of vital importance that the provision of open spaces and parklands, floral baskets, spring bulb displays and extensive tree planting be continued and expanded so that Belfast becomes an increasingly attractive city for future generations.

# Department of Client Services

# Parks and Ameneties Section

*Belfast Parks* *offer a wide range of facilities for you to enjoy, including :*

**Malone House** at Barnett Demesne, with rooms available for conferences, wedding receptions, seminars, meetings, etc., **Barnett Restaurant** (Open Tue - Sat 10.00 a.m. - 4.30 p.m. and Fri, Sat from 7.00 p.m.) and **Higgin Art Gallery**.
Tel (01232) 681246

**Belfast Castle**, in the centre of **Cave Hill Country Park**, also has rooms for hire and the **Cellar Restaurant**, (Open Mon - Sat 11.00 a.m. - 10.00 p.m.) and **Cave Hill Heritage Centre**.
Tel (01232) 776925
Adjacent Castle gardens and **Adventure Playground** for under 14's.

Why not visit **Belfast Zoo**, open every day with free car parking and the **Ark Restaurant**.
Tel (01232) 776277

Enjoy a stroll through **Grovelands** at Stockman's Lane, the **Rose Gardens** at **Sir Thomas and Lady Dixon Park** or the Victorian **Botanic Gardens** where it's summer all year round in the **Palm House** and **Tropical Ravine**.

For details of programme of events (walks, tours, band performances, shows, etc.) and further information, contact
**Belfast Parks and Amenities Section**
The Cecil Ward Building, 4 - 10 Linenhall Street, Belfast.
Tel (01232) 320202

Belfast, like the rest of Ireland, is proud of its artistic tradition. The arts have always been strong in this part of the world but in recent years they have been going from strength to strength thanks to considerable investment in new and upgraded venues, and continuing financial support from the public and private sectors.

The most significant development is the construction of the Belfast Waterfront Hall which is due for completion around the end of 1996 and is certain to attract even more artists of world renown to the city (see page 50 for more details).

The cultural highlight of the year is undoubtedly the Belfast Festival at Queen's which normally lasts for two to three weeks each November. This is a world class festival which attracts many international performers from the world of theatre, dance, music, and comedy. The timing of the festival means that it is also able to stage many of the fringe acts which have enjoyed success at the Edinburgh Festival.

## THEATRES

### ARTS THEATRE
**Botanic Avenue**  `p12 G6`
**Phone 324936**
The Belfast Civic Arts Theatre, to give it its full name, stages a wide range of popular drama, comedy, music and variety acts.

### GRAND OPERA HOUSE
**Great Victoria Street**  `p1 G7`
**Phone 241919**
The Opera House is home to Opera Northern Ireland but it is much more than a venue for opera - it stages a wide variety of theatre, music, dance, comedy, and even pantomime. Many international stars from the world of entertainment have played to packed audiences since the theatre was restored to its Victorian splendour back in 1980. There are special facilities for wheelchair users and an induction loop system relays non-musical performances to hearing aid users.

### GROUP THEATRE
**Bedford Street**  `p2 G7`
**Phone 323900**
The Group Theatre forms part of the Ulster Hall complex which is operated by Belfast City Council. The theatre seats 240 and stages a large number of productions, performed mainly by local dramatic societies.

### LYRIC THEATRE
**55 Ridgeway Street**  `p19 G5`
**Phone 381081(Box Office) or 669660(Admin)**
The Lyric Theatre is Northern Ireland's only repertory theatre, presenting a broad range of classical and contemporary plays with a particular emphasis on Irish work. Now in its 26th year, the theatre aims to fulfil a broad role, offering fifty weeks a year of varied programming ranging from live music, dance and comedy events to co-productions with local theatre companies and the best of Irish theatre. Situated on the banks of the Lagan in the heart of Stranmillis village, the theatre is only two miles from the city centre on a major Citybus route. The theatre is accessible for patrons with special needs and is equipped with a loop induction system.

### OLD MUSEUM ARTS CENTRE
**College Square North**  `p1 G8`
**Phone 235053**
A recent addition to the arts scene, the Old Museum Arts Centre has already earned a reputation for staging experimental theatre and has courted some healthy controversy on occasions.

## OPERA

For somewhere as small as Northern Ireland, we are lucky to have two very fine operatic companies. Opera Northern Ireland has co-operated very successfully with the Ulster Orchestra to stage some very lavish productions at the Grand Opera House, and their efforts have been rewarded with national critical acclaim.

The Castleward Opera Company provides one of the social events of the year when they stage

*Designed by Rodney Miller Associates, Belfast. Photography by Jonathan Howe.*

LYRIC PLAYERS THEATRE

their annual festival of opera at Castleward, a National Trust property on the shores of Strangford Lough. This is the Northern Ireland version of Glyndebourne - black tie and picnic hamper are the order of the day - and all performances are normally sold out well in advance of the event which lasts for about three weeks in June. Phone 661090 for details.

## CINEMA

For many years the number of Belfast cinemas seemed to be in inexorable decline, but the advent of the multiplex has reversed this trend and there are now dozens of screens to choose from around the city. Most concentrate on the mainstream Hollywood releases and, as a consequence, many cinemas end up showing the same film. The Queen's Film Theatre is the main exception to this rule, catering to followers of European cinema as well as screening many current and past cult classics.

The 'Entertainment' section of the Belfast Telegraph is a good place to find out what is showing and where, or you can phone the appropriate number below.

**CINEWORLD**
**Falls Road**            `p11 E7`
**Phone 600988**
Five screen multiplex located in the Kennedy Shopping Centre.

**CURZON**
**Ormeau Road**           `p20 H6`
**Phone 641373**
Old style independent cinema now adapted to five screens.

**GLENGORMLEY MOVIE HOUSE**
**Glenwell Road**         `p3 E15`
**Phone 833424**
New multiplex in the north of the city.

**MGM**
**Dublin Road**           `p2 G7`
**Phone 245700**
New eight screen multiplex situated close to

many of the city's most popular restaurants and pubs and ideal, therefore, if you are intending to make a night of it.

**QUEEN'S FILM THEATRE**
**University Square Mews**    `p12 G6`
**Phone 244857**
Financial support from the Arts Council and Queen's University allows the QFT to screen some alternatives to the usual box office hits. The only place in Belfast where you have any chance of seeing a foreign language film. Two screens.

**STRAND**
**Holywood Road**         `p14 L8`
**Phone 673500**
The oldest cinema in Belfast but now adapted to four screens.

**YORKGATE MOVIE HOUSE**
**York Street**           `p9 H9`
**Phone 741746**
Modern multi screen which is part of the Yorkgate shopping complex, located close to the start of the M2 motorway.

## MUSIC

Belfast is steeped in musical tradition and includes Van Morrison, James Galway and Barry Douglas among its famous sons. The city is regularly included on the itinerary of these and countless other celebrated international artists and entertainers.

For lovers of classical music, the Ulster Orchestra performs a series of concerts throughout the year at the Ulster Hall. The orchestra continues to grow in reputation, both at home and abroad, and has performed several times at the Henry Wood Promenade Concerts in London's Royal Albert Hall. It also enjoys a successful relationship with Opera Northern Ireland which stages its productions at the Grand Opera House. For details of concerts and recordings, contact the ticket office at the BBC Shop in Arthur Street or telephone 233240.

It may come as no surprise to learn that Belfast

**GRAND OPERA HOUSE**

pubs provide the main platform for local bands and musicians. There are dozens of such venues and most of them are listed in the 'Pubs' section on pages 74-78. A good choice of rock, jazz, folk and blues is usually on offer and, once again, the 'Entertainment' section of the Belfast Telegraph is a good place to find out what's on.

Most of the major concerts in Belfast currently take place at one of the three venues listed below. The Grand Opera House, Dundonald Ice Bowl and one or two of the city's leisure centres are also used from time to time. Belfast Waterfront Hall will be an important addition to this list when it opens for business in early 1997.

## ULSTER HALL
**Bedford Street** `p2 G7`
**Phone 323900**

The Ulster Hall is a 19th century building which houses the magnificent Mulholland Organ which has recently benefited from a major overhaul. In addition to being the home of the

Ulster Orchestra, the hall provides a venue for a wide range of concerts and recitals, from classical to rock and pop.

## WHITLA HALL
**University Road** `p12 G6`

The Whitla Hall belongs to Queen's University and is often used for concerts, recitals, and occasionally for drama. The Student Union also has a large hall which is used as a venue for live bands.

## KINGS HALL
**Lisburn Road** `p18 E4`
**Phone 665225**

The King's Hall is Belfast's largest indoor arena and tends to be used, therefore, when the top rock and pop performers visit the city. A wide variety of exhibitions and events also take place in the hall throughout the year, including the Motor Show, the Ideal Home Exhibition, the Royal Agricultural Society Show, and major boxing contests.

There are hundreds of restaurants to choose from in Belfast but this guide will attempt to select about 50 of the best. This process is bound to be subjective but no apologies are made for that. After all, how many times have you eaten at a restaurant for the first time because it happened to be recommended to you by somebody else?

All the restaurants featured have been tried out, often frequently, by somebody connected with the Belfast Street Atlas & Guide. They have been selected by people who enjoy good food and drink in stimulating surroundings, while bearing in mind price, location and diversity. These places are the ones that we have enjoyed most, the ones that we recommend to friends and relations. They don't always agree, and perhaps you won't either, but that's what being subjective is all about!

Few people would argue that the face of Belfast's restaurants and pubs has been transformed over the past ten years. Choice and quality have improved tremendously, and this trend looks set to continue. In terms of culinary diversity, we can't compete with a cosmopolitan city like London, but most of the major cuisines are available, and Belfast's restaurants can more than hold their own in terms of quality, price, and atmosphere.

Many are mentioned in the growing array of Irish and British food guides. These publications all have their good points but, invariably, one area of contention is their attempts to estimate the likely cost of a meal. We have all had the experience of going somewhere, supposedly "cheap and cheerful" , to find that a couple of drinks and a shared bottle of wine can do strange things to the bill. On the other hand, there are occasions when you may have taken advantage of a very reasonable fixed price menu at an expensive restaurant, and left with both your conscience and the contents of your wallet largely intact!

When you add in the "businessman's lunch", the "early evening specials", Sunday lunches and happy hours, attempts to estimate price often tend to be in vain. The system adopted for this guide, therefore, is rather broad-brush in its approach, attempting to categorise a restaurant as expensive, middling or cheap.

"Expensive" restaurants are those where you can expect the final bill to exceed £20 per head. If you eat somewhere categorised as "cheap", you will, more often than not, escape for under a tenner. The final bill at a restaurant falling into the "middling" category should come to somewhere between £10 and £20, bearing in mind all the caveats mentioned earlier.

Finally, the golden rule when using this guide is to phone first! All the information included was gathered during June 1995 but restaurants come and go, change hands, chefs, menus, opening hours and much else, so it is best to check with the restaurant before turning up.

## PRICE RATING

£     **Cheap (usually under £10 per head)**

££     **Middling (between £10 and £20)**

£££     **Expensive ( £20+)**

## ANTICA ROMA
**67/69 Botanic Avenue**    `p12 G6`
**Phone 311121 Fax 310787**
**Price Rating : £££**
*Opening Times : Mon-Fri 12noon-2.30pm;*
*Mon-Sat 6pm-11pm; Sun 5pm-10pm*
Under the same ownership as Villa Italia and Speranza, both of which also appear in this guide, Antica Roma retains the Italian cuisine but takes a step decidedly up-market. Most often noted for its dramatic decor (murals that don't quite rival the Sistine Chapel), the food is as good as any Italian restaurant in Belfast and rates a mention in virtually all of the good food guides. The atmosphere is lively, especially at weekends. All in all, a fashionable place to see and be seen.

## ASHOKA
**363/365 Lisburn Road** `p19 F6`
**Phone 660362  Fax 660228**
**Price Rating: ££**
*Opening Times: Mon-Fri 12noon-2pm; Mon-Sat 5.30pm-11.30pm; Sun 5.30pm-10.30pm*
Self proclaimed "restaurant to the stars", this popular and long-established Indian restaurant offers a comprehensive menu which includes a good choice of vegetarian dishes, and even includes something for the maverick in the party who insists on eating European food when everybody else is looking forward to a "good Indian". Excellent value fixed-price menus.

## THE ATTIC
**54 Stranmillis Road** `p19 G5`
**Phone 661074**
**Price Rating : ££**
*Opening Times : Mon-Sat 11am-3pm & 5pm-10.30pm; Sun 11am-3pm & 4.30pm-9pm*
Small, intimate restaurant occupying the two upper floors of a Victorian terrace. The focus is on good European cooking rather than a wide ranging menu. Unlicensed but you are welcome to bring your own wine.

## AUBERGINES & BLUE JEANS
**1 University Street** `p12 G6`
**Phone 233700**
**Price Rating : ££**
*Opening Times : Mon-Sat 12noon-11pm; Sun 12noon-10pm*
Sister restaurant to Saints & Scholars which is next door but aimed more at the casual diner. Bistro menu and lively atmosphere. May have to queue at weekends.

## BANANAS
**4 Clarence Street. Phone 244844** `p2 G7`
**Price Rating : ££**
*Opening Times : Mon-Fri 12noon-3pm; Mon-Sat 5pm-11pm*
Bananas shares a kitchen with its more upmarket sister, Restaurant 44, which is next door. Modern international cuisine and colonial style decor - there's even a stuffed gorilla, although it isn't

on the menu!

## BELFAST CASTLE RESTAURANT
**Antrim Road. Phone 776925** `p5 F13`
**Price Rating : ££**
*Opening Times : Mon-Sat 11am-11pm; Sun 11am-5pm*
Perched high up on the slopes of Cave Hill with spectacular views over Belfast, few restaurants enjoy a setting to rival Belfast Castle. Formerly the home of the Marquis of Donegall, the castle is now in the hands of the City Council and has become a successful conference venue not least because of its reputation for fine food. Photograph on page 73.

## BENGAL BRASSERIE
**339 Ormeau Road. Phone 647516** `p20 H6`
**Price Rating : ££**
*Opening Times : Mon-Fri 12noon-2pm; Mon-Sat 5.30pm-11.15pm; Sun 5.30pm-10.15pm*
Highly rated Bengali cooking in recently refurbished restaurant. Wide choice includes list of daily specials such as Tandoori Duck and Indian River Fish.

## BISHOPS RESTAURANT
**34 Bradbury Place. Phone 311827** `p1 G7`
**Price Rating : £**
*Opening Times : Mon-Sun 11am-3am*
Belfast's answer to Harry Ramsden. Quality fish and chips to set you up for a good night on the town. Unlicensed.

## BLEECKERS
**42 Malone Road. Phone 663114** `p19 F5`
**Price Rating : £**
*Mon-Sat 5pm-11.30pm; Sun 4pm-10pm*
American style restaurant, popular with local student population and families with children.

## CAFE POIROT
**51 Fountain Street** `p2 G8`
**Phone 323130**
**Price Rating : £**
*Opening Times : Mon-Sat 7.45am-5.15pm*
French style cafe which is very popular with

**Malone House**

shoppers and office workers. Expect to queue at lunchtime. Take away service, and tables outside, weather permitting!

## CHEZ DELBART
**10 Bradbury Place** `p1 G7`
**Phone 238020**
**Price Rating : ££**
*Opening Times : Mon-Sun 5pm-11.30pm*
Known locally as Frogties, this was a popular French restaurant back in the days before the 'Golden Mile' really became established. Two floors but not a lot of space, so don't be surprised if you have to queue in order to sample the fine food and authentic bistro atmosphere.

## CHICAGO PIZZA PIE FACTORY
**1 Bankmore Square** `p2 G7`
**Phone 233555**
**Price Rating : £**
*Opening Times : Mon-Thur 12noon-11pm; Fri-Sat 12noon-1am; Sun 12noon-10.30pm*
Part of a successful international chain, the formula is all-American. Separate bar and restaurant, both handy to the MGM cineplex which is next door.

## CLARE CONNERY AT MALONE HOUSE
**Barnett Demesne** `p25 F2`

**Phone 681246 Fax 682197**
**Price Rating : ££**
*Opening Times : Tue-Sat 10am-4.30pm; Fri-Sat from 7pm*
A Georgian mansion set in the heart of Lagan Valley Regional Park, only Belfast Castle can rival Malone House for the beauty of its setting. The chef, Clare Connery, is a highly regarded 'TV cook' and the food lives up to her reputation.

## CUTTERS WHARF
**Lockview Road. Phone 663388** `p19 G5`
**Price Rating : ££**
*Opening Times : Mon-Fri 12noon-10.30pm; Sat 6pm-10.30pm*
The restaurant, like the bar below, has a boathouse feel to it which fits in nicely with its riverside location. Modern European cuisine with extensive choice. Cutter's Wharf is one of the busiest bars in Belfast and a lively atmosphere is likewise guaranteed in the restaurant.

## DRAGON PALACE
**16 Botanic Avenue** `p12 G6`
**Phone 323869**
**Price Rating : ££**
*Opening Times : Mon-Sun 12noon-2pm & 5pm-12midnight*
This may not be a very inspiring Chinese restaurant from the outside but the food is very highly rated and it's difficult to argue with a two course lunch for £3.70!

## ESPERANTO
**Dublin Road** `p2 G7`
**Price Rating : ££**
*Opening Times : Mon-Fri 5pm-11pm; Sat 4pm-11pm; Sun 4pm-10pm*
Fashionable newcomer to the area. International cuisine and lively atmosphere.

## EUROPA HOTEL
**Great Victoria Street** `p1 G7`
**Phone 327000 Fax 327800**
**Price Rating : ££**

*Opening Times : Mon-Sun 6am to 1.30am*
For the past generation the Europa has been known mainly for the frequency with which it was bombed. Rebuilding work following the last explosion, however, has transformed the hotel. Gone are the security barriers to reveal an impressive new neo-classical facade which is certainly more inviting than before. The diner can choose between the all-day Brasserie and the Gallery Restaurant. The latter comes under the 'expensive' category but the cuisine is all that you would expect from a top class hotel.

## FOUR WINDS
**111 Newton Park** `p26 J3`
**Phone 401957**
**Price Rating : £££**
*Opening Times : Mon-Sat 12noon-2.30pm & 7pm-10pm*
Long established, family-run bar and restaurant. Located out in the suburbs but remains popular due to its strong reputation for good food.

## FRIAR'S BUSH
**159 Stranmillis Road** `p19 G5`
**Phone 669824**
**Price Rating : ££**
*Opening Times : Tues-Sat 7pm-10pm*
European cuisine served in intimate surroundings. Unlicensed but you can bring your own wine. Four course set menu £13.95 (Tues-Fri).

## FITZY'S
**27 University Road** `p12 G6`
**Price Rating : £**
*Opening Times : Mon-Sat 5pm-11.30pm; Sun 4pm-10pm*
New restaurant in university area, proving to be an instant success judging from the queues. Varied menu includes pizzas and pasta dishes.

## THE GREEK SHOP
**43 University Road** `p12 G6`
**Phone 333135**
**Price Rating : ££**
*Opening Times : Mon-Fri Noon-3pm, Tues-Sat*

*6pm-10pm*
Belfast's only Greek taverna. A small, family run establishment where plate smashing is definitely frowned upon! Unlicensed but you can bring your own retsina.

## HARVEY'S `p1 G7`
**95 Great Victoria Street. Phone 233433**
**Price Rating : £**
*Opening Times : Mon-Sun 5pm-12midnight*
Combination of pizzeria and American style restaurant.

## JHARNA
**133 Lisburn Road** `p19 F6`
**Phone 381299 Fax 381299**
**Price Rating : ££**
*Opening Times : Mon-Sat 12noon-2pm & 5.30pm-11.30pm; Sun 5.30pm-11pm*
Indian restaurant with a good reputation for seafood dishes (the Fish Badami is so good that a company in England recently placed a take

away order and had it flown to Bournemouth at a cost of £1500). Three course lunch for £4.95.

## LA BELLE EPOQUE
**61/63 Dublin Road** `p2 G7`
Phone 323244
Price Rating : £££
*Opening Times : Mon-Fri 12noon-11.30pm; Sat 6pm-11.30pm*
Authentic French cuisine which rates a mention in many of the good food guides.

## LA BOHEME
**103 Great Victoria Street** `p1 G7`
Phone 240666 Fax 240040
Price Rating : £££
*Opening Times : Mon-Fri 12noon-12midnight; Sat 6pm-12midnight*
Another highly rated French heavyweight at the heart of the Golden Mile.

## LARRY'S PIANO BAR
**34 Bedford Street** `p2 G7`
Phone 325061
Price Rating : ££
*Opening Times : Tues-Sat 5pm-1am*
Without doubt the most raucous atmosphere of any restaurant in Belfast. Larry's is a popular choice for stag and hen nights, and other large groups wishing to let their hair down. The piano gets plenty of use and it is not unusual for the staff to 'do a turn'. Don't be surprised if you see dancing on the table, or the occasional body sliding under it!

## MALONEY'S
**33/35 Malone Road** `p19 F5`
Phone 682929 Fax 683272
Price Rating : ££
*Opening Times : Mon-Fri 12noon-11.30pm, Sat 12noon-12midnight, Sun 12noon-10pm*
Fashionable restaurant close to Queen's University. Bare brick interior but the atmosphere is warm and friendly and the menu is varied, with a mixture of continental and traditional cooking. Table d'hote menu (Mon-Fri) at £11.95 offers excellent value.

## MANOR HOUSE
**47 Donegall Pass** `p2 G7`
Phone 238755
Price Rating : ££
*Opening Times : Mon-Sat 12noon-2.30pm & 5pm-12midnight; Sun 1pm-12midnight*
At first glance, a traditional Chinese restaurant but the menu reveals a few surprises that help the Manor House to stand out from the pack. Fish head, duck's web, eel - all cooked in an authentic Chinese style which has brought the restaurant to the attention of most of the good food guides. Good value set menus both at lunch and dinner, and an excellent selection of vegetarian dishes.

## NICK'S WAREHOUSE
**35 Hill Street** `p2 H8`
Phone 439690 Fax 230514
Price Rating : ££
*Opening Times : Mon-Fri 12noon-2.30pm; Tues-Sat 6pm-9pm*
Redeveloped warehouse in what used to be a rather unfashionable part of town near to St Anne's Cathedral. Nick's pioneering spirit was quickly rewarded with a large and loyal following, especially among the business community who frequent it both at lunchtime and after work. The building is divided between a wine bar which serves food downstairs and a restaurant upstairs; both are intimate yet informal. The food is excellent and gets an enthusiastic mention in most of the good food guides.

## THE OTHER PLACE
**133 Stranmillis Road** `p19 G5`
Phone 664644
Price Rating : £
Open all day, and very popular both as a place to eat and as somewhere to pop into for a coffee. Bring your own wine. Sister restaurant in Botanic Avenue.

## PIERRE VICTOIRE
**30 University Road** `p12 G6`
Phone 315151

**Price Rating : ££**

*Opening Times : Mon-Sat 12noon-3pm & 6pm-11pm*

Lively French bistro in the heart of the university area. Good value set lunch.

## PLANKS
**Lisburn Road** p19 F6
**Price Rating : £**

*Opening Times : Lunch & Dinner*

Some restaurants inadvertently resemble a building site but at Planks the look is intentional. Good value food, friendly service, and bring your own wine policy, attracts a lively young crowd.

## PONTE VECCHIO
**73 Great Victoria Street** p1 G7
**Phone 242402**
**Price Rating : ££**

*Opening Times : Mon-Sat 5pm-11.30pm; Sun 5pm-10pm*

Busy Italian restaurant offering good value for money.

## RESTAURANT 44
**44 Bedford Street Phone 244844** p2 G7
**Price Rating : £££**

*Opening Times : Mon-Sat 12noon-3pm & 6pm-11pm*

Colonial style brasserie serving Anglo French cuisine. Despite a change of ownership, Restaurant 44 remains highly rated and continues to be a popular choice both for lunch and dinner, especially when somebody else is paying.

## ROSCOFF
**Lesley House, Shaftesbury Square** p1 G7
**Phone 331532 Fax 312093**
**Price Rating : £££**

*Opening Times : Mon-Fri 12.15pm-2.15pm; Mon-Sat 6.30pm-10.30pm*

For Roscoff, read great scoff - if you are only in Belfast for one meal, this is the place to eat. From outside, the premises could be mistaken for a bookmaker's shop, but behind its opaque

windows the decor is light and modern. Chef, Paul Rankin, trained under Albert Roux at the internationally renowned La Gavroche in London before returning home with his American wife, Jeanne, to open their own restaurant. The emphasis is on creative cooking and the menu is constantly changing. Despite their growing fame (several books and two TV series) it is still possible to eat reasonably cheaply by taking advantage of the set menus at lunch and dinner, £14.50 and £21.50 respectively. Roscoff is guaranteed a mention in all the good food guides and it is the first restaurant in Northern Ireland to receive a Michelin Star.

## SAINTS & SCHOLARS
**3 University Street** p12 G6
**Phone 325137 Fax 323240**
**Price Rating : ££**

*Opening Times : Mon-Sat 12noon-11pm; Sun 12.30pm-2.30pm & 5.30pm-9.30pm*

Popular bistro offering a combination of excellent food and good service. Children are welcome but the clientele is mainly professional - John Major ate here on his last visit to Belfast, but was unavailable for comment.

## SALVO'S
**16 Shaftesbury Square** p1 G7
**Phone 247891**
**Price Rating : £**

*Opening Times : Mon-Sat 5pm-11.30pm*

Small, bustling Italian restaurant. Chef's special every night. Bring your own wine.

## SKANDIA
**50 Howard Street** p1 G7
**Phone 240239**
**Price Rating : £**

*Opening Times : Mon-Sat 9.30am-11pm*

As the opening times suggest, the Skandia caters for every meal from breakfast through to after-theatre supper! It is ideal for family dining with special menus for children. Its location, close to the Grand Opera House yet near to the city centre, makes it a popular choice with both

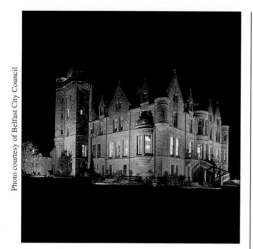

**Belfast Castle**

shoppers and theatre goers. Its sister restaurant in Callendar Street is right in the heart of the city's shopping district and has revived many a flagging bargain hunter over the years. Both restaurants are unlicensed but you are welcome to bring your own wine.

## SPERANZA
**16/17 Shaftesbury Square** `p1 G7`
**Phone 230213 Fax 236752**
**Price Rating : £**
*Opening Times : Mon-Sat 5pm-11.30pm*
Although a bit easier on the pocket than her sister restaurants, Villa Italia and Antica Roma, the family likeness remains. A large bustling restaurant, Speranza concentrates more on pizzas and pasta. The atmosphere is lively and informal, and children are made welcome.

## THE STRAND
**12 Stranmillis Road** `p19 G5`
**Phone 682266 Fax 663189**
**Price Rating :**
*Opening Times : Mon-Sun 12noon -11pm*
The Strand is a restaurant cum wine bar that places a strong emphasis on quality which helps to explain why it has remained one of Belfast's

more popular restaurants for so long. The menu is wide ranging and ever changing - food is served throughout the day and there is always a good choice of 'specials' offering very good value.

## TERRACE RESTAURANT
**255 Lisburn Road** `p19 F6`
**Phone 381655 Fax 663185**
**Price Rating : ££**
**Opening Times : Mon-Sun 12noon-10.30pm**
Restaurant with winebar downstairs. French cuisine with Californian influence, and a good selection of fish dishes. Live music at weekends.

## VILLA ITALIA
**39/41 University Road** `p12 G6`
**Phone 328356 Fax 234978**
**Price Rating : ££**
*Opening Times : Mon-Sat 5.30pm-11.30pm; Sat 4pm-11.30pm; Sun 4pm-10.30pm*
Villa Italia has taught Belfast quite a bit about the art of queuing over the years, but its popularity remains undimmed despite the arrival of some nearby competition. Its success is based on a formula of reasonably priced Italian food served by attractive staff in one of the liveliest spots in town.

## WELCOME
**22 Stranmillis Road** `p19 G5`
**Phone 381359 or 381465 Fax 664607**
**Price Rating : ££**
*Opening Times : Mon-Sun 12noon-2pm & 5pm-11.30pm*
With a pagoda roof over the entrance and an abundance of dragons, screens and lanterns inside, there is no mistaking this Welcome for anything other than a Chinese one. Established over twenty years ago, the highly rated cooking is a combination of Cantonese, Pekinese and Szechwan and the choice of dishes is exhaustive. The indecisive among you (not to mention the tight) will appreciate the set lunch priced at £4.95.

*Photo courtesy of Belfast City Council*

It seems that wherever you go in the world these days, an Irish pub will not be far away. Ireland rightly has a reputation for great pubs and Belfast certainly upholds this tradition.

There are many historic pubs and some very good modern ones. It can be difficult to distinguish between pubs, clubs and bars as many of Belfast's watering holes fit comfortably into all three categories, but the listings below try to indicate where you are likely to find live music and the sort of crowd that you might encounter. Many of the pubs that do provide music are split into more than one bar thereby allowing the customer to opt for a drink with a bit more chat. The 'Entertainment' section of the Belfast Telegraph is a good source of information or alternatively you can phone the pub or club on the numbers listed below.

Opening hours are NOT listed as they are often subject to extensions which vary according to what's on. Licensing laws have been relaxed in Northern Ireland in recent years, especially in relation to Sunday drinking but pubs are normally open from 11.30am to 11pm from Monday to Saturday. Sunday opening is now optional but is usually restricted to between 12.30pm & 2.30pm and 7pm to 10pm.

Beer consumption is dominated by two major breweries, Guinness and Bass, although a local real ale alternative is provided by Hilden which is brewed in Lisburn. Finally, a cautionary word to visiting spirit drinkers, Northern Ireland measures are 50% bigger than those served in English pubs!

## BOB CRATCHIT'S
**38 Lisburn Road. Phone 332526**   `p19 G6`

The Bob Cratchit theme seems to begin and end with a rather spooky model of the Dickens character which occupies pride of place in this spacious bar which is located in the Russell Court complex, a former hotel which was bombed out of business many years ago. Its proximity to the City Hospital helps to keep Bob Cratchit's busy both at lunchtime and at night, and Russell's Nightclub is a popular choice if you are looking for 'a bit of a bop'.

## BOTANIC INN
**23 Malone Road**   `p19 G6`

To describe a pub as a heap of rubble would normally be deemed libellous, but not so where the 'Bot' is concerned as the bulldozers have recently moved in. But this is not an obituary for what was a very busy watering hole in the university area - the 'Bot' will be back, bigger and better no doubt, to quench the thirst and distract the mind from work and study.

## BRITANNIC
**Amelia Street. Phone 249476**   `p1 G7`

The Britannic is located above the Crown but it uses a separate entrance at the side of the building. Named after the sister ship of the Titanic, the Britannic is a cosy lounge bar fitted out on a nautical theme with original timbers from its namesake.

## CLARENCE   `p2 G8`
**18 Donegall Square East. Phone 238862**

More of a bar-cum-restaurant than a pub, the Clarence is located in attractive basement premises just across the road from the City Hall. The focus is on food, with a menu that changes daily, making it a popular place to meet for a working lunch.

## CRESCENT BAR
**179 Sandy Row. Phone 320911**   `p1 G7`

Not a very fashionable area of town, but the Crescent is a honeypot for students and followers of the club scene. House music, indie & new wave are all on offer.

## CROWN LIQUOR SALOON   `p1 G7`
**46 Great Victoria Street. Phone 249476**

More has been written about this pub than any other in Belfast, and deservedly so. John Betjeman, a former Poet Laureate, described it as the 'jewel in the crown' of British pubs and, perhaps fittingly, it is owned by the National Trust. The pub dates from 1826 but the opulent decor for which it is famed is attributable to the skills of Italian craftsmen who came to Belfast much later in the century to work on the famous

liners being built at Harland & Wolff shipyard. The decor is a magical combination of stained glass, mosaic tiling and intricate wood carving. There are ten wooden snugs, somewhat reminiscent of old railway compartments, with some delightful attention to detail such as gas lighting and an original Victorian bell system for summoning service. The pub is a popular stop on the tourist trail but the clientele remains fairly local. If you are visiting from outside Ireland and find yourself ordering your first ever pint of Guinness, you might as well go the whole hog and try a bowl of their excellent Irish stew.

## CUTTER'S WHARF
**Lockview Road. Phone 662501**   `p19 G5`
A very welcome addition to Stranmillis, an area strangely devoid of pubs, the Cutter's Wharf has been built on the banks of the River Lagan. One of the few Belfast pubs to offer the fair weather drinker the chance to sip something cool out of doors, the interior has been designed along the lines of a boat house - stone flagged floors and lots of bare wooden beams. Crowded most days of the week, especially so at weekends. Jazz brunches are a popular feature on Sundays, and the restaurant upstairs is highly rated. The yuppie era may be dead and gone but the news has failed to reach the regulars at the Cutter's Wharf.

## DEER'S HEAD   `p2 G8`
**1 Lower Garfield Street. Phone 239163**
Nicely refurbished pub, tucked away a little bit, but its proximity to CastleCourt and the city's main shopping area makes it a popular stop for a bite of lunch.

## DEMPSEY'S TERRACE & THE ELBOW
**43 Dublin Road. Phone 234000**   `p2 G7`
A combination of bar, restaurant and nightclub, this large complex was at the forefront of revitalising Belfast nightlife back in the 1980's. Its recent change of name followed a major refurbishment which briefly made Dempsey's Terrace King of the city's theme bars until the rebuilding of Robinson's. For the record, you can choose from five 'flavours' of bar -

Georgian, Edwardian, Spanish, Irish and Elizabethan! Disco for "the over 25's" every night of the week except for Sundays.

## DOME & LIMELIGHT
**17 Ormeau Avenue. Phone 325942**   `p2 G7`
Bar and one of Belfast's busiest nightclubs where the main focus is a diet of house and techno music for the young and energetic! Club nights at the Limelight include 'Shag', a students' disco every Tuesday.

## DUKES HOTEL
**65 University Street. Phone 236666**   `p16 P9`
Relatively new hotel near to Queen's University and Botanic Gardens. Victorian exterior belies an ultramodern interior design. The bar is a good choice if you are looking a quiet drink in a relaxed atmosphere.

## DUKE OF YORK   `p2 G8`
**3 Commercial Court. Phone 241062**
One of the oldest pubs in Belfast, the Duke of York is tucked away up a side street close to Saint Anne's Cathedral. Although recently refurbished, the pub retains its old world charm. Live music several nights a week.

## EGLANTINE INN
**32 Malone Road. Phone 381994**   `p19 G6`
Many pubs in Belfast are spoken of in reference to another. So it is with the 'Egg' and the 'Bot', two of the busiest pubs in town, situated across the road from each other close to the university. The 'Egg', which is divided into bars on three floors, was virtually rebuilt from within a few years back, and now the 'Bot' has gone one step further by choosing demolition and a total rebuild. One thing is for sure, the 'Egg' will be even busier in the meantime. Live music upstairs.

## ELK INN   `p16 Q8`
**793 Upper Newtownards Road. Phone 480004**
Relatively new pub, situated close to Stormont. Popular choice for lunch with the thousands of civil servants and medical staff who work in this

area of the city.

## ELMS
**36 University Road. Phone 322106** `p19 G6`
Busy pub near to Queen's University which caters to the student population with plenty of live music.

## EMPIRE
**42 Botanic Avenue. Phone 328110** `p2 G6`
It was a long time in coming but it was the Empire that introduced live comedy to Belfast's pubs. Local boy made good, Paddy Kielty, comperes a showcase of talent from near and far every Tuesday night. Get there early if you want a table but bear in mind that you might be drinking for a couple of hours before you see the first act. This seems to affect people in one of two ways: either they suddenly find that everything in life is unbelievably funny, or they discover that they were born to heckle. Whether it's comedy or live music another night, a good time is usually guaranteed.

## ERRIGLE INN
**320 Ormeau Road. Phone 641410** `p20 H6`
Popular bar with the locals and, for many years, one of Belfast's leading venues for live music. Rock, pop, and blues all regularly on the menu.

## EUROPA HOTEL `p1 G7`
**Great Victoria Street. Phone 327000**
Lively public bar on the ground floor and quieter lounge bar on the first floor where a pianist plays nightly. The hotel's nightclub, Paradise Lost, is probably the most upmarket nightclub in the city and is open Friday, Saturday, and Sunday.

## THE FLY
**5 Lower Crescent. Phone 246878** `p1 G7`
Smallish bar on two floors of a converted Georgian terrace in the heart of the university area.

## FRONT PAGE
**106 Donegall Street. Phone 324924** `p2 G8`
So called due to its location in the heart of the

city's newspaper district, the Front Page is a busy bar which stages a live band most nights of the week - rock, folk and blues are all on offer. Also known as a venue for live comedy, although getting a laugh from the audience here can be a tougher proposition than at the Empire.

## GARRICK
**29 Chichester Street. Phone 321984** `p2 H8`
Historic city centre pub named after one of its former patrons, David Garrick, the world-famous 18th century actor, who used to pop in for a pint during rehearsals!

## KELLY'S CELLARS
**30 Bank Street. Phone 324835** `p2 G8`
Another city centre tavern steeped in history, the founding Kelly was Hugh, who first got the drink flowing back in 1720. Downstairs still has an authentic 18th century feel about it. The pub has had many famous patrons over the centuries and will continue to have a few more over the years to come. Live music is mostly Irish traditional and blues.

## KING'S HEAD `p16 P9`
**829 Lisburn Road. Phone 660455**
Originally a Victorian mansion, the pub has managed to retain many of the original features including a civilised atmosphere. The layout is split into several rooms, one being a library lined with books should you happen to run out of conversation. The large conservatory, which has been added in recent years, is used for live music.

## KITCHEN BAR
**16 Victoria Square. Phone 324901** `p2 H8`
Small traditional bar dating back to 1859, its city centre location and great pub grub mean that you need to get there early if you want a table for lunch. Live folk music.

## LAVERY'S GIN PALACE
**12 Bradbury Place. Phone 327159** `p1 G7`
At the risk of over-using the word, Lavery's really is a Belfast institution. It's very popular with students, but all forms of life are here to

**A bit of 'diddly-dee'**

behold, often packed in like sardines. Don't be surprised if you step inside only to find that you are making your way along the bar without your feet touching the floor. A good spot to study life but not so good if you are looking for a quiet drink. Loud music upstairs every night of the week except for Sundays.

## MANHATTAN
**23 Bradbury Place. Phone 233131**   `p1 G7`

Brash new kid on the block, this large bar cum club is expensively fitted out with items of Americana. Caters to a younger crowd with resident DJ's every night of the week except for Sundays.

## MORNING STAR   `p2 H8`
**17 Pottinger's Entry. Phone 323976**

Hidden down a narrow alleyway right in the heart of the city's main shopping district, this listed building dates back to the early 18th century. Although very much a traditional pub, it is perhaps best known for the adventurous cooking offered on Gourmet Nights which are held on the last Saturday of each month.

## MORRISON'S
**21 Bedford Street. Phone 325061**   `p2 G7`

Morrison's may look old - it is themed on a turn

of the century spirit grocers - but it has been around for only a couple of years. Having replaced the Linen Hall (now closed) as a second home for some of the hacks from the BBC across the road, you may get to spot a few local 'celebs'. Very popular bar which can get uncomfortably packed at weekends. Live music upstairs.

## PARLIAMENT BAR
**Dunbar Link**   `p2 H8`

Another bar with a heavy emphasis on music. Very popular with the gay community.

## PAT'S BAR   `p9 H9`
**19 Prince's Dock Street. Phone 744524**

One of a few traditional dockside bars known for their friendly atmosphere and live traditional music.

## REGENCY HOTEL
**13 Lower Crescent. Phone 323349**   `p1 G7`

Smart lounge bar with piano player. Nightclub upstairs.

## RENSHAWS HOTEL
**75 University Street. Phone 333366**   `p12 G6`

Another new hotel in the heart of the university area, Renshaws was formerly a Tutorial College. Very pleasant bar which is a popular choice for a quiet drink or a bite to eat.

## ROBINSON'S   `p16 P9`
**38 Great Victoria Street. Phone 247447**

The 'Troubles' are hopefully over but their legacy lives on. Robinson's, situated almost next door to the Crown, had long been a Belfast landmark when it was burnt to the ground a few years ago. Two million pounds later, it looks much as it did from the outside, but the inside has been reincarnated under various themes. The front bar has been painstakingly restored in keeping with the Victorian original but the back bar, now known as Fibber Magees, has been laid out as a 19th century general merchant's store. Even more themes feature throughout the other two floors making it possible to do a pub crawl without actually leaving Robinsons! On top of

all that, there's a wide variety of live music on offer.

## ROTTERDAM BAR
**54 Pilot Street. Phone 746021** `p9 H9`

The Rotterdam is not going to catch much in the way of passing trade, being tucked away in the docks area of Belfast, but it is well worth going that little bit out of your way for. Currently undergoing major refurbishment, which will hopefully do nothing to detract from its very traditional atmosphere, it is a thriving venue for live music, mostly folk and blues.

## RUMPOLE'S `p2 H8`
**81 Chichester Street. Phone 232840**

Rumpole's is a pub with a bit of a split personality. As its name might suggest, it is very close to the Law Courts and a popular watering hole with the legal fraternity, both at lunchtime and after work. By early evening the legal eagles are usually making other plans, however, and the pub reverts to the status of a 'local'. Disco for the "over 30's!" on Friday and Saturday nights.

## SHAFTESBURY INN
**739 Antrim Road. Phone 370015** `p5 G13`

Well established and popular north Belfast bar and restaurant.

## THOMPSON'S GARAGE
**Patterson's Place** `p1 G8`

Situated close to the City Hall, the aptly named Garage is a bar with club nights on Thursdays, Fridays & Saturdays.

## VICO'S `p2 G7`
**10 Brunswick Street. Phone 321447**

Pizzeria which has established itself firmly as part of the club scene. Club nights are Thursdays, Fridays & Saturdays - music includes rock, house, garage, acid jazz, funk & soul.

## THE WAREHOUSE
**Pilot Street** `p9 H9`

Situated in the docks area of town, the

The Crown Bar

*Photo courtesy of Northern Ireland Tourist Board*

Warehouse stages live bands virtually every night of the year.

## WASHINGTON
**15 Howard Street. Phone 241891** `p1 G7`

The 'Wash' is a large city centre bar on two floors which caters mainly to a lively young crowd. Music upstairs.

## WELLINGTON PARK HOTEL
**21 Malone Road. Phone 381111** `p19 G6`

The Welly Park, as it is affectionately known, is a bit of a hybrid. Ostensibly, it is a quiet 50 bedroomed hotel situated close to the university. Come Friday and Saturday nights, however, it is commandeered by a legion of Belfast's young (and not so young) professional types, who tend to end up at the Welly for a late drink to round off a good night's crack.

## WHITE'S TAVERN
**Winecellar Entry. Phone 243080** `p2 G8`

Like the Morning Star, White's Tavern is an historic bar tucked away up a narrow alleyway in the heart of the city's main shopping district. This is the oldest pub in town - a popular spot for lunch since the 17th century! Live traditional music on Thursdays.

## BELFAST CITY COUNCIL LEISURE CENTRES

**B**elfast City Council Leisure Services have responsibility for the operation of 15 leisure centres as well as a large number of playing fields, a nine hole golf course (see "Golf" on page 80), the Ulster Hall and the Arts Theatre (see "Theatre, Music, Cinema" on pages 63- 66). The number of leisure centres and the standard of provision is sure to remain the envy of most other UK cities. The centres are all marked on the street maps and their page and map references are given below.

### ANDERSONSTOWN LEISURE CENTRE
**Andersonstown Rd. Phone 625211** `p18 D5`
Facilities include : Main Hall (32 x 26m), 3 Swimming Pools, Minor Hall (20 x 11m), 2 Squash Courts, Weights Room, Saunas, Sunbeds, Lounge, Cafeteria & Social Area, Handball Alley, Committee Room, Outdoor Floodlit Pitch, Conference Facilities.

### AVONIEL LEISURE CENTRE
**Avoniel Road. Telephone  451564** `p14 K7`
Facilities include : Main Hall (32 x 26m), 25m Swimming Pool, Sauna and Sunbed Lounge, 2 Squash Courts, Weights Room, Fitness Suite, Steam Room, Spa, Cafeteria & Social Area, Committee Room, Outdoor Floodlit Pitch, Conference Facilities, Car Park.

### BALLYMACARRETT RECREATION CENTRE
**Connswater St. Telephone 458828** `p14 K8`
Facilities include : Main Hall (24 x 16.5m) Social Area, Fitness Room, Committee Room.

### BALLYSILLAN LEISURE CENTRE
**Ballysillan Rd. Telephone 391040** `p7 E10`
Facilities include : Main Hall (32 x 26m), 25m Swimming Pool, Cafeteria & Social Area, Squash Court, Fitness Suite, Outdoor Floodlit Synthetic Pitch, Conference Facilities.

### BEECHMOUNT LEISURE CENTRE
**Falls Road. Telephone 328631** `p11 E7`
Facilities include : Main Hall (37 x 17m), Minor Hall (18 x 12.6m), 2 Squash Courts, 2 Handball Alleys, Cafeteria & Social Area, 6 Tennis Courts, 5-a-Side Pitch, 3 Hard Porous Pitches, Athletics Tracks, Mini Park, Conference Facilities.

### BELFAST INDOOR TENNIS ARENA
**Ormeau Embankment. Tel 458024** `p2 H7`
Facilities include : 4 Full Size Indoor Tennis Courts, Climbing Wall, Laser-Gun Labyrinth, All-Weather Pitch.

### FALLS SWIM CENTRE
**Falls Road. Telephone 324906** `p11 E7`
Facilities include : Major Pool (20.1 x 7.3m), Minor Pool (20.8 x 11.4m), Minor Hall, Fitness Suite.

### GROVE LEISURE CENTRE
**York Road. Telephone 351599** `p9 H10`
Facilities include : Gala Pool (25 x 12.8m with capacity for 800 spectators), Diving Facilities, Minor Pool (22.5 x 10.8m), Funtasia Play Area, 2 Saunas, Solarium, Committee Room, Cafeteria & Social Area, Steam Room, Fitness Suite, Conference Facilities and Residential Accommodation.

### LOUGHSIDE RECREATION CENTRE
**Shore Road. Telephone 781524** `p6 H12`
Facilities include : Main Hall (24 x 17m), Social Area, Weights Room, Committee Room, Sauna, Sunbed, Floodlit All-Weather Pitch, 2 Grass Football Pitches and Changing Accommodation (Parks Dept.).

### MAYSFIELD LEISURE CENTRE
**East Bridge St. Telephone 241633** `p2 H7`
Facilities include : Main hall (37 x 32m), 25m Swimming Pool, Hi-tech Fitness Room, 2 Squash Courts, Saunas and Solarium Lounge, Long Hall, Minor Hall (14.7m x 12.1m), Cafeteria & Social Area, Committee Room, Outdoor 5-a-Side Pitch, Conference Facilities, Car Park.

### OLYMPIA LEISURE CENTRE
**Boucher Road. Telephone 233369** `p18 E6`
Facilities include : Main Hall (23.5 x 16.5m), 25m Swimming Pool, Social Area, Snack Bar, Conditioning Room, Playroom/Craft Room, Sauna, Sunbeds, Outdoor Floodlit Synthetic Pitch, Conference Facilities, Play Centre (Parks Dept.), Community Centre (Community Services Dept.).

## SHAFTESBURY RECREATION CENTRE
**Balfour Avenue. Telephone 329163** `p2 H7`
Facilities include : Main Hall (24 x 16.6m), Committee Room, Cafeteria & Social Area, Private Snooker Room, 7-a-Side Floodlit Hard Porous Pitch.

## SHANKILL LEISURE CENTRE
**Shankill Road. Telephone 241434** `p2 H7`
Facilities include : Main Hall (36 x 32m), Free Form Swimming Pool with Wavemaker, Sauna and Sunbed Lounge, 4 Squash Courts, Fitness Room, Snooker Room, Weights Hall, Cafeteria & Social Area, 2 Outdoor Games Areas, Conference Facilities.

## WHITEROCK LEISURE CENTRE
**Whiterock Road. Telephone 233329** `p18 E6`
Facilities include : Main Hall (24 x 17m), 25m Swimming Pool, Social Area, Fitness Room, Sunbed, Infants' Play Area, Outdoor Floodlit Football Pitch, Conference Facilities, Community Centre (Community Services Dept.), Play Centre (Parks Dept.).

## OTHER SPORTS!

As you can see from the exhaustive list above, the city's leisure centres cover a multitude of different sports and activities but a brief outline is given below of a few more.

### ATHLETICS

International meetings are held at the Mary Peters Track which is in the Malone Playing Fields, just off the Upper Malone Road. The track is in the care of the City Council and is available for public use. Phone 602707.

### BOXING

Barry McGuigan may have hung up his gloves but Barney Eastwood still manages several champion boxers and Belfast plays host to regular international fight nights. The main venue is the King's Hall.

### FOOTBALL

Several Belfast teams play in the Irish League including Linfield who play at Windsor Park, Glentoran who play at the Oval in Parkgate Drive, Cliftonville who play at Solitude in Cliftonville Street, and Crusaders who play at Seaview in Saint Vincent Street. International matches are played at Windsor Park.

### GAELIC GAMES

The main venue for watching Gaelic football and hurling is Roger Casement Park on the Andersonstown Road.

### GOLF

There are many fine golf courses in Belfast. The City Council operate a municipal course out at Mallusk (phone 843799) but most courses are in private hands, although visitors are welcome subject to certain restrictions. It is always advisable, therefore, to phone before turning up to play. Malone (Malone Road - phone 612758) and Belvoir Park (Church Road - phone 646714) are arguably the two finest courses in Belfast but there are several others to choose from including Knock (Upper Newtownards Road - phone 482249), Shandon Park (Shandon Park - phone 793730) and Fortwilliam (Downview avenue - phone 776798). If you just want to hit a few balls, a new driving range has recently opened at the bottom of New Forge Lane.

### HORSE RACING AND RIDING

Northern Ireland has two racecourses. Downpatrick hosts the Ulster Harp National in March, and Down Royal, near Lisburn, hosts the Ulster Harp Derby in July. Both have meetings throughout the year.

If you prefer riding them to betting on them, try the Lagan Valley Equestrian Centre on the Upper Malone Road. Phone 614265.

### ICE SKATING

Dundonald Ice Bowl on the Old Dundonald Road has a rink which is capable of hosting international competitions.

### TEN PIN BOWLING

There are ten pin bowling alleys at Dundonald Ice Bowl, Belfast Superbowl in Clarence Street, and at the Valley Leisure Centre on Church Road.

# B E L F A S T

## THE LEISURE CITY

Belfast has given everyone a chance to become involved in sport
and physical recreation! From its embryo, Belfast City Council Leisure
Services has striven to provide a quality service for all sections of the
community. To date, it boasts a total of 15 Leisure & Recreation
Centres and the Ulster Hall/Group Theatre which caters
for performers.

~

Belfast is 'Leading Leisure through the Nineties' and beyond.
Strategic Planning recently found the city to have some of the most well
equipped and well used centres in Northern Ireland, and perhaps the
United Kingdom. The latest high technology fitness equipment and single
station multi-gymn machines can be found in centres such as Maysfield,
Avoniel, Olympia, Andersonstown, Ormeau, Ballysillan, Ballymacarrett,
Falls and Grove Leisure Complexes. All centres are going through the
process of being refurbished and tastefully decorated. Indeed, some of our
leisure centres can bear a strong resemblance to a 'PRIVATE' Health Club
or 'UPMARKET' facility which is readily available to the customer at a very
reasonable price, offering 'LEISURE' as a great value for money service.

A warm welcome is always guaranteed in any of the Belfast Leisure
Centres, and most centres have facilities to have a cup of coffee and
a chat or even a main meal or function. Most centres can provide
concert/conference facilities and any of the centre managers will be
delighted to discuss your requirements when booking.

New developments or projects to be noted are :-

A 'WATER WONDERLAND'
at Shankill Leisure
Centre provides the latest
features in water based
activities and is sure
to offer lots of FUN FILLED
ENJOYMENT FOR ALL THE
FAMILY.

The BELFAST INDOOR TENNIS
ARENA has just opened for
'service' at Ormeau Embankment.
Four full-size indoor courts, a
climbing wall with four graded
climbs, fitness suite and laser-gun
labyrinth are among the features of
the new complex.

The Grove Leisure Centre
has recently become a
SWIMMING CENTRE OF
EXCELLENCE and now
hosts many MAJOR
INTERNATIONAL EVENTS.

If you really take your LEISURE or PLEASURE seriously and want
further information on Belfast City Council Leisure Services, contact
THE CECIL WARD  BUILDING, 4 - 10 LINENHALL STREET,
BELFAST, BT2 8BP - Tel : **320202**

~

Belfast has shopping facilities which would be the envy of many other UK provincial cities. The main shopping area around Donegall Place and Royal Avenue remains pedestrianised despite the removal of security barriers, and the absence of traffic makes for a hassle-free shopping environment.

The city centre has benefited from hundreds of millions of pounds of retail investment in recent years, the largest project being the opening of the CastleCourt shopping complex back in 1990. Other developments such as Ross's Court and Spires have followed, and economic confidence has remained high despite the recent recession which has affected high streets in other parts of the UK.

## OPENING HOURS

This confidence is reflected in a recent extension to the opening hours of city centre shops. Normal opening times are from around 9a.m. to approximately 6p.m., Monday to Saturday. City centre shops have traditionally stayed open late on Thursdays until 9p.m. but late opening has now been extended to Fridays when closing time is 8p.m. Sunday opening has been introduced to a limited extent but is widespread during the run-up to Christmas.

## PARKING

The problems generally associated with finding a city centre parking space seem to have largely disappeared in Belfast. In addition to the 1600 spaces provided by CastleCourt, there are several other car parks, all of which are marked in blue on the face of the maps on pages 1 & 2. A 'Pay & Display' system operates to the south of the City Hall where there are several hundred on-street parking places available with prices starting at 30p for half an hour.

The central location of the two main bus stations and the imminent opening of a new train station on Great Victoria Street mean that many shoppers heading for Belfast choose to leave their car at home.

## MONEY AND BANKS

The currency in Northern Ireland is the British pound (sterling) but, with the recent influx of visitors from the Republic of Ireland, many shops now accept payment in Irish pounds (punts) at the prevailing exchange rate. All local banks handle foreign exchange transactions.

The four main high street banks in Northern Ireland are the Ulster Bank, the Northern Bank, the Bank of Ireland, and First Trust. Opening hours vary but are generally 9.30am-3.30pm, Monday to Friday. The most convenient way to get hold of some spending money is to make use of the cash dispensers which are available at most city branches. Customers who bank locally can make withdrawals from any of the banks' dispensers but transactions by customers of British banks may be restricted, although most dispensers will accept Visa or Mastercard or both.

## SHOPS

If you are used to shopping on the British high street you will be familiar with most of the large retail outlets in Belfast. The city centre branches of **Marks & Spencer** and **Debenhams** are among the most successful of any in their respective chains. Other department stores within the pedestrianised area around Donegall Place and Royal Avenue are **C & A**, **British Home Stores** and **Littlewoods**. Anderson & McCauley, the last of the locally based department stores, is no longer with us but **Habitat** now occupy a large part of the building with a very stylish store selling their lines of household goods and home furnishings.

When it comes to ladies' fashion, once again the British multiples have a strong presence but they are backed up by many locally based outlets. **Next** have branches in Donegall Place and at CastleCourt, **Jaegar** have a store in Royal Avenue, **Wallis** have an outlet in Castle Place and, **Benetton** are at CastleCourt along with **Dorothy Perkins**, **Laura Ashley** and **Miss Selfridge**. There are dozens more ladies' fashion outlets within the central shopping area.

# *The Bank at your fingertips.*

Ulster Bank Servicetill,
24 hours a day,
7 days a week.

♻ **Ulster Bank**

**Propaganda** in Arthur Street sells designer labels for younger women, while a significant number of designer outlets which cater for all ages can be found in the Bloomfield Avenue area, about one mile east of the city centre. Fans of the Irish designer, **Paul Costello**, will be interested to know that he has recently opened an outlet in Bradbury Place.

The situation is similar for menswear. British multiples include **Burton** in Donegall Place and at CastleCourt, **Next** in Donegall Place and **Principles for Men** at CastleCourt. There are quite a few locally based outlets which deal in designer labels. These include **Carter** in Upper Queen's Street and **Bogart** in Ann Street.

If it's sports goods that you are looking for, the **Athletics Stores** in Queen Street is the largest outlet in the city centre. Outdoor specialists include **Jackson Sports** in High Street and **Surf Mountain** in Brunswick Street.

For books and records we return to the household names. **Waterstones** have a great bookshop on Royal Avenue and **Dillons** have an equally good outlet in Fountain Street. **Easons,** who provide Ireland's answer to WH Smith, have stores in Ann Street and at CastleCourt. The giants of music retailing are here too. **Virgin** have one of their Megastores at CastleCourt, which is also a good place for buying concert tickets, and **Our Price** have a large outlet in Donegall Place.

Electrical retailing is dominated by **Dixons** in Donegall Arcade and by their branches of **Currys Superstores** which tend to be in out of town locations.

When it comes to giftware and souvenir hunting there are some interesting outlets and much of the product range is locally produced. **Equinox** on Howard Street concentrates mainly on designer tableware and is a good place to go in search of wedding presents, or a good cup of coffee for that matter. **Hoggs** on Royal Avenue specialise in china and glass and is a good place for picking up a piece of Tyrone crystal or Belleek pottery. For something a little bit different, try the **Craftworks Gallery** in Linenhall Street.

## CASTLECOURT

CastleCourt is an 8.5 acre retailing development located right in the heart of Belfast's city centre.

The scheme consists of 77 shops and services, a 1600 space 6 level multi-storey car park and, on the roof, an office building which is the headquarters of the Department of Social Services.

CastleCourt is one of the most successful shopping centres in the UK with over 250,000 people visiting its shops every week. It has won many prestigious awards since it opened in April 1990, including the Civic Trust Award, the British Council of Shopping Centres' Excellence in Marketing Award, and the Northern Ireland Electricity BETA Award.

CastleCourt's car park is the largest in Northern Ireland and is easily accessible from the Westlink route which connects the M1 and M2 motorways, as well as all other city centre incoming routes.

CastleCourt has a superb choice of shops, many of which are not found elsewhere in the province. A full list appears opposite.

No visit to Northern Ireland is complete without a visit to the province's premier shopping centre - CastleCourt - right in the heart of Belfast.

# If You Haven't Been To CastleCourt, You Haven't Been To Belfast

## No visit to Belfast is complete without a visit to CastleCourt.

With over 70 shops and services and a 1600 space car park - all under one roof, it's little wonder that CastleCourt is one of the UK's largest and most modern shopping centres catering for all your shopping needs.

### For the best in Belfast - come to CASTLECOURT, right in the heart of the city.

Adams / Antone Michael / Bay Trading Company / Bargain Books / Benetton / Betty Barclay / Bijou / Birthdays / Body Active / Boots / Burtons / Hall of Cards / Debenhams / Dolcis / Donuttree / Dorothy Perkins / Early Learning Centre / Easons / Esprit / Evans / Exhibit / Ferguson Flowers / Fruit of the Loom / Fosters / Games Workshop / Gap / Globe / Halifax / Hobsons Sport/Travel / Charles Hurst / Index / Jeffrey Rogers / Just Fresh / Knickerbox / Laura Ashley / Lifestyle / Lunn Poly / Menarys / Michael deLeon (Bellart) / Miss Selfridge / Morgan / Next / Northern Bank / Options / Orchard / Paco Sweaters / Parks / Perfume Shop / Petal / Phillipa Charles / Photoland / Pretty Woman / Shoe Express / Principles for Men / H. Samuels / Saxone / Sheldon / Sisley / Spoils / Stewarts World of Wine / Stylo Barratt / Sunglass Hut / T K Maxx / Tom Jones / Virgin / Vision Express / Whitsitt (Denby) / Tennessee Secrets / Rediscovered Originals / The Gadget Shop

## CASTLE COURT
### BELFAST

## The Centre at the Heart of Belfast

Belfast is not over endowed with hotels but this situation is being remedied with several recent openings and quite a few new projects due to come on stream over the next couple of years.

All of the main hotels in and around the city are listed below. All are licensed and have their own restaurant facilities, and most bedrooms are ensuite with television and telephone.

The Northern Ireland Tourist Board grades each hotel on the basis of the facilities, service and cuisine which it provides. The number of stars after the hotel name below indicates its grading, four stars being the highest rating.

Price depends mainly on the timing of your stay. The average cost during the week is somewhere in the region of £70 to £80 per person per night for bed and breakfast, but weekend rates are substantially cheaper.

Guest houses are a more economic option. Once again, the Northern Ireland Tourist Board allocates a grading and this is included after the name of each establishment below.

## HOTELS

**ALDEGROVE AIRPORT HOTEL** ***
**Belfast International Airport**
Phone (01849) 422033 Fax (01849) 423500
108 bedrooms. Situated within one hundred yards of the terminal building. Fitness suite, sauna and free parking for guests.

**BALMORAL HOTEL** **
**Black's Road**    p23 C4
Phone 301234 Fax 601455
44 bedrooms. Located in the south of the city. Recently refurbished and extended.

**BEECHLAWN HOUSE HOTEL** ***
**4 Dunmurry Lane**    p24 D2
Phone 612974 Fax 623601
34 bedrooms. Close to Dunmurry Golf Course and Lagan Valley Equestrian Centre.

**CHIMNEY CORNER HOTEL** ***
**630 Antrim Road, Newtownabbey**
Phone 844925 Fax 844352
63 bedrooms. Convenient to Belfast International Airport.

**CRAWFORDSBURN INN** ***
**15 Main Street, Crawfordsburn**
Phone (01247) 853255 Fax (01247) 852775
33 bedrooms. The oldest inn in Ireland, located in a picturesque village 10 miles outside Belfast.

**CULLODEN HOTEL** ****
**142 Bangor Road, Cutra**
Phone 425223 Fax 426777
92 bedrooms. Former bishop's palace, situated about 15 minutes drive from Belfast city centre. Leisure facilities include a swimming pool, gymnasium, squash and tennis courts.

**DUKES HOTEL** ***
**65/67 University Street**    p19 G6
Phone 236666 Fax 237177
21 bedrooms. Victorian exterior belies an ultra-modern interior. Gymnasium and sauna.

**DUNADRY INN** ****
**2 Islandreagh Drive, Dunadry**
Phone (01849) 432474 Fax (01849) 433389
67 bedrooms. Converted linen mill in tranquil setting. Facilities include a swimming pool, gymnasium, on site fishing, croquet and bowls.

**EUROPA HOTEL** ****
**Great Victoria Street**    p1 G7
Phone 327000 Fax 327800
184 bedrooms. Belfast's leading hotel, situated close to the city centre, and convenient for theatres, pubs and restaurants.

**FORTE CREST HOTEL** ***
**300 Kingsway**    p23 B2
Phone 612101 Fax 626546
82 bedrooms. Formerly the Conway, facilities include a mini-gymnasium and a squash court.

**GLENAVNA HOUSE HOTEL** ***
**588 Shore Road, Newtownabbey**
Phone 864461 Fax 862531

32 bedrooms. Former 19th century gentleman's residence standing in 6 acres of gardens.

## LA MON HOUSE HOTEL *
**41 Gransha Road, Castlereagh**
**Phone 448631 Fax 448026**
38 bedrooms. Situated in the Castlereagh Hills about 5 miles out of Belfast. Facilities include a swimming pool and gymnasium.

## LANDSDOWNE COURT HOTEL ***
**657 Antrim Road** `p5 G12`
**Phone 773317 Fax 370125**
25 bedrooms. Recently refurbished hotel in the north of the city.

## MALONE LODGE HOTEL **
**60 Eglantine Avenue** `p19 G6`
**Phone 382409 Fax 382706**
33 bedrooms. New hotel in the university area.

## PARK AVENUE HOTEL **
**158 Holywood Road** `p14 L8`
**Phone 656520 Fax 471417**
65 bedrooms, not all ensuite. Situated a couple of miles east of the city centre.

## PLAZA HOTEL **
**15 Brunswick Street** `p12 G7`
**Phone 333555 Fax 232999**
72 bedrooms. Modern city centre hotel convenient for shopping and nightlife.

## REGENCY HOTEL **
**8 Lower Crescent** `p12 G7`
**Phone 323349 Fax 320646**
14 bedrooms. Conveniently located for shopping, nightlife and the university.

## RENSHAWS HOTEL *
**75 University Street** `p12 G6`
**Phone 333366 Fax 333399**
20 bedrooms. Former Tutorial College in the heart of the university area.

## STORMONT HOTEL ***
**587 Upper Newtownards Road** `p15 N7`

**Phone 658621 Fax 480240**
106 bedrooms. Modern hotel located in the east of the city close to the old parliament building.

## TEMPLETON HOTEL **
**882 Antrim Road, Templepatrick**
**Phone (01849) 432984 Fax (01849) 433406**
20 bedrooms. New hotel conveniently located for Belfast International Airport.

## WELLINGTON PARK HOTEL ***
**21 Malone Road** `p19 G6`
**Phone 381111 Fax 665410**
50 bedrooms. Located in the university area, the hotel foyer and bars are a busy meeting place on Friday and Saturday nights.

## GUEST HOUSES

## CAMERA GUEST HOUSE (A)
**44 Wellington Park** `p19 G6`
**Phone 669565**
11 bedrooms, 7 ensuite. Large Edwardian terrace in university area.

## HELGA LODGE
**7 Cromwell Road** `p12 G7`
**Phone 324820 Fax 320653**
12 bedrooms, all ensuite. Large terraced property close to Botanic rail station and university.

## STRANMILLIS LODGE (A)
**14 Chlorine Gardens** `p19 G6`
**Phone 682009 Fax 682009**
6 bedrooms, all ensuite. Large detached house in residential south Belfast, close to university.

## WINDERMERE HOUSE (A)
**60 Wellington Park** `p19 G6`
**Phone 662693**
8 bedrooms, 2 ensuite. Close to university.

## HOSTELS

## BELFAST YOUTH HOSTEL
**22 Donegall Road** `p12 F7`
**Phone 324733 Fax 439699**
Modern 38 room youth hostel situated close to the hub of the city's night life.

'The more you look, the more you see' - that is the National Trust's motto in Northern Ireland. From the breathtaking beauty of **Slieve Donard** in the Mourne Mountains, to the industrial archaeology of **Patterson's Spade Mill**, and the treasure trove of historic houses, the National Trust has a rich diversity of places to visit in Northern Ireland.

County Down is a hive of activity : **Castle Ward**, a unique 18th century mansion, is set in a 700 acre estate on the shores of Strangford Lough. The house has two different facades, one Gothic, the other Classical, and in the estate you will find a working cornmill, laundry, dairy and a wildlife centre.

**Mount Stewart**, also on the shores of Strangford Lough, offers an historic house set in one of the most spectacular gardens in the British Isles. Another must for garden lovers is **Rowallane** near Saintfield. This magnificent garden stretches for 52 acres providing refuge for exotic plants. Famed for their spring colour, both gardens have delights and attractions in every season.

**Victorian dressing room at Castle Ward**

County Tyrone is the county of National Trust curiosities housing two excellent examples of industrial heritage. The 18th century **Gray's Printing Press** in Strabane, has a display of early printing presses and an audio visual exhibition, explaining Gray's American connections - it is said that John Dunlop, printer of the American Declaration of Independence learned his trade here. At **Wellbrook Beetling Mill** near Cookstown, the final process in the manufacture of linen is demonstrated with the aid of a working water wheel.

Standing in the heart of County Armagh, the Orchard County of Ulster, **Ardress** is a gentleman farmer's house with fine examples of Irish furnishings. A special treat for children is the cobbled farmyard complete with rare poultry and a saddleback pig. **The Argory**, overlooking the River Blackwater, is a house in a time capsule with everything as it was at the start of this century.

County Fermanagh is calm serenity. One of the finest jewels in the Region's crown must surely be **Castle Coole** in Enniskillen, which ranks as one of the finest neo-classical houses in Ireland. **Florence Court** boasts a dramatic location, overlooking the surrounding countryside. Its grounds are a haven for plant

**Newcastle and the Mourne Mountains**

and wildlife alike, and tucked away like a prize possession is a beautiful walled garden.

Unsurpassed for its scenic beauty is one of the Trust's best kept secrets, **Crom Estate** on the shores of Upper Lough Erne. There are excellent holiday cottages at both Crom and Florence Court, some of which are adapted for less able visitors.

On one hand the Trust can offer magnificent grandeur but on the other, it can offer modesty. **Hezlett House** at Castlerock, County Londonderry, is a thatched cottage, with an unusual cruck truss roof construction. Across the county lies **Springhill**, a 17th century Plantation house. Ten generations of the one family lived here so it is no surprise that many say a ghost roams the corridors at nightfall.

Much of the coast and countryside is also protected by the National Trust in Northern Ireland, not least along the spectacular North Antrim coast. Often referred to as the 'Eighth Wonder of the World' is the **Giant's Causeway**

**Castle Coole**

- volcanic formations just oozing with myth and magic. If that's not dramatic enough, just try the **Carrick-a-Rede** rope bridge for size! The trick is not to look down at the crashing waves and craggy cliffs below!

For further details, contact the Public Affairs Department at the National Trust, Rowallane, Saintfield, County Down. Telephone 01238 510721.

**Carrick-a-Rede**

Although Belfast is located on the east coast of Northern Ireland, the province's excellent road network means that nowhere is more than a couple of hours away by car. There is much to see and, even if you are without your own transport, Ulsterbus and Northern Ireland Railways will get you there (see pages 51 to 55).

There are six counties in all, Antrim and Down being the closest at hand. Northern Ireland has not had as many visitors as it has deserved over the past twenty five years but the tourism infrastructure is firmly in place and visitors making their first trip here are usually impressed by the high standard of facilities and the variety of things to do and see.

It is impossible to do justice to the multitude of attractions in the spaceof two pages but a brief flavour of all six counties is given below which will hopefully encourage you to visit the nearest Northern Ireland Tourist Board Information Centre before setting out to explore.

## COUNTY ANTRIM

Nobody visiting Northern Ireland for the first time should leave without seeing the spectacular north Antrim coastline which includes Northern Ireland's most famous tourist attraction, the **Giant's Causeway.** Legend has it that the Causeway was built by Finn McCool, an Irish giant who used it to cross to Scotland. Geologists, on the other hand, have a theory that the thousands of hexagonal basalt columns were formed 55 million years ago as a result of volcanic activity combined with the cooling effect of the sea. The audio visual show at the award winning **Causeway Visitors' Centre** will help you to draw your own conclusions.

There are many other attractions nearby and, with good planning, you should be able to see several of them in one trip. The first stop after the Causeway for many people is the **Carrick-a-Rede** rope bridge (picture on page 90) which provides spectacular views of the coastline.

Other points of interest along the coast include the ruins of **Dunluce Castle.** The castle dates from around 1300 but paid dearly for its precarious location in 1639 when the kitchen fell into the sea while dinner was being prepared!

This area is a mecca for golfers. As well as **Royal Portrush,** which has staged the British Open and is rated as one of the finest courses in the world, **Castlerock** and **Portstewart** are other top class seaside courses.

**Bushmills** boasts the oldest Whiskey distillery in the world and **Glenariff Forest Park** offers some beautiful views of the **Glens of Antrim.** If it's wildlife that you are looking for, then the **Causeway Safari Park** is also nearby.

Another popular destination is **Portrush**, one of the province's main seaside resorts which has an amusement park and indoor **Waterworld** complex to keep children busy, whatever the weather.

## COUNTY DOWN

County Down has much to offer and everything is within an hour's drive of Belfast. The two most popular areas to visit are the Ards Peninsula and the Mourne Mountains.

The Ards Peninsula is an area of great natural beauty with the Irish sea on one side and Strangford Lough on the other. **Bangor** is a major seaside resort with plenty to amuse the family, especially since the opening of **Pickie Fun Park. Scrabo Tower,** a 19th century memorial to the third Marquess of Londonderry, is a couple of miles from Bangor and offers some of the finest views anywhere in Ireland. **Strangford Lough** is a centre for sailing and one of the most important areas for birdlife in the British Isles. The peninsula is dotted with quiet sandy beaches and is the location for several historic houses - the National Trust properties at **Mount Stewart** and **Castle Ward** are well worth a visit. **Portaferry** is a picturesque village at the southern tip of the Ards Peninsula and is home to **Exploris,** a state of the art public aquarium with some very impressive live displays, a Touch Tank, and excellent educational facilities.

**Newcastle** is where the '**Mountains of**

**Mourne** sweep down to the sea' and is another of the province's main seaside resorts. Once again, there is plenty to keep the family amused including a beautiful beach, an indoor water complex and amusement arcades. For the golfer, there is **Royal County Down**, consistently rated among the top ten courses in the world. Perhaps the best way of seeing the mountains is to visit one of the nearby forest parks at either **Castlewellan** or **Tollymore**, or visit the **Silent Valley Reservoir** which was created in 1933 by damming and flooding a large area of the Mournes.

**Downpatrick,** about 15 miles from Newcastle, provides the final resting place of **Saint Patrick** in the grounds of **Down Cathedral**. Seaforde is also nearby and attracts many visitors to its **Tropical Butterfly House** where you can see hundreds of free-flying exotic butterflies as well as live displays of insects and reptiles from around the globe.

## COUNTY ARMAGH

**Armagh** city is less than an hour's drive from Belfast and is one of the best preserved Georgian cities in the British Isles. It is also the ecclesiastical capital of Ireland, seat of both the Protestant and Catholic Archbishops and famous for its twin cathedrals. The history of the city and the county are chronicled in two museums and the **Palace Stables Heritage Centre**. The most popular visitor attraction, however, is the **Armagh Planetarium** which houses a giant telescope and other astronomical instruments, and uses computers to produce impressive celestial effects for its popular **Star Shows** .

Just to the west of Armagh city lies **Navan**, the ancient capital of Ulster. Remains of its famous hill fort are open to the public and the nearby **Navan Centre** provides a high-tech interpretation of the history and archaeology of the area.

## COUNTY LONDONDERRY

Like Armagh, **Londonderry** (also known as Derry) is a very historic city with two cathedrals. It is most famous for its ancient walls which still encircle it today having withstood several sieges over the centuries, the most celebrated lasting for 105 days in 1688/89. The one mile walk around the top of the walls affords many fine views over the city and the Foyle estuary. The **Tower Museum** outlines the history of the area from prehistoric times to present day and, beyond the city, there is some spectacular coastline and many fine beaches.

## COUNTY FERMANAGH

Fermanagh is the lake district of Northern Ireland, a paradise for fishing, boating and other water based activities. **Lough Erne** is dotted with dozens of islands and surrounded by spectacular scenery which makes it ideal for cruising. **Enniskillen**, the county town, is located right on the lough and is the natural starting point for lakeland excursions. Other attractions in the area include **Belleek Pottery** which has been producing world famous china since 1857, and the **Marble Arch Caves,** one of Europe's finest showcaves which allows visitors to explore a fascinating underworld of rivers, waterfalls, winding passages and lofty chambers.

## COUNTY TYRONE

Tyrone is a sparsely populated area but, like the rest of Northern Ireland, it has natural beauty in abundance. The countryside of the **Sperrin Mountains** is a major attraction for followers of outdoor pursuits but the county has much else to offer the visitor.

The **Ulster-American Folk Park** near Omagh details the story of 200 years of emigration from Ireland to North America, recreating the conditions of the time. The **Ulster History Park**, also near Omagh, goes back even further in time, detailing the history of Ulster from 8,000 BC to the end of the 17th century. Returning to the present day, the **Tyrone Crystal Factory** in Dungannon is another popular attraction offering the visitor a chance to see how the world famous crystal is hand-blown.

Listed below are some of the events which take place annually in Belfast and farther afield. The Northern Ireland Tourist Board will be happy to supply further details together with up to the minute information on everything else that's going on. You can call into their new Tourist Information Centre at 59 North Street or telephone 246609.

## JANUARY

**New Year Viennese Concerts played by the Ulster Orchestra at various venues**
Coca-Cola International Cross-Country Athletics at Mallusk

## MARCH

**Ulster Harp National - steeplechase at Downpatrick Racecourse**
Opera Northern Ireland Spring Season at the Grand Opera House
**Belfast Music Festival at Balmoral**

## APRIL

**Circuit of Ireland Motor Rally**
Tour of the North Cycle Race
**City of Belfast Spring Flower Festival**

## MAY

**Royal Ulster Agricultural Society Show at Balmoral**
Belfast Marathon
**Belfast Civic Festival & Lord Mayor's Show**
North West 200 Motorcycle Road Races at the Portstewart circuit
**Taste-Fest food festival in Botanic Gardens**

## JUNE

**Proms Concerts featuring the Ulster Orchestra at the Ulster Hall**
Belfast to Dublin Maracycle
**Belfast Folk Festival**
Castleward Opera
**Northern Ireland Game Fair, Shane's Castle**

## JULY

**City of Belfast International Rose Trials at Lady Dixon Park (until end of September)**
Ulster Senior Hurling Championship Final at Casement Park
**Northern Ireland Amateur Golf Championship at Royal Portrush**
Ulster Harp Derby at Down Royal Racecourse near Lisburn
**International Ulster Motor Rally**

## AUGUST

**Ulster Motorcycle Grand Prix at Dundrod**
Oul' Lammas Fair at Ballycastle

## SEPTEMBER

**Ideal Home Exhibition at the King's Hall**
Royal Ulster Academy of Arts Exhibition at the Ulster Museum, Belfast
**Opera Northern Ireland Autumn Season at the Grand Opera House**
Belfast Championship Dog Show at Balmoral

## NOVEMBER

**Belfast Festival at Queen's. One of the best arts festivals in Europe. Lasts for 3 weeks.**

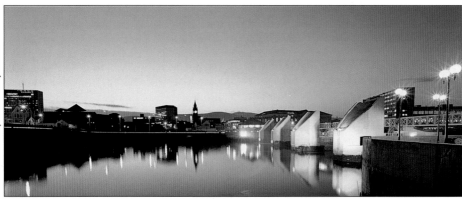

Photo courtesy of Belfast City Council

**River Lagan by Night**